Linux Install and Configuration

Little Black Book

Dee-Ann LeBlanc

Isaac-Hajime Yates

President, CEO
Keith
Weiskamp

Publisher
Steve Sayre

Acquisitions Editor
Stephanie Wall

Marketing Specialist
Tracy Schofield

Project Editor
Dan Young

Technical Reviewer
Dennis Groves

Production Coordinator
Laura Wellander

Cover Design
Jesse Dunn

Layout Design
April Nielsen

Linux Install and Configuration Little Black Book

Limits Of Liability And Disclaimer Of Warranty

Trademarks

The Coriolis Group, LLC
14455 N. Hayden Road, Suite 220
Scottsdale, Arizona 85260

480/483-0192
FAX 480/483-0193
http://www.coriolis.com

Library of Congress Cataloging-in-Publication Data
LeBlanc, Dee-Ann
    Linux install and configuration little black book/by Dee-Ann LeBlanc and
    Isaac-Hajime Yates
        p. cm.
    Includes index.
    ISBN 1-57610-489-3
    1. Linux. 2. Operating systems (Computers). I. Yates, Isaac-Hajime II. Title.

QA76.76.O63 L432 2000
005.4'469–dc21   99-043504
                                                            CIP

Printed in the United States of America
10 9 8 7 6 5 4 3 2 1

14455 North Hayden Road, Suite 220 • Scottsdale, Arizona 85260

Dear Reader:

Coriolis Technology Press was founded to create a very elite group of books: the ones you keep closest to your machine. Sure, everyone would like to have the Library of Congress at arm's reach, but in the real world, you have to choose the books you rely on every day *very* carefully.

To win a place for our books on that coveted shelf beside your PC, we guarantee several important qualities in every book we publish. These qualities are:

- *Technical accuracy*—It's no good if it doesn't work. Every Coriolis Technology Press book is reviewed by technical experts in the topic field, and is sent through several editing and proofreading passes in order to create the piece of work you now hold in your hands.

- *Innovative editorial design*—We've put years of research and refinement into the ways we present information in our books. Our books' editorial approach is uniquely designed to reflect the way people learn new technologies and search for solutions to technology problems.

- *Practical focus*—We put only pertinent information into our books and avoid any fluff. Every fact included between these two covers must serve the mission of the book as a whole.

- *Accessibility*—The information in a book is worthless unless you can find it quickly when you need it. We put a lot of effort into our indexes, and heavily cross-reference our chapters, to make it easy for you to move right to the information you need.

Here at The Coriolis Group we have been publishing and packaging books, technical journals, and training materials since 1989. We're programmers and authors ourselves, and we take an ongoing active role in defining what we publish and how we publish it. We have put a lot of thought into our books; please write to us at **ctp@coriolis.com** and let us know what you think. We hope that you're happy with the book in your hands, and that in the future, when you reach for software development and networking information, you'll turn to one of our books first.

Keith Weiskamp
President and CEO

Jeff Duntemann
VP and Editorial Director

This book is dedicated to the Linux community, for making it all work.
—Dee-Ann LeBlanc
&

This book is dedicated to Chatida, Bao, Dr. Keating, friends, and family:
Thank you for challenging me to excel while standing by me when
I needed you the most.
—Isaac-Hajime Yates
&

About The Authors

Dee-Ann LeBlanc is a technical writer and trainer currently specializing in Linux. She is a Red Hat Certified Engineer and teaches a variety of courses through ZDU, including regular stints with Introduction to Unix and Unix System Administration.

Dee-Ann is also the author of *Running A Perfect Internet Site With Linux*, and the lead author for *General Linux I Exam Prep* coming from The Coriolis Group, and has also written books on Internet tools.

Dee-Ann enjoys exploring new avenues of Linux, Unix, and the use of computers as tools to achieve what needs to be done out in the "real world." See what she is up to today, including the latest contact information, at **www.rainsoft.com/dee/write**.

Isaac-Hajime Yates is an IT Technician for iMALL Inc. where he troubleshoots end-user problems in the corporate office, evaluates utility software, analyzes computing issues, and develops strategies to create and implement batch files and programs.

Isaac also works as a Computer Lab Instructional Specialist for Santa Monica College where he supervises student workers and supports anywhere from 70 to 200 workstations on a given day.

He has been working in the computing field since 1995 and has dabbled with Windows, Linux, and several other Unix flavors, Mac OS, DOS, programming, HTML, and networking, among others.

Acknowledgments

Every new computer book brings about a fresh set of challenges. In a book such as this one, the challenge is to try to think of everything I can that people might want to do, or might run into as they install and configure a Linux box. In addition to my own experience, having a steady stream of students ensures that I am always discovering new aspects of Linux that cause people problems. I would like to thank my students as well as those people who have helped me instruct others, as well as those who have added their knowledge to mine to provide a broader range of experience for students. These people are Clay Lawrence, Charles Hays, and Garv Austin.

I would also like to thank the very supportive team at The Coriolis Group who made this book possible. Stephanie Wall and Dan Young made my experiences with The Coriolis Group pleasant, and they also were a good cheering section down the stretch. Special thanks to Dennis Groves who helped find the items I missed in each chapter.

Thanks also to my husband, Robert, for putting up with my weird moods and hours, and to all those friends who are still willing to talk to me after I vanished for a month or so.

—*Dee-Ann LeBlanc*

I'd like to thank everyone at The Coriolis Group for giving me an opportunity to help write this book. Special thanks to Dee-Ann LeBlanc who provided me with advice when I needed it. It is a huge honor for me to work with her on this book.

Family and friends have played an enormous role in inspiring me to push myself forward in both my work and personal life. I've always been grateful for both the big and little things people have done to look out for me along the way. So by helping to write this book, I am expressing my thanks.

—*Isaac-Hajime Yates*

Contents At A Glance

Table Of Contents

Chapter 3
Installing Caldera 27

Chapter 7
Window Managers And Desktop Environments 133

Chapter 8
Creating User Accounts 149

Chapter 9
The Linux File System 165

Chapter 10
Compiling The Kernel 175

Chapter 12
Integrating Into Windows Networks With Samba 233

Chapter 16
Installing New Software 303

Chapter 17
C Programming Tools 313

Introduction

What Is Linux?

Linux is a free version of the Unix operating system, distributed under the GNU Public License (GPL). This operating system is available both on the Internet from many download sites and from distributions which charge for a combination of conveniences like packaging onto a CD-ROM, installation programs, manuals, and technical support.

The Linux operating system is prized for the amount of control a system administrator has over the details of its operation, and how the source code for the OS and most of its tools is available for modification. A high number of Internet and intranet server machines are run using Linux, and thanks to a growing number of packages such as office tool suites, may soon become more popular in the desktop market as well.

While there is much documentation available for Linux on the Internet and on the CD-ROMs (which the Linux distributions come on), these files are written for a variety of levels of users and scattered throughout the world. The *Linux Install and Configuration Little Black Book* aims to give you a more centralized location for finding the information you need to install and run Linux to your specifications.

Assumptions About You

This book assumes that you have already decided to install Linux. The only decisions you should have left to make at this point are whether to use the Red Hat or Caldera distributions, and assembling the right combination of hardware if this step has not already been done. You should have experience administering other operating systems that have helped you learn the basics of hardware issues, the Internet, and the various applications available to you. All you want to do now is get started.

Some Background About Linux

The Linux operating system was born back in 1991 when Linux Torvalds, a student at the University of Helsinki in Finland, decided to make his own version of the Unix operating system as a hobby project. As the basics for the OS slowly came together, he began offering the code for viewing to the community that currently was using Minix, which was a small Unix OS written by Andy Tanenbaum.

Soon the Linux OS became a hobby for the readers of the Usenet **group comp.os.minix** and with their collective minds and efforts Linux grew and grew until, in 1992, Linux version 1.0 was officially released. As the Linux kernel gained more ground it became the choice of the GNU (Gnu's Not Unix) project's goal to create a full operating system replete with tools such as compilers, editors, network services, a GUI, and more.

In many ways Linux has become synonymous with GNU's "free" software approach. The free referred to here does not refer to cost, as GNU software can certainly be packaged and sold with value-added services. GNU is the forerunner of what has now become the Open Source movement. This movement states that people should have access to the source code for the software and operating system so that they can modify it if necessary and even share those modifications.

There is more to this movement. If you are interested, check out **www.gnu.org** for further information.

What You'll Learn In This Book

The *Linux Install and Configuration Little Black Book* concentrates on the installation and configuration of the Caldera and Red Hat Linux distributions on PC hardware. This book also presents to you what options are available and whether they would be useful. Services such as Samba, NFS, packet filtering firewalls and anonymous FTP are often mentioned in Linux circles but are only necessary if your particular setup requires them.

You'll learn the benefits of being a Linux setup expert and configuring a machine to do exactly what you want. Knowing what is possible and what isn't is a valuable step toward getting the most out of your Linux box or LAN.

You'll also learn these essential Linux administrative skills:

• Fine-tuning system security.

- Customizing what networking services run at startup.
- Setting up networking services for your site and your users.
- Adding and administering user accounts.
- Shell programming.

How This Book Is Organized

Chapters 1 through 4 handle the process of getting started with and installing Linux. The topics include choosing one distribution over another, how to obtain the distribution, how to ensure that Linux will run with your hardware, partitioning hard drives, and installing each distribution.

Chapters 5 through 9 cover the basics of using Linux and initially setting it up. You'll learn how to use Linux at the command line level, configure the X Windowing System, choose and install a window manager for your GUI, create user accounts according to your specifications, and work with the Linux file system.

Chapters 10 through 14 cover the more advanced portion of using and configuring Linux. Topics such as compiling the kernel—the operating system itself—configuring your LAN, setting up your Internet connection, and configuring both network and Internet services are presented.

Chapters 15 through 16 cover adding additional items specific to your Linux box. How to handle the different types of packages available in the Linux world and installing these packages is covered in depth.

Chapters 17 through 19 cover programming issues such as where to find and how to install the C programming packages on the distribution CD-ROMs, and how to write both shell and Perl scripts.

Chapters 20 through 21 cover the issues that come up once all the rest is said and done. The first of these is setting up a backup routine for your system. The second is heightening system security to keep unwanted intruders out.

How To Use This Book

Use the *Linux Install and Configuration Little Black Book* as best suits your needs. Since this book is designed to be a reference, it is not necessary to read it cover to cover. Instead, you can read the chapters that interest you and look up the specifics on other relevant items. Or, never read any of the full chapters, though reading Chapters 1 and

2, and then 3 or 4 are all highly recommended if you have never used Linux before. Each chapter conveniently contains a jump table which acts as a quick reference to where you can find the solutions to a number of installation and configuration issues.

We welcome your feedback on this book and are available by email for questions and comments. You can reach Dee-Ann LeBlanc at **dee@renaissoft.com** and Isaac-Hajime Yates at **iyates@excite.com**.

Getting Started With Linux

In Brief

Everywhere you look at computer news today, you see Linux mentioned. It's hard enough to follow discussions about a new operating system, and worse when you have to try to separate hype from fact. Even worse, you can't just walk into a store and buy "Linux". More than one distributor offers specially packaged versions with individual focuses and features. In this chapter you'll find the information you need to decide whether Linux is right for you, and to help you choose the distribution—between Red Hat and Caldera—and hardware that are appropriate for your purposes.

What Is Linux?

Linux is a version of the Unix operating system inspired by the two long-standing Unix variants, BSD and System V. At its heart it is a command-line-oriented operating system because Unix, its predecessor, was designed to be a tool used by programmers to build further tools. Even if you aren't a programmer and don't intend to use the operating system for this purpose, it is important to know how to deal with Linux at the command-line level. On a machine that provides intensive server functions, it is a waste of RAM and processor time to use a graphical user interface (GUI). However, although Linux has had a GUI for some time, both Red Hat and Caldera have included more and more useful graphical tools for working with the system. Learn to use both the command line and the GUI, and you have access to Linux's full range of capabilities.

Why Is Linux Special?

Linux is in the news so much partly because of the approach embraced by those who develop the operating system. Certainly the idea of peer review is nothing new in the scientific community, but in today's software development world, which is rife with the buzzwords "proprietary code," it is somewhat of a retroactive revolution. It is retroactive because the open source movement takes programming back to the computer science part of programming via the scientific method.

The development of the operating system and the tools available for it is an international effort, by its community of users along with Linus Torvalds, the initial author of the Linux kernel. On the tool front, Linux is currently gaining support from major developers. IBM and Corel, for example, are in the process of porting their commercial products to Linux, and even without these items there are thousands of programs and tools available for use under Linux. Many of these tools were ported, or translated, by Linux users from other Unix flavors.

For its user community, one of the most exciting facets of Linux is that the operating system is open source, meaning that all of the source code for it is available. Not only is this a boon for those who are developing software for the operating system, it also means that users have the ability to configure their system to as deep a level as they need to, limited only by their talents and the abilities of the software and the operating system itself.

NOTE: *Many industry pundits are predicting that other operating systems may follow suit and go open source eventually, offering their code for peer review and enhancement. Whether this will happen in practice, only time will tell.*

Linux Distributions

One of the biggest issues raved about during media coverage of Linux is that it is "free". And yet, a number of commercial distributions are available. So how can it be both?

Linux is covered under the GNU Public License (GPL). A number of Linux distributions—all sharing the standard Linux kernel, though sometimes it is slightly modified—are available for download on sites on the Internet, though the operating system is so large today that most people would rather buy it on CD-ROM (see the section "Finding Inexpensive CD-ROMs For Linux" for more information). Each distribution is slightly different, with the differences usually being in the installation-routine packages included, or a specific focus on security or usability. Packaged Linux, meaning the kernel and accompanying tools and packages, is called a distribution. The Linux distributions discussed in this chapter are Caldera and Red Hat.

Linux is free if you download it from the Internet, or borrow a CD-ROM from someone. A typical download is about 500MB. On a 33.6 kbps modem this download can take up to twenty-four hours. As the OS got larger and more tedious to download, the Linux distributions became more prominent. At first, they were primarily companies that packaged the OS on CD-ROMs with value-added features such as programs to help with installation and preconfigured services. Today, companies like Red Hat and Caldera package large distributions with complex installation programs; extra software, such as commercial demos; printed manuals; and technical support. Their distributions are still freely available for download—though Caldera's does not come with the full installation program for the download—and users with high speed connections and CD-ROM burners are happy to use this, but even people with such equipment may not want to go to the trouble.

Who Uses Linux?

Linux has finally begun to make strides toward general acceptance. However, it is not yet quite the operating system for the masses that the media would have everyone believe. The learning curve with Linux is steep for those who are used to today's point and click operating systems. It is like learning a new language. There are a whole new set of commands to learn, and new ways of doing and approaching things that have long been taken for granted. Having more control over the environment you work in requires a greater understanding of it, and how to manipulate it without causing problems. However, this level of control is exactly what makes the operating system perfect for system administrators and people who work with servers and LANs. For those who have Unix experience, Linux is much simpler to learn.

Linux also requires you to be familiar with your system hardware. Power users, system administrators, and developers often have an easier time learning Linux than general users. However, even for these groups a large dose of patience and dedication toward learning and experimenting with the subject is required.

Choosing Between Red Hat And Caldera

Both Caldera and Red Hat offer complete Linux solutions with technical support. The specific needs of your setup will eventually dictate which distribution to choose, or make it apparent that neither is significantly better or worse than the other in your case, at which point other factors such as price come into play. What follows is the information necessary to make the decision: Red Hat or Caldera?

When comparing the two Linux distributions, the first thing one notices is that they share many of the same advantages, although perhaps in different forms. Both of the distributions have configurable GUIs with tools to simplify many common tasks, a certain amount of hardware detection to make the installation process faster and less tedious, long lists of video cards and monitors to prevent most users from having to look up hardware statistics, testing of the GUI settings before completing installation, and more. In fact, in most cases programs can easily be used on either distribution, sometimes with minor tweaking if the necessary files are kept somewhere else. Both also allow you to partition the drive during the installation process, rather than having to have anticipated this issue.

Red Hat provides a wide variety of installation methods. It is possible to install the operating system from the CD-ROM on your local machine, or over a LAN or even an Internet connection from an FTP or Web server. Many product comparisons choose this Linux distribution for operating server machines. Every part of the Red Hat main distribution is open source as well, meaning that from the GUI to the installation program, you can edit the source code and make adjustments if you choose to. Finally, Red Hat gives you more control over what packages to install initially, although both distributions make it fairly simple to add and remove packages after installation.

Caldera's installation program is more polished, allowing testing of keyboard and mouse options, addition of user accounts while packages are installed, and even a game to play while waiting for the rest of the installation to complete. Many product comparisons choose this Linux distribution for desktop use and for those who need to dual boot, and those who are uncomfortable with disk partitioning are delighted to have Partition Magic included in the bundle.

In the end, however, the choice between the two operating systems comes down to personal preference. They both have a slightly different look and feel, especially if you choose their default GUIs, which are not the same. Installing either of them can be simple or a mess, depending on the combination of hardware in the machine and what settings you choose. For many people, the answer comes down to how many others they know who are using a specific distribution and could offer them assistance at a later date, or to trying both and seeing which works best with their hardware setup.

Related solution:	Found on page:
Deciding What Partitioning Program Tool To Use	20

Preparing For Linux

After deciding to install Linux, is it relatively easy to get. Both distributions are available in many computer stores and bookstores and on the Internet—and it is possible to download either for free. If you think you will want technical support, be sure to purchase the CD-ROMs from Red Hat or Caldera themselves, or from another distributor that offers support. Otherwise, there are places to order inexpensive CD-ROMs (see the section "Finding Inexpensive CD-ROMs for Linux" for more details).

Understanding Linux Equipment Needs

Linux is quite generous in terms of its minimal requirements. Most modern-day PCs meet the minimal needs, which are shown in Table 1.1.

The above listing assumes you want the bare minimum of what Linux has to offer. If you also want development tools, GUI, email and Web browsing, networking, services, and such features, the system requirements go up depending on how many features you want to have. In general, the speed of the CPU is not as important as how much RAM is installed within it. The more memory your computer has, the better it will run with Linux.

On the flip side from this issue, Linux is one operating system for which it can be better to have equipment that's been around for a while. Linux supports most hardware for the PC, but not all. Bleeding-edge devices (brand new items that use new technology which has not been used enough by the general public to be fully supported or mature) often take a bit of time to be supported by Linux. For example, brand new leading-edge video and sound cards tend to be a problem. To find out the status of certain hardware technologies under the Linux

Table 1.1   Minimum system requirements for Caldera and Red Hat Linux.

Hardware Component	Caldera	Red Hat
MB RAM	32	16
MB hard drive space	300	500
CPU	80386 or better	80386 or better for the standard boxed set
Floppy	Yes, if CD-ROM is not bootable	Yes, if CD-ROM is not bootable
CD-ROM	Yes	No, if alternate install types are available

distributions discussed in this book, go to **www.redhat.com** or **www.caldera.com**. Also, keep in mind that, although the new features may not be available for use under the operating system, sometimes generic options are available that at least make the hardware useable, if not at its maximum capability.

Plug and Play (PNP) devices can work under Linux, although some cope better than others. Configuring a PNP device to work under Linux varies in difficulty, depending on whether or not there are jumpers available to turn PNP off. Otherwise, you may be able to use the various PNP tools Linux contains to get the device to work. One type of PNP device that will not work with Linux, however, is the Winmodem. These particular modems are specifically made for use with MS Windows; they do not even work with MS-DOS.

Related solutions:	Found on page:
Launching The Installer From A Boot Disk	59
Launching The Installer From The CD-ROM	33
Launching The Installer From Floppy Disks	38

Determining If You Have The Right Equipment

Both Red Hat and Caldera support a large amount of hardware. However, they don't support everything. Before you make the leap into purchasing either, it is important to look at what you have now or want to purchase, and whether drivers for Linux are available for it. Every piece of hardware in your system is important. Fortunately, both distributions offer a hardware compatibility list via their Web site, as detailed in "Immediate Solutions."

WARNING!   It is important to look over the hardware compatibility lists and be sure your hardware is supported before you get started. Otherwise, you can run into difficulties getting Linux up and running.

Immediate Solutions

Finding Your System Information Using Windows 95/98/NT

Windows conveniently stores much of your system's information in the Control Panel. To get this information, do the following:

1. Click the Start button and select the Settings menu.

2. Click Control Panel in the Settings submenu. Figure 1.1 shows what the Control Panel looks like under Windows NT, and Figure 1.2 shows the Control Panel under Windows 98.

3. The most important information to gather for running the GUI is on your video card and monitor. Click on the Display icon in the Control Panel to access the information shown in Figure 1.3.

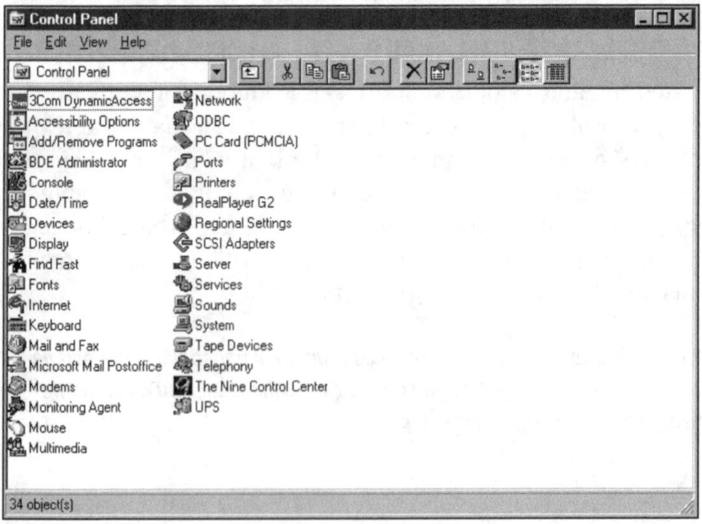

Figure 1.1   The Windows NT Control Panel.

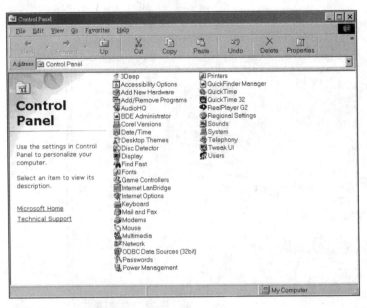

Figure 1.2   The Windows 98 Control Panel.

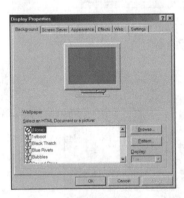

Figure 1.3   The Display Properties information obtained from the
Control Panel, at the Background tab.

4. Click on the Settings tab, shown in Figure 1.4.

5. The Settings tab contains the exact brand and model of your
   monitor and video card. Begin writing down the information
   you see; it will be useful later.

6. What happens from here depends on which version of Windows
   you are running:

   • If you're using Windows 98, click on the Advanced button to
     open the video card Properties dialog box shown in Figure 1.5.

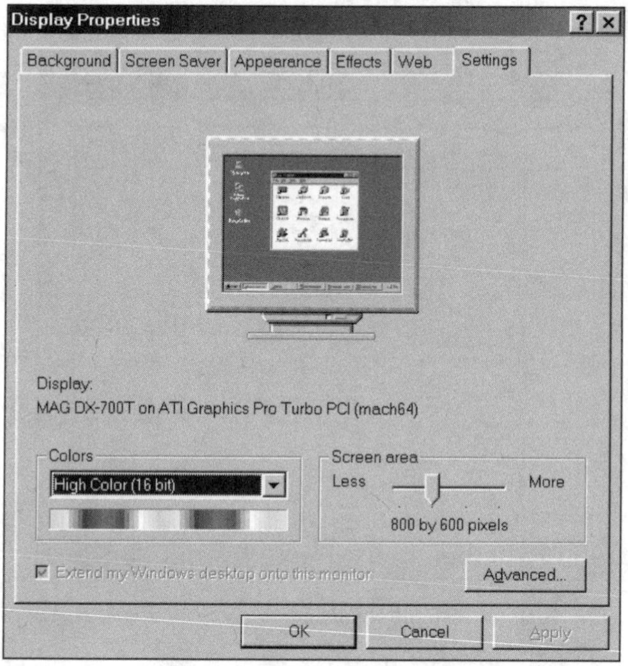

Figure 1.4   The Display Properties information obtained from the
Control Panel, at the Settings tab.

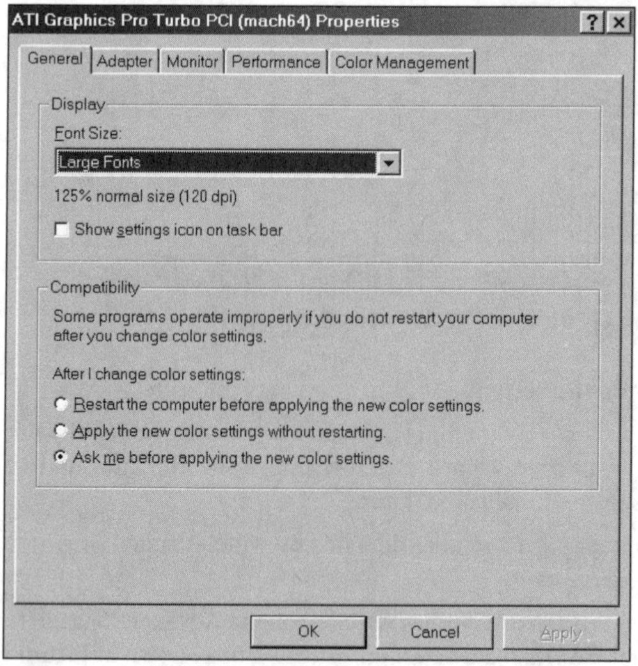

Figure 1.5   The Windows 98 Video Card Properties dialog box, General tab.

- If you're using Windows NT, click the Display Type button to open the Display Type dialog box shown in Figure 1.6. In Windows 98, click on Advanced to gather more information. The more information you have about your video card, the better.

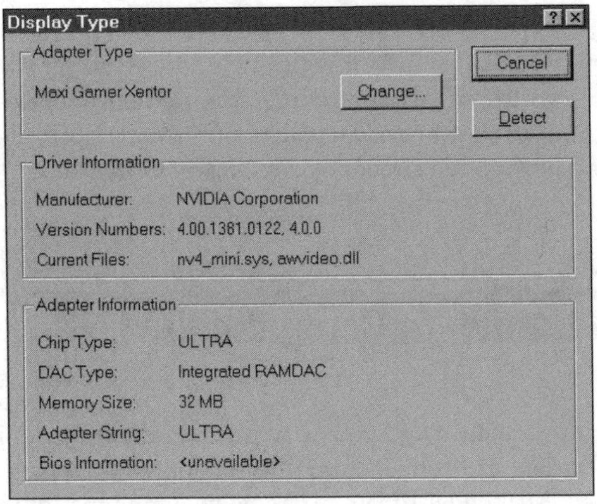

Figure 1.6   The Windows NT Display Type dialog box.

7. After gathering the information on your video card capabilities, close the Display Properties dialog box.

8. To get further information on the hardware on your machine:

   - If you are using Windows 95 or 98, open the System program in the Control Panel, and then click on the Device Manager tab. Navigate the device listings to get information on the various components in your system.

   - To get some information in Windows NT, open the Devices program in the Control Panel and scan through the driver list.

9. If you still aren't sure about everything in the machine, you may have to open it up and take a look. Or dig through that old pile of manuals in the closet.

Finding The Hardware Compatibility List For Red Hat

Red Hat's main site is **www.redhat.com**.

The main page posts news and articles that pertain to Red Hat, as well as other Linux news and other links to look at. To access the hardware compatibility list, go to **www.redhat.com/support**. Red Hat does a good job of keeping on top of bug fixes, updates, frequently asked questions (FAQs), and news in the Linux field, among other things.

Finding The Hardware Compatibility List For Caldera

Caldera OpenLinux's main page is at **www.calderasystems.com**. Caldera sells a variety of products and offers bundled packages as well. As with Red Hat, Caldera's site offers news pertaining to both OpenLinux and the Linux field. To access the hardware compatibility list, click on the support link or go to **www.calderasystems.com/ products/openlinux/hardware.html**. Caldera's support page provides a wealth of information and is your place to go if you plan to use Caldera.

Finding Inexpensive CD-ROMs For Linux

Linux is an inexpensive operating system, but anyone who is trying to save some money can go to these sites to save even more:

- **www.cheapbytes.com**
- **www.linuxmall.com**

Finding The Latest News On Linux

To keep up with the latest news on Linux, point your Web browser to these sites:

- www.linuxtoday.com
- www.linuxjournal.com
- www.linuxgazette.com
- www.redhat.com
- www.linux.com
- www.linuxhq.org
- www.freshmeat.net
- www.slashdot.org
- www.gnu.org

Determining Whether Linux Can Do What You Want

To determine whether Linux can achieve the results you require from it without first purchasing Linux, consider the following process:

1. Get onto the Web.

2. Look through the Linux How-To list at the Linux Documentation Project's Web site (**http://metalab.unc.edu/LDP/**). This list is a collection of documents on how to accomplish specific tasks with Linux. Although it is not important to understand them at this point, if there is one for what you need to accomplish, then it can be done.

3. Go to the Red Hat (**www.redhat.com**) and Caldera (**www.calderasystems.com**) sites and read the product sales literature, FAQs, and manuals.

4. Use a news-archiving site, such as Dejanews (**www.dejanews.com**), to search in the comp.os.linux.* Usenet hierarchy for the type of task you want to accomplish.

Partitioning Hard Drives

In Brief

Partitioning hard drives is one of the most nerve-wracking processes many people new to Linux encounter. Fortunately, both distributions discussed in this book come with tools to accomplish this task without needing to resort to the cryptic *fdisk*, unless you choose to do so. This chapter covers many of the issues you will encounter while preparing partitions, and then creating them.

Before You Partition

As with any operating system, Linux needs space to inhabit that is formatted with its own file system type. In order to give Linux a home, you need to create two or more partitions for it. Imagine a hard drive as a piece of pie, and each partition as a slice of that pie. Before you partition your hard drive, you need to understand the limitations inherent in creating partitions, and have a sense of how much space you want for Linux.

NOTE: *In fact, there is a method of installing Linux inside a Windows partition, but not only is it incredibly awkward to set up, it also runs slowly.*

Partition Limitations

There are certain limitations on a PC for how many partitions you can create. Some of these limitations depend on the type of partition in question. There are three types of partitions possible: primary, extended, and logical. A primary partition is the most straightforward form, and there can only be four of them on a drive regardless of how large it is. So, continuing with the pie reference, see Figure 2.1.

An extended partition is not actually used by itself. Instead, you convert one of the logical partitions to an extended partition. The reason for this is that a logical partition contains data, whereas an extended partition contains other partitions. Using these combinations allows you to have more than four partitions on a single drive. Figure 2.2 shows one way of dividing the pie so you can have two different extended partitions.

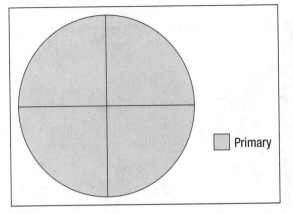

Figure 2.1   You can create up to four primary partitions on a drive.

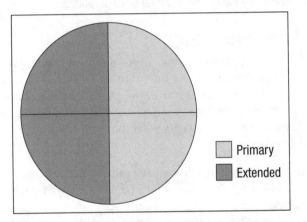

*Figure 2.2   You can create up to four primary and extended
partitions, total, on a drive.*

Once you've created an extended partition, you can then place up to
12 logical partitions inside it. Sometimes people use these because
they run into a situation where they need more partitions. At other
times more planning is involved when setting up a new computer,
and extended partitions are created for each operating system to help
locate groups of logical partitions later. This factor is especially true
for the larger drives that have enough room to support numerous
operating systems and partitions that are available today. Figure 2.3
shows one method in which the drive could be divided using a combination of the three partition types.

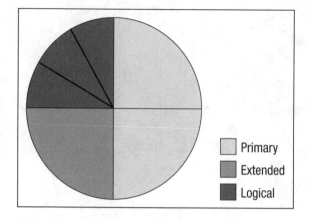

Figure 2.3   *By combining primary, extended, and logical partitions,
you can reach a maximum and total of 16 partitions.*

How Much Space To Assign

The simple but annoying answer to the question of how much space
to assign to Linux involves what you intend to do with it. If the machine is intended to be a server of some sort, then usually it should
only contain the Linux operating system. A desktop machine can be
set up to dual-boot and so can have its partitions split between multiple operating systems.

The Red Hat and Caldera distributions have minimum requirements
of 500MB and 300MB, respectively, but let's be a little more realistic.
You may want programming tools, graphical user interfaces, games,
text editors, graphics tools, Internet programs, and then some. Perhaps your ultimate goal is to set up a LAN that, along with supporting
a number of users, also stores mission-critical data. For such instances,
the drive space required grows into the Gigabytes.

It is a good idea to have Linux on a separate hard drive instead of sharing a hard drive with another operating system, if you can afford to do
so. With hard drive prices continually falling, a new hard drive could be
a wise and inexpensive investment. For the features and flexibility Linux
has to offer, the extra space could prove worth it. However, Linux can
peacefully coexist with other operating systems, whether on the same
hard drive or on separate ones. The main reason for separating operating systems is that if something goes drastically wrong with one, or
with the hard drive itself, not everything is affected.

Related solutions:	*Found on page:*
Deciding On A Removable-Rack Hard Drive System	371
Configuring LILO To Boot Multiple Operating Systems	71

Deciding How Many Partitions To Make

You must have at least two partitions to run Linux. The first is the root (/) partition, which is where all of the files necessary to use Linux are placed (if there are only two partitions), and the second is the swap partition. A swap partition supplements the RAM in your machine to smooth out the tasks it needs to run. This concept is similar to the virtual memory used in Windows. However, swap space is not nearly as fast as actual RAM. A good rule in general to follow is to make the swap space approximately equal to how much RAM you have, within the limitations of the kernel.

The more intensively the machine will be used as a server or administration box, the more important it becomes to separate the file system (the Linux file system is discussed in greater detail in Chapter 9) out into a number of partitions. How many are necessary is a function of what the computer's job will be. However, it is smart to create some special partitions, such as:

- A separate /boot partition, so that if something happens to the main root (/) partition, you can still boot the machine.

- A separate /var/log partition, so that if the system log files run wild they cannot overrun the main partition and crash the machine.

- A separate /tmp partition, so that if programs begin creating ridiculous numbers of temporary files, or if users abuse the directory, the rest of the file system is safe. This portion of the file system is also under the most wear and tear and so is likely to fail faster than other portions.

- A separate /home partition, to allow enforcement of disk quotas for users or groups and to keep from overwriting home data if upgrading or installing a new version of a Linux distribution.

TIP: *People who are used to Windows are often confused when they try to understand the concept of partitions with directory names. To Linux, anything that contains files is part of its file system. Whether that item is a different hard disk partition, a floppy disk, a Zip disk, or a CD-ROM, there are commands for adding that item to the file system. As an example, take the home partition. In Windows the partition might be called E:, but in Linux it's assigned a more meaningful name so it can be plugged directly into the file system. Instead of having home on the root (/) partition, the home partition is plugged into the file system itself as the home directory as well.*

Related solution:	Found on page:
Mounting Onto The File System	168

Deciding What Partitioning Tool To Use

Numerous factors come into play when looking at partitioning tools. The primary issue is whether there is an existing Windows partition that needs to be resized to make room for a Linux partition, or whether there is sufficient unpartitioned drive space available. If there is sufficient space, then any of the partitioning programs will do. Choosing between them is mostly a matter of what interface makes the most sense to you. If you are highly familiar with disk partitioning, then any of the tools will do nicely. If this is the first time you have ever needed to partition disk drives, then avoid programs like *fdisk*, which are powerful but bare-bones.

If you need to rearrange a hard drive and the Windows partitions on it to make room for Linux, the situation gets more complicated. See the section "Adjusting-Partitions Nondestructively With FIPS."

Additional commercial programs are also available to create, delete, or even nondestructively alter partitions. Some of the more popular partitioning tools are:

- Partition Commander, available at **www.v-com.com**.
- Partition Magic, available at **www.powerquest.com**.
- Partition It, available at **www.quarterdeck.com**.

Immediate Solutions

Adjusting Partitions Nondestructively With FIPS

If there are existing Windows partitions on the hard drive, you should also want to add Linux. You can use the First NonDestructive Interactive Partition Splitting (FIPS) utility to resize the current partitions without losing data. Do the following to accomplish this task:

1. Back up important data and programs from the Windows partitions. Although FIPS is a nondestructive tool, there is no guarantee that everything will run smoothly. Even if the re-partitioning goes well, something could go wrong later during the install process and you could lose access to your Windows data. It is best to err on the side of caution.

2. Locate the FIPS program and its documentation:

   - On the Red Hat CD-ROM, the program can be found in \dosutils. Also inside this directory is \fipsdocs, which contains all of the documentation for the program.

   - On the Caldera CD-ROM, the package can be found in \col\tools\fips.

   - On the Internet, the latest version of FIPS and its documentation are available from the creator at **http://bmrc.berkeley.edu/ people/chaffee/fips/fips.html**. A FAQ is also included at this address.

3. Read the included documentation. Because the goal is to adjust existing partitions with data you would likely rather avoid having to reinstall from backups, it is important to read the documentation and be sure you understand what each option presented will do.

4. Follow the process outlined in the FIPS documentation. Be sure to include every step, such as defragmenting the hard drive and backing up the boot sector. These items are included for your data's protection.

NOTE: *FIPS 1.5 does not support FAT32 partitions. To get support for FAT32, you need version 1.5c or higher, which is available on the FIPS Web site.*

Adding Partitions With Red Hat's Disk Druid

Red Hat's installation program includes a piece of software called "Disk Druid." The process of making a partition with this tool is as follows:

1. Work through the Red Hat installation program until you are given the option of partitioning tools. Choose Disk Druid.

NOTE: *It often helps with more complex drive setups to go into Windows, if it is already installed, and make a note of the sizes of the drives or partitions you want to keep and the drives or partitions you want to delete. Doing this can be of great help when you are trying to guess later which partition you want to wipe.*

---

2. Examine the partitions currently listed. It is important to know which you want to keep and which you need to delete. Some combinations of actions might be:

   • If you intend to give all hard drive space to Linux, delete all existing partitions.

   • If you bought a brand new hard drive for Linux and put it in your machine alongside a Windows drive, you need to determine which is which. Look in the Type column for which drive has the "DOS" label. The other one is the one you will create Linux partitions on. If it is currently marked as one large partition, delete it.

   • If you have more than one Windows drive and are giving one of them over to Linux, you need to determine which is which. Linux sees drives in alphabetical order, so the IDE hard drive on the first controller is hda, the second is hdb, and so on—if the drive is SCSI, then sda, sdb, and so on. Partitions are then numbered in order, so the first partition on the first IDE drive is hda1. Knowing the size of the item you want to clear for Linux also helps in narrowing down which one. Once you have determined which drive to clear, delete all partitions on it.

   • If you have cleared space on a Windows drive with a program like FIPS, or saved space on it for Linux, then there is no need to delete anything.

3. Choose the option "Add a new partition". Because of the need to have the boot sector before the 1024th cylinder, it is often a good idea to add the root or boot partition first, depending on whether you have chosen to include a separate boot partition. Now, to fill in the options.

4. The Mount Point text box refers to where within the Linux file system the partition belongs. The root partition is /. The boot partition is /boot. A swap partition has no mount point at all, so if that's what you are creating, skip it.

5. Enter the size you want the partition to be in the Size (Megs) text box.

6. If you want the partition to stay its current size, make sure there is no asterisk (*) in the Grow to fill disk? box. Instead, if you would like Disk Druid to calculate what room is left once all the partitions are created and give this particular partition extra space out of what is left, then make sure there is an asterisk there.

7. If there are multiple allowable drives listed, be sure that there is no asterisk (*) on a drive you don't want to put Linux partitions on.

8. Choose the Partition Type. The two choices for Linux partitions are Linux Swap and Linux Native. Only choose Swap for the actual swap partition. The rest should be Native.

9. Choose OK to return to the main Disk Druid window.

10. Set the next new partition, or choose OK to complete the partitioning process.

Related solutions:	*Found on page:*
Launching The Installer From A Boot Disk	59
Launching The Installer From The CD-ROM	60

Clearing Space And Adding Partitions With Partition Magic

A version of Partition Magic comes with Caldera. It has some of the same capabilities as FIPS, meaning that it can be used to resize the existing Windows partitions on your hard drive to make room for Linux. To accomplish this and then create the Linux partitions, do the following:

1. Install Partition Magic (PM) on the system in question. At the end the system will reboot.

2. Caldera's version of PM runs automatically as the machine comes back up.

3. If you need to resize a drive, and if PM has the wrong Windows partition or drive selected to resize, click the Select Partition button. Also click this button if you don't want to resize but want to make a partition into a Linux partition.

4. Choose the appropriate partition.

5. Click OK to return to the main screen.

6. Choose the size to assign to the Linux partition from among the radio button options.

7. Click OK. PM creates the partition.

Adding Partitions With Caldera Disk Partition Program

If you choose not to use PM before beginning the Caldera installation, do the following:

1. Follow through the Caldera installation process until you reach the screen labeled Installation Target.

2. Choose one of the following, according to your needs:

   • If you want to use the whole hard drive space on the system for Caldera, choose the Entire Harddisk option.

   • If you have already prepared Linux partitions, or just want to install on top of an old version of Linux, deleting it, choose the Prepared Partition(s) option.

   • If you want to create partitions at this point, choose the Custom option. The Partition Hard Disk(s) screen opens.

3. Examine the partitions currently listed. It is important to know which you want to keep and which you need to delete. Some combinations of actions might be:

   • If you intend to give all hard drive space to Linux, delete all existing partitions.

   • If you bought a brand new hard drive for Linux and put it in your machine alongside a Windows drive, you need to determine which is which. Look in the System column for which drive has the "DOS/Windows" label. The other one is the one you will create Linux partitions on. If it is currently marked as one large partition, delete it.

- If you have more than one Windows drive and are giving one of them over to Linux, you need to determine which is which. Linux sees drives in alphabetical order, so the IDE hard drive on the first controller is hda, the second is hdb, and so on—if the drive is SCSI, then sda, sdb, and so on. Partitions are then numbered in order, so the first partition on the first IDE drive is hda1. Knowing the size of the item you want to clear for Linux also helps in narrowing down which one. Once you have determined which drive to clear, delete all partitions on it.

- If you have cleared space on a Windows drive with a program like FIPS, or saved space on it for Linux, then there is no need to delete anything.

4. Click the Add logical button to add a new logical partition. Now, to fill in the options.

5. The Mount Point text box refers to where within the Linux file system the partition belongs. The root partition is /. The boot partition is /boot. A swap partition has no mount point at all, so if that's what you are creating, skip it.

6. The partition size is defined in terms of sectors. First, choose the beginning sector. Often it is best to just choose the first one available.

7. Next, choose the ending sector. If you have difficulties computing how sectors relate to size, let the program do it for you. Choose an ending point and the program will calculate how large it is in megabytes. Keep going until you have the size you want.

8. Choose the Partition Type. The two choices for Linux partitions are Linux Swap and Linux Native. Only choose Swap for the actual swap partition. The rest should be Native.

9. Choose OK to return to the main Partition Hard Disk(s) Window.

10. Set the next new partition, or choose OK to complete the partitioning process.

Installing Caldera

In Brief

Now that you have made your preparations and understand some of the basics behind the install process, it is time to install the operating system. It is important not to skip the preparations in Chapters 1 and 2 before proceeding. If you do, you might have to go back later to learn how to partition your hard drive or how to clear space and repartition a drive that was originally designated as a Windows-only single partition.

The Caldera install program, LIZARD, is heavily automated and graphical. However, this does not mean that it is completely intuitive. The solutions in this chapter offer assistance with the decisions you need to make as you proceed through the installation process.

The Install Process

As you go through the Caldera install process, it is important to carefully read the screen at each stage. Be sure you understand what the installer is asking about or, if not, make the best guess you can and be prepared to have to fine-tune or reinstall later. Remember that you can correct many mistakes later once you understand Linux more, by doing one of the following:

- Reinstalling Linux itself
- Adding or removing software packages
- Re-configuring software that is already installed
- Adding or removing modules from the kernel
- Recompiling the kernel

TIP: *Many people reinstall Linux at least once, if not multiple times, to fix strange problems that crop up after the initial install or to take advantage of understanding the installer questions more thoroughly after the initial installation. You may want to consider the first install as a practice run.*

LIZARD is kind enough to provide you with a *Tetris*-like game to play while it installs all of the packages you selected. However, this is also a good time to have other things to do because this transfer of data to the hard drive can take quite a while. The progress bar will keep you up to date on how much longer you have to wait.

TIP: *If you plan to reinstall your system or just are unsure if you will need to or not, it is a good idea to create a separate /home or /temp partition. Then, when you reinstall later, you will not format this specific partition—which means it will keep all of the files you don't want to lose from one installation to another. This procedure requires you to save or copy any files you want to keep onto the partition you don't intend to format during the reinstall.*

Related solution:	*Found on page:*
Moving An Existing Directory To A New Partition	173

Caldera's Installation Options

One of the choices offered during the install process involves which packages are installed. These choices are broken into four groups:

- Minimum set

- All recommended

- All recommended plus commercial

- All packages

Although some information is given toward the right-hand side of the screen about what is involved with these choices, a more detailed description is offered here so you can make a more educated decision. The only options that are listed as available are the ones you have the hard drive space to support.

Minimal Install

The minimal install takes approximately 160MB of disk space. It is by far the fastest of the options to install, but that is because it installs the least amount of material. What you get with this install are the basic tools that come with Linux and KDE (the GUI). Any additional packages, such as Netscape, games, graphics tools, or other applications, are not included in this installation option.

This option is best for machines where you know you are going to heavily customize what software is installed and what is not. This is the option to use if you don't intend to use the GUI and plan on disabling it. That is common for a server machine, which would only be slowed down by the GUI and whose disk space would be wasted by a lot of extra GUI tools.

TIP: *With any of the installation options, if you don't want the machine to automatically boot into the GUI, set your startup runlevel to be three. This setting will boot you directly to the command line.*

All Recommended Packages

The recommended packages installation takes approximately 500MB of disk space. What you get with this install is a large number of tools, games, and applications that you may find useful or interesting. These applications include Netscape, graphics editors, multimedia tools, and a wider range of utilities than are available in the minimal install.

This option is best for those who want to try out Linux and the tools that commonly come with it, but not the commercial packages they would have to buy in order to keep them longer than the trial period.

All Recommended Packages Plus Commercial

The recommended plus commercial packages installation takes approximately 800MB of disk space. This install includes everything from the recommended version and, also, such commercial packages as WordPerfect and the StarOffice suite of applications.

This option is best for those who want to try a full-fledged desktop machine, including word processing and office packages.

All Packages

The full install takes approximately 1.4GB of disk space. This option installs every package that comes with Caldera OpenLinux. These packages include all of the graphics manipulation, office, and software development tools.

This is the best option for those who want to try Caldera OpenLinux with every feature available and give it a serious test run. It's also good for people who know they want to use a lot of the tools advertised by Caldera, but are not yet sure which ones. You can test what you want and then remove anything you're not interested in using.

TIP: *Remember that you can remove or add packages at a later date, regardless of which install option you choose in the beginning.*

Considerations For Configuring Graphics

The most important devices to configure correctly are your video display devices—the monitor and video card. You can recover from misconfigurations of other hardware, but you might not be able to recover if you have incorrect display settings. Take care to do this segment of the installation correctly.

WARNING! *You can damage your hardware by using video settings that are higher than it can handle.*

Video Cards

If you went through the preparations outlined in Chapter 1, you should already have the necessary information about your video card. Here are some tips to help you set up these devices properly during the install process:

- Let LIZARD do most of the work for you. It can autoprobe your video card and get all of its settings that way. Just click the Probe button in the Select Video Card configuration segment.

- If you need to configure the video card manually, look in the manuals for the detailed information necessary.

- If you can't find the video card's manuals, look on the manufacturer's Web site.

- This information is important to get correct. It's worth tracking it down through Web searches, a letter to the manufacturer, or phone calls.

- If you can't locate the manufacturer, it may be because the company changed names or merged with another company. Or it might be a subsidiary listed under a larger company's Web site. Web searches can help with this problem. Search for the model name and number.

- If you can't find any information, err on the side of caution.

Monitors

Many of the same configuration considerations apply to monitors that apply to video cards, such as hunting down the correct data about the capabilities if you can manage to do so. However, there is no autoprobe feature for the monitor itself. There are three different ways you can choose the monitor settings to use:

- Scroll through the manufacturer listing and see if you can find your monitor's maker. If so, click on the plus (+) next to the entry to see the list of models. Choose the model for your monitor, then click the Next button.

- If your monitor is not listed for some reason but you have the data for it, fill in the horizontal and vertical sync ranges at the bottom of the screen. Give the monitor a name as well, then click the Next button.

- If you do not have data for your monitor available anywhere, be very careful. Go to the top of the listing and look at the generic monitor options. Choose the one most appropriate for your setup. It is best to guess low if you are unsure.

Video Modes

The Caldera installer's video mode selection feature is configured to automatically offer you only the modes that your hardware can support. It is not recommended to change it to show you every possible mode. Otherwise, you may accidentally choose a mode that is not compatible with your hardware, which could damage it.

It is recommended to use the mode testing feature before moving on to the next step in the installation process. To do this, click the "Test this mode" button and see how it looks on your screen.

Installing Multiple Operating Systems

Many people who want to use Linux at home or on a desktop at work also want to run another operating system on the machine—for example, Windows. Linux can share a hard drive with another operating system so long as the installs are handled carefully. The primary issue is the install order. Linux should be installed after the other operating system(s) when at all possible.

TIP: Be sure to create boot disks for any other operating systems on the machine before installing Linux. This step improves the odds that you can get back to them if something goes wrong during the Linux install. Instructions for making MS Windows boot disks are given in the section "Creating A Windows Boot Disk." Also, remember that there is no guarantee that your data will survive your adding another operating system to the hard drive. Be sure to make backups of important files and programs!

Immediate Solutions

Launching The Installer From The CD-ROM

The preferred way to install Caldera OpenLinux is from the CD-ROM itself. Most modern machines can accommodate this, but not all machines are capable of it. You can determine if yours will or will not by following through the process.

TIP: *If you're installing Caldera on a machine that it has to share with Windows, consider following the instructions in "Installing Caldera From Windows" instead.*

To install Caldera from a CD-ROM, do the following:

1. Reboot your machine and press the appropriate key to enter the BIOS at the beginning of the boot process.

2. Enter the segment of your BIOS that controls which drive order the system checks while booting. In some versions of BIOS this menu option is "BIOS FEATURES SETUP."

3. Change the boot order of the drives so that CD-ROM comes first in the listing. If the only drives that are offered are floppies and hard drives, then your BIOS does not support booting from the CD-ROM and you will need to use one of the other boot options, either "Installing Caldera From Windows" or "Installing Caldera With Boot Disks."

4. Make sure the Caldera CD-ROM 1 is in the CD-ROM drive.

5. Save, then exit the BIOS.

6. As the machine reboots, the install program starts automatically.

Installing The Caldera Windows Tools

If you already have Windows installed on the machine you intend to share between it and Linux, Caldera OpenLinux provides tools that make this type of installation easier. To prepare to make use of these tools, do the following:

3. Installing Caldera

1. Boot into Windows if necessary.

2. Put the Linux CD-ROM 1 into your CD-ROM drive.

3. The Caldera program autolaunches. If it does not do so on your machine, open the CD-ROM in the file manager of your choice and enter the Winsetup directory. Run the Setup program to launch the Caldera program.

NOTE: Carefully read all dialog boxes and screens presented to you. Otherwise, you might miss information that applies specifically to your situation.

---

4. To begin the install process, click the menu option "Install Products."

5. To go directly to the install, choose the language you want to use under "Full Install Preparation." If you need to address disk partition issues first, see Chapter 2.

6. The Install Wizard launches and walks you through the installation process. The components installed by the end are:

   • Install disk creation tools

   • README file with last-minute changes that may not have made it into the OpenLinux documentation

   • A program to repartition your hard drive (Partition Magic is discussed in detail in Chapter 2)

   • A program to set up your machine to give you a menu to choose Windows or Linux at boot time

Related solution:	*Found on page:*
Clearing Space And Adding Partitions With Partition Magic	23

Determining Which Install Disks Are Necessary

Caldera OpenLinux has a number of install disk options. Determining which you need is somewhat a matter of trial and error:

1. Are you unable to install directly from the CD-ROM or from Windows? If so, you will definitely need to create an Installation boot disk.

2. Are you installing with hardware that many people don't have on their machines, such as over a laptop PCMCIA device or SCSI drives? If so, you may need a Module diskette, which supplies the extra drivers necessary for you to go through with the install process. Otherwise, if your install fails and you are using only the Installation boot disk because of not having the proper drivers, try adding a Module disk to the mix and see if that fixes the problem.

3. If for some reason the LIZARD installation program will not display properly on your monitor, you will need to use the LISA install and module disks instead. LISA is the installation program used for previous versions of Caldera.

Making Install Disks

There are two different types of installation disks available for Caldera OpenLinux, as well as two supplementary disks. See the section "Determining Which Install Disks Are Necessary" if you are unsure of which ones you need. In order to make the disks, you need to have installed the Caldera Windows tools. See the section "Installing The Caldera Windows Tools" for more information.

NOTE: *If the version of Caldera you have came with installation disks, try them first.*

Making A LIZARD Installation Disk

To make a LIZARD installation disk to install Caldera OpenLinux, do the following:

1. Boot into Windows if you haven't already.

2. Format a blank 3 1/2 inch floppy if you don't have one at hand.

3. Open the Windows Start menu.

4. Open the Programs submenu.

5. Open the OpenLinux submenu.

6. Choose the option Create Install Diskette.

7. Type the drive letter you have the floppy in (for example, "a") and then press Enter.

8. A progress bar lets you track the disk creation process. Once it's done, remove the disk; it's ready to use.

Making A LIZARD Module Disk

To make a LIZARD module disk to provide extra hardware drivers during the Caldera OpenLinux installation process, do the following:

1. Boot into Windows if you haven't already.

2. Format a blank 3 1/2 inch floppy if you don't have one at hand.

3. Open the Windows Start menu.

4. Open the Programs submenu.

5. Open the OpenLinux submenu.

6. Choose the option Create Module Diskette.

7. Type the drive letter you have the floppy in (for example, "a") and then press Enter.

8. A progress bar lets you track the disk creation process. Once it's done, remove the disk; it's ready to use.

Making A LISA Installation Disk

To make a LISA installation disk because the LIZARD installer will not work properly on your hardware, do the following:

1. Boot into Windows if you haven't already.

2. Format a blank 3 1/2 inch floppy if you don't have one at hand.

3. Open the Windows Start menu.

4. Open the Programs submenu.

5. Open the OpenLinux submenu.

6. Choose the option Create LISA Install Diskette.

7. Type the drive letter you have the floppy in (for example, "a") and then press Enter.

8. A progress bar lets you track the disk creation process. Once it's done, remove the disk; it's ready to use.

Making A LISA Module Disk

To make a module diskette to go with your LISA installation disk because you need the extra device drivers, do the following:

1. Boot into Windows if you haven't already.

2. Format a blank 3 1/2 inch floppy if you don't have one at hand.

3. Open the Windows Start menu.

4. Open the Programs submenu.

5. Open the OpenLinux submenu.

6. Choose the option Create LISA Module Diskette.

7. Type the drive letter you have the floppy in (for example, "a") and then press Enter.

8. A progress bar lets you track the disk creation process. Once it's done, remove the disk; it's ready to use.

Creating A Windows Boot Disk

If you're preparing to share a hard drive or a machine between both Windows 9x and Caldera, it's smart to create a Windows boot disk before beginning your Caldera installation. To create this boot disk, do the following:

1. Click the Start button in Windows 9x to open the Start menu.

2. Click the Settings option on the Start menu to open the Settings submenu.

3. Click the Control Panel option to open the Control Panel window.

4. Double-click the Add/Remove Programs icon to open the Add/Remove Programs Properties dialog box.

5. Click the Startup Disk tab to bring that selection to the front.

6. Click the Create Disk button to begin creating your startup disk.

NOTE: *You might at this point be told to insert your Windows 9x CD-ROM.*

---

7. A progress bar appears and moves as Windows prepares the necessary files. When it's ready, it displays a dialog box telling you to label a floppy as your startup disk and insert it into the floppy drive. Be sure to label this disk. Depending on the specific installation process you follow, you may have a pile of disks by the time you are ready to install; they could easily get out of order if they aren't labeled.

8. Once the floppy is in the drive, click OK.

9. Windows creates your startup disk. When it is finished, click OK to close the dialog box.

NOTE: *Usually, the disk creation process monopolizes the whole computer. Don't plan to be able to multitask while making this disk.*

---

10. Put your Windows startup disk, clearly labeled, in a safe place.

Launching The Installer From Floppy Disks

When you are ready to install Caldera and need to use an install and perhaps a module disk to do so, do the following:

1. Decide which install disks you'll need by reading the section "Determining Which Install Disks Are Necessary."

2. Make the install disks according to the instructions in the section "Making Install Disks."

3. Make any boot disks (for example, a Windows boot disk) and backups that you feel are necessary.

4. Place your install disk in the floppy drive and reboot the computer.

5. The installation program launches automatically.

Assigning IP Addresses For A Private, Local Network

If you are setting up an isolated LAN or machine, consider using the sets of IP addresses shown in Table 3.1, which are reserved for just such a purpose.

Table 3.1   *IP addresses for private local networks.*

IP Class	Address Range
A	10.0.0.0 - 10.255.255.255
B	172.16.0.0 - 172.31.255.255
C	192.168.0.0 - 192.168.255.255

> **TIP:** *Using this addressing scheme makes adding Internet access later fairly painless. If you pull IP numbers out of the air that happen to be owned by someone else on the Internet, then adding Internet access becomes a huge hassle down the road.*

Recovering NT From A Boot Manager Failure

If you're trying to have both Linux and NT on the same machine and you become unable to access NT, do the following:

1. Boot with your NT Setup Disk 1 in the floppy drive.

> **TIP:** *If you don't have a problem of this type now, but are sharing Linux and NT on the same box, it is a good idea to read this section and make sure you have all of the necessary materials handy "just in case."*

2. Insert Disk 2 when instructed to do so.

3. Choose the repair program by typing the letter R.

4. The repair program will do all checked tasks. Uncheck any task you don't want it to perform.

5. Click Continue.

6. Insert Disk 3 when instructed to do so.

7. Insert your Emergency Repair Disk when instructed to do so.

8. Remove the repair disk and press Enter to reboot when instructed.

Making A Custom Linux Boot Disk

To make a boot disk that will work with your system after it's installed, instead of launching the installation program, do the following:

1. Log in as **root**.

2. Type "uname -r" to get the kernel version.

3. Insert a blank floppy into the floppy drive.

4. Type "mkbootdisk *version*", then press Enter. For example, if the kernel version is 2.2.17-9, then you would type "mkbootdisk 2.2.17-9".

5. Press Enter again after being prompted for the disk.

6. When the disk is made, remove it from the drive.

7. Label the disk clearly as your Linux boot disk.

8. Store the disk in a safe place.

Setting Up To Boot Into Caldera

How you boot your machine is partly determined by what operating systems you have on it. If you have a combination of Windows 9x and Caldera on the system, refer to the section "Installing Boot Magic." If you are only using Caldera on the computer, refer to the section "Installing LILO."

TIP: *Sometimes things go wrong with boot loaders. Follow the instructions in the section "Making A Custom Linux Boot Disk" before rebooting your Caldera installation.*

Installing Boot Magic

If you plan to share your machine between Caldera and Windows, do the following:

1. Follow the instructions in "Installing The Caldera Windows Tools" before you install Caldera.

TIP: *If you have already installed Caldera, don't worry: you can skip to Step 3 and then follow the instructions in Step 1, then go down to Step 4.*

2. Install Caldera according to the method that works best for you.

3. When the install is finished and Caldera starts up, click the Shutdown button.

4. In the dialog box that comes up, click the "Shutdown and Restart button".

5. The machine reboots. Be sure to pull any installation disks out of the floppy drive, or if you installed from the CD-ROM be prepared to pull up the BIOS and return its settings to boot in the order of floppy first, then hard drive—usually A, C.

6. Click the Start menu.

7. Click the Programs submenu.

8. Click the OpenLinux submenu.

9. Click the BootMagic item to start up the BootMagic program.

10. Configure your BootMagic installation.

Installing LILO

You don't need to install LILO by hand if you have installed Caldera with LIZARD. It is automatically installed for you.

Booting Into Caldera

When booting into Caldera, you have to deal with a boot loader whether or not the machine shares space with another operating system. If Linux is sharing a hard drive with Windows, the Boot Magic operating system selection screen comes up for you to choose which operating system to boot into.

Otherwise, if Linux has the hard drive all to itself, the LILO (LInux LOader) prompt appears as

```
LILO boot:
```

Press the Tab key to see what operating system labels are available. If you do nothing, then LILO will boot you into Linux after several seconds, automatically.

Diagnosing Boot Hangs During LILO

When LILO displays on your screen, each letter stands for a part of the boot process. Table 3.2 lists the meaning of each error that can occur during this process. Table 3.3 is a partial list of error codes and their causes.

Table 3.2   Using LILO to diagnose a boot hang.

LILO Stage	Diagnosis and Suggestions
Blank	LILO did not start to load. It was either not installed or not on an active partition. Go back into Partition Magic and be sure your Linux root (/) partition is bootable.
L *Error Code*	The first stage of LILO loaded properly, but the second could not. The hex error code is a clue toward the problem. The disk parameters may not be what LILO was expecting. See the section "Determining Disk Parameters" for help with this issue.

(continued)

Table 3.2   Using LILO to diagnose a boot hang (continued).

LILO Stage	Diagnosis and Suggestions
LI	The first stage of LILO loaded properly, and the second loaded but could not be run. It is likely that the LILO files are not installed in the proper places. See the section "Running LILO" for how to fix this; if the problem persists, see the section "Determining Disk Parameters."
LIL	The second stage of LILO loaded and ran properly, but could not load all of its data. The boot sector of the hard disk may be bad, or it doesn't properly understand the physical makeup of the hard drive. See the section "Determining Disk Parameters" for help with this issue.
LIL?	The second stage of LILO loaded at an incorrect address. Try re-running LILO, or setting the disk parameters (see the section "Determining Disk Parameters").
LIL-	The descriptor table was corrupted. Try re-running LILO, or setting the disk parameters (see the section "Determining Disk Parameters").
LILO	LILO loaded and ran properly.

Table 3.3   LILO disk error codes.

Code	Code Definition	Potential Solutions
0x00	Internal error	Re-run LILO (see "Running LILO").
0x01	Illegal command	Make sure LILO is installed (see "Running LILO"). Make sure the hard drive is properly set in the BIOS and be sure that you do not have too many drives installed for the machine's BIOS to handle.
0x02	Address mark not found	Try rebooting several times. If the problem persists, see "Running LILO."
0x04	Sector not found	LILO encountered unexpected disk parameters. See the section "Determining Disk Parameters."
0x06	Change line active	Try rebooting several times. If the problem persists, see "Running LILO."
0x08	DMA overrun	Try rebooting several times. If the problem persists, see "Running LILO."
0x09	DMA attempt across 64K boundary	Remove the "compact" option from LILO's configuration file (see the section "Edit LILO").

(continued)

Table 3.3   LILO disk error codes (continued).

Code	Code Definition	Potential Solutions
0x0c	Invalid media	Try rebooting several times. If the problem persists, see "Running LILO." There may be a physical problem with the hard disk.
0x10	CRC error	Try rebooting several times. If the problem persists, see "Running LILO." There may be a physical problem with the hard disk.
0x20	Controller error	Try rebooting several times. There may be a problem with the hard drive controller. Try moving the drive's connection to another controller.
0x40	Seek failure	Try rebooting several times. If the problem persists, see "Running LILO." There may be a physical problem with the hard disk.
0x80	Disk timeout	Try rebooting several times. There may be a problem with the hard drive. Open the machine and put your hand against it (be careful to make sure it's not burning hot) and see if the drive spins up properly during the boot process, or if it spins erratically.

WARNING!   Always be careful when opening a machine and working with it while the power is on.

Restoring Your Master Boot Record

If you need to clear either Boot Magic or LILO from the MBR, log on as **root** and type "fdisk /mbr".

Running LILO

To run LILO so it updates itself and its map files, log on as **root** and type "/sbin/lilo".

Editing LILO

To edit LILO's configuration file, log on as root and edit the file /etc/lilo.conf with your preferred text editor. Make the changes you want to make, save and close the file, then re-run LILO (see the section "Running LILO") to activate the changes.

For example, if using the **vi** text editor, the steps would be:

1. Log in as **root**.

2. Type "vi /etc/lilo.conf" to edit the file.

3. Use the arrow keys to move the cursor to where you want to add text.

4. Press i to enter **vi**'s Insert mode.

5. Make the desired changes.

6. Press the ESC key to exit Insert mode.

7. Press the colon (:) key to enter Colon mode.

8. Type "wq" and press Enter to save and exit the file.

Determining Disk Parameters

If at any point you see an error involving disk parameters or geometry, you may have a disk that is set up in a way the kernel was not expecting.

TIP: *Before you continue, first see the section "Edit LILO." In the global section type in the word "linear", save and exit the file (see the section "Running LILO"), and then reboot. This sequence just might fix your problem.*

To enter your disk geometry, do the following:

1. Write down the hex BIOS code for your hard drive. This code is given as part of the error message that led you to this point. It probably said something like one of the following examples:

```
geo_query_dev HDIO_GETGEO (dev 0x50)
Device 0x50: Got bad geometry 24/48/248
```

TIP: *If the error message comes in the second format, the last three numbers are actually sectors/heads/cylinders. Write these down and skip directly to Step 5.*

---

2. Boot into MS-DOS.

3. Run the following under MS-DOS:

```
DPARAM.COM Hex Error Code
```

For example,

```
DPARAM.COM 0x50
```

4. Write down the results of **DPARAM**.

5. Boot into Linux with an emergency boot disk.

6. Open your LILO settings file (see the section "Editing LILO").

7. Create a disk declaration to tell LILO what file system device your hard drive is. For example, for the second IDE drive the statement would be:

```
disk /dev/hdb
```

8. Within the disk declaration, define the geometry with the data you have gathered. You need to enter statements for the BIOS, sectors, heads, and cylinders. For example, with the numbers obtained in step 1 you might create the statement:

```
disk /dev/hdb
  bios 0x50
  sectors 24
  heads 48
  cylinders 248
```

9. Save your settings, run LILO (see "Running LILO"), and reboot (see "Shutting Down Your System"). If LILO still does not boot, continue to the next step.

10. Insert a partition statement into the declaration under the disk line. This should be the exact partition LILO resides on, which is the root (/) partition. For example, for the first partition on the second IDE drive it might be

```
partition /dev/hdb1
```

11. The only information left that could be of use is the sector the partition starts on. This data can be gleaned with a tool such as fdisk (discussed in detail in Chapter 2). An example might be

```
start 2048
```

12. Save your settings, run LILO, and reboot.

Adding A Boot Delay To Allow Time To Choose An Operating System In LILO

Add a new line beneath the boot line at the beginning of /etc/lilo.conf. The timeframe is listed in tenths of a second. To have a delay of, for example, three seconds, you would add "delay 30" and then re-run LILO (see "Running LILO").

Reinstalling LILO

If you decide you would benefit from a fresh LILO install, first make sure you have emergency boot disks available. Then do the following:

1. Log on as **root**.
2. Delete the current LILO installation, as called for in "Removing LILO."
3. Edit your /etc/lilo.conf file to reflect the settings you want, if desired (see "Editing LILO").
4. Run LILO to place the new information in the MBR (see "Running LILO").

Removing LILO

To uninstall LILO, type "lilo -u".

Shutting Down Your System

To shut down your system cleanly, use the **shutdown** command. You can use a number of variables, depending on what you intend to do. To shut down in order to shut the machine off, log on as **root** and type "shutdown -h".

If you want the machine to reboot when it's finished shutting down, type "shutdown -r".

Either of these commands by itself terminates all processes, including logging out users. However, you can add additional flags to customize the command's behavior. If you want to reboot quickly the next time, shut off file system checking for the next boot by adding the -f flag. For example, to shut the machine off for maintenance that does not involve the hard drive and thus avoid the hard drive check as it comes back up later, type "shutdown -hf".

If you have additional users on the system, you may choose to give them some time (in minutes) to save their work and log out. To add a time delay and custom message to, say, reboot the system, use the following format:

```
Shutdown -rft 5 Quick maintenance reboot
```

3. Installing Caldera

TIP: *If you always use the -f flag, you will eventually be forced by the operating system to do a file system check.*

Installing Red Hat

In Brief

Now that you have done the preliminary work, it is time to install the operating system. It is important not to skip the preparations in Chapters 1 and 2 before proceeding. There are too many issues that can otherwise catch you off-guard. Issues such as hardware not supported by the distribution, or placing the first stage of LInux LOader (LILO) above the 1023rd cylinder on your hard drive can make installation a miserable experience if you are not prepared.

The Red Hat 6.0 Linux distribution comes with an installation program that walks you through the procedure. This chapter focuses on making the most out of the options provided, and dealing with any problems you might encounter. Even though the install can be a straightforward process for some people, specific conditions can make it more complex. Whether these complexities come from hardware or configuration issues this chapter leads you through how to resolve them.

The Install Process

When going through the installation process, it is important to read through the options. The ease with which you can later set up services is determined by what packages you choose at this stage. Any mistakes you make here can, however, be corrected after the install through a variety of methods:

- Reinstalling Linux.
- Adding or removing software.
- Additional configuration of software and Linux.
- Adding or removing modules from the kernel.
- Recompiling the kernel.

TIP: *Many people reinstall at least once, if not multiple times, in an effort to fix persistent problems or fine-tune after they understand Linux more thoroughly. You may want to consider your first install and setup as a practice run.*

Once you reach the point where the installer is building your file system, you may want to have something else to occupy yourself with. This process moves fairly quickly, though there is no progress bar to keep you updated.

TIP: *If you intend to use the system but think you might need to reinstall to fine-tune, one trick is to create a separate /home partition that you keep in subsequent installs. This allows you to keep all of the files in the /home partition while wiping everything else. Or, you could simply create a separate partition that you use to store items you don't want to lose, naming it something like /temp. Just don't make a new file system (reformat) on the partition you're trying to save during the new install and you can keep it intact.*

Red Hat's Install Classes

Install classes are a feature introduced in Red Hat's 5.2 release and are available in subsequent releases. There are three install classes available:

- Workstation
- Server
- Custom

Each class has its strengths and weaknesses. It's important to choose the one most suited to your needs.

The Workstation Class

If you want to do a minimal practice run, the Workstation class is a good choice. It is a helpful option for beginners who are unsure about partitioning issues. Some things to keep in mind with the Workstation install class are:

- It installs LILO on your Master Boot Record (MBR), whereas you may want it instead on the Linux partition or a boot disk. If MS Windows is already installed on the system, LILO is automatically configured to dual boot.

- It erases all existing Linux partitions on your hard drive, whether or not they are Red Hat Linux, and then uses all unpartitioned space that is left on the drive.

- It chooses which packages to install. You have no input in the matter.

The Workstation class uses approximately 600MB of space to create the following partitions:

- 64MB swap for swap space.
- 16MB /boot for the first stage of LILO and the kernel.
- 600MB or larger—expands to fill all available free space on the drive—root (/).

The Server Class

If you intend to dedicate an entire machine to Linux, then the Server install can be a good choice—especially as a practice run for setting up a server of your own. You may find that the default installation for this class is perfect for your situation, or you may decide once you have a handle on using the machine that you'll go back and do a Custom install.

Related solutions:	Found on page:
Finding The Hardware Compatibility List For Red Hat	12
Deciding How Many Partitions To Make	19
Compiling A Kernel	184

This install class assumes that you intend to make the machine an actual server, so treats it as such. Some things to keep in mind with the Server install class are:

- It wipes all existing partitions and creates its own, each holding a different segment of the Linux file system.

- It erases your entire hard drive, so only use the Server class if it's the only thing you want on that machine.

- It chooses which packages to install. You have no input in the matter.

The Server class uses approximately 1.6GB of space to create the following partitions:

- 64MB swap for swap space.
- 16MB /boot for the first stage of LILO and the kernel.
- 256MB root (/) partition.
- 256MB /var partition.
- 512MB or larger /usr partition.
- 512MB or larger /home partition.

These last two partitions will grow to fill all available space left on the drive.

The Custom Class

Those who want to have more control over their installations should choose the Custom install. This install class allows you to determine where LILO will be installed, if you even wish to use it. You can also set up partitions the way you feel most suits your needs.

The primary issue to keep in mind with this install class is that it does not handle most issues for you. A more thorough understanding of the issues is required to use this install class. If you become unsure, you can go with the defaults, or choose the Everything option and install all components if there is enough disk space available. The sum total of Everything comes to 1GB just in packages.

NOTE: *Remember that you can install more packages at any time if it turns out you have forgotten something.*

LILO, The LInux LOader

LILO is a boot manager (a program that allows you to choose which operating system you want to use at boot time). LILO—or another boot manager, as listed in Table 4.1—must be installed regardless of whether you have only Linux, or have multiple operating systems installed. This is because your computer cannot boot with Linux unless it knows where to find the kernel, which is in many ways the OS itself. LILO gives your computer this information.

You have several options of where to install LILO on your system. Each option has its own advantages and disadvantages. If you are running other operating systems aside from Linux on the same machine, be sure that you have emergency boot disks available for each of them. Even if you never need them, having these disks available usually means you can rest easy if something goes wrong with the LILO install.

WARNING! *If you intend to dual-boot Linux on a computer that also contains NT, it is imperative that you create an updated Emergency Repair Disk before installing Linux. This way, if something happens to the boot sector during the install, you can recover your NT system.*

If you have Linux and NT sharing a computer, you can use NT's boot manager instead of LILO. The same goes for OS/2 and its boot manager.

Table 4.1   Alternative boot managers.

Boot Manager	Source
System Commander	**www.v-com.com**
NT OS Loader	NT Distribution Disks
OS/2 Boot Manager	OS/2 Distribution Disks
Partition Magic	**www.powerquest.com**

The Master Boot Record

For some, the simplest option is to install LILO on the primary hard drive's MBR. This location is especially straightforward for those who are only using the computer in question as a Linux machine.

WARNING!   If the same computer you are installing Linux on is also intended to run MS Windows, this OS also places information on your MBR. Installing MS Windows after installing Linux will wipe out LILO if it is already installed on your MBR. This situation can be repaired if you created an emergency boot disk for Linux. See the section Running LILO for more details. Whenever possible, install MS Windows operating systems first and Linux last.

The Linux Root Partition

Those who have multiple operating systems installed on the same hard drive, or each on its own drive, often choose to install LILO on Linux's root partition. Installing LILO on this location can help to avoid any conflicts between your operating systems over which uses the MBR.

WARNING!   You must make the Linux root partition bootable with the program you used for partitioning if that is where you want to install LILO.

A Floppy Disk

If you are heavily concerned about potential problems from installing LILO on your hard drive, it is best to install LILO to a floppy disk. This allows you to only invoke the boot manager when you have the floppy in the drive, which is a good solution for those who do not intend Linux to be their primary OS.

WARNING!   Be sure to make a backup of your LILO floppy and keep it in a safe place.

Considerations For Configuring Video Options

If you did the preparation outlined in Chapter 1, you should have the information on your video card and display already available. Here are some tips to help you fill out the required data:

- Often the information you need is available in the hardware manuals.

- If you can't find the manuals, locate the manufacturer's Web page. Many video card and monitor manufacturers publish the relevant data on their Web sites.

- This information is important enough to contact the manufacturer by email, postal mail, or phone if that is what is required to get the data.

- If you cannot locate the manufacturer, more research may be necessary. The maker may have merged with another company, or may be a subsidiary that is listed under a larger company's Web sites.

- Err on the side of caution where you are unsure. It's better to not utilize the full range of features than to burn out your hardware.

WARNING!   You must fill out video card and monitor data accurately, or damage to your hardware can result when you try to start the GUI.

Services Available At Boot Time

At one point in the install process you are shown a list of services that can be started at boot time. Pressing F1 while the cursor is on the service brings up a short description of the service. Here is useful information to help you determine which you want to use:

- apmd is a power management daemon used on laptop computers. If you are installing Linux on a desktop machine that does not rely on battery power, do not run this daemon by default.

- atd tracks jobs created with the **at** command. The **at** command allows users and system administrators to schedule a one-time job to run at a specific time.

- crond tracks regularly-run jobs scheduled by editing the system-wide cron files, or created by users with crontab.

- gpm allows limited mouse-based features to be used in a non-GUI session. These features are generally limited to the ability to select and copy text between screens, and use pop-up menus. If the machine involved will not have a mouse attached to it, do not start this service automatically.

- keytable loads the keymap selected during the install process. The system's keymap is a file that tells Linux which characters appear when which keys and key combinations are pressed. It is a good idea to leave this service on to start at boot.

- linuxconf is what allows system administrators using GUI to call up the Linuxconf program at any time during a GUI session to manipulate their system's setup.

- lpd is the print server. If the machine will not be connected directly or via a LAN to a printer then don't start this service at startup.

- netfs is the networking mounting file system enabler. If you need to mount any drives across network connections such as NFS or Samba be sure this is enabled. If you are installing on a stand-alone machine then disable it.

- network is an important option if you will be using any network interfaces.

- pcmcia is used for laptop devices that use a PCMCIA slot.

- random manages the tools Linux uses to generate random numbers. It is recommended that random remains turned on.

- sendmail handles the email you send from one machine to another. It is a good idea to keep it running unless you are setting up a single user, standalone machine.

- sound is a utility that ensures that your sound card mixer settings are not lost between boot sessions. It is safe to shut off this process if the machine has no sound card.

- syslog is a tool that various daemons and other processes use to write data to the system logs. Leave this one on.

Installing Multiple Operating Systems

Often people who want to use Linux at home install it on a machine that also runs another operating system. As a general rule, it is often best to install Linux last. Doing this prevents LILO (or an alternate boot loader) from being erased from the MBR.

TIP: *Also remember to create boot disks for each of the operating systems involved in case something goes wrong. Instructions for MS Windows are given in the section "Creating A Windows Boot Disk".*

Immediate Solutions

Determining Which Install Disks Are Necessary

The install disk that comes with Red Hat Linux is good for standard installs where nothing fancy is required. However, if you need to do a network install or are installing on a laptop, you might just need to create an extra disk or two before you can get started.

To determine which install boot disk(s) you need, do the following:

1. Are you installing on a laptop through a PCMCIA device such as an external CD-ROM? If so, you need to create a supplemental disk with the file supp.img to go along with one of the boot images.

2. Are you doing an install that requires use of networking? Such installs are NFS network installs, or installing from an FTP or HTTP server. They require bootnet.img.

3. If you don't need any of the above, you still need boot.img if you don't have the general install boot disk.

Creating A Linux Install Boot Disk

Once you've determined which boot disks you need, creating them each involves the same process:

1. Open an MS-DOS shell or boot into MS-DOS.

2. Change to the directory where you have **rawrite.exe**.

3. Run the rawrite program.

4. At the prompt, enter the path for the boot image you want to write.

```
Enter disk image source file name:
```

5. Place a blank, MS-DOS formatted floppy in your floppy drive.

6. At the prompt, enter the location of your floppy drive.

```
Enter target diskette drive:
```

7. The boot image is now written to the floppy sector by sector, as it needs to be done.

Downloading The Latest Boot Images

If you did not receive a boot disk with the installation CD-ROMs, or you downloaded Red Hat from the Internet, you need to create a boot disk before beginning the install (discussed in the section Creating A Linux Install Boot Disk). To get the latest boot disk image:

1. Point your Web browser to **www.redhat.com/errata**.

2. Download the most recent boot.img file for the distribution you have.

3. Either place the installation CD-ROM in your CD-ROM drive or point your browser or FTP client to Red Hat's FTP site (**ftp.redhat. com/**).

4. If using the CD-ROM, change to the directory \dosutils. If you don't have access to the CD-ROM, download rawrite.exe from **http://metalab.unc.edu/pub/Linux/distributions/redhat/ current/i386/dosutils/**.

Creating A Windows Boot Disk

To create a boot disk for MS Windows 95 and later, do the following:

1. Click the Start button in MS Windows to open the Start menu.

2. Click the Settings option on the Start menu to open the Settings submenu.

3. Click Control Panel to open the Control Panel window.

4. Double-click the Add/Remove Programs icon to open the Add/ Remove Programs Properties dialog box.

5. Click the Startup Disk tab to bring that section to the front.

6. Click the Create Disk button to begin creating your startup disk.

You may be told at this point to insert your Windows CD-ROM.

7. Windows prepares the necessary files, giving you a progress bar. When ready, it displays a dialog box telling you to label a floppy as your startup disk and insert it into the floppy drive.

8. Once the floppy is in the drive, click OK.

9. Windows creates your startup disk. When all is finished, click OK to close the dialog box.

   The startup disk creation is a processor-intensive task. You will not be able to do much else with the computer while this happens.

10. Put your startup disk, clearly labeled, in a safe place.

Launching The Installer From A Boot Disk

You can launch the installation program from a floppy one of two ways. If you purchased Red Hat Linux and received a boot floppy with the distribution, that is the one you want to use. Or, you can create a boot disk yourself (first see the section "Determining Which Install Disks Are Necessary," earlier in this chapter).

To start the installation, put the disk in your floppy drive and then (re)boot the computer. This should automatically begin the install process. If it does not, there may be one of several issues to deal with:

- Check your BIOS and make sure the floppy is the first drive accessed in the boot sequence.

- The boot disk supplied may be faulty, or may not have the necessary drivers to support your setup. You can create a new, updated boot disk following the instructions in the section "Create A Linux Install Boot Disk."

- There may be a hardware problem. If you have the luxury of having multiple machines, you can test hardware by moving it into another computer and seeing if it functions properly there.

- You may not be able to install from a floppy on that machine. Examine the network installation options available to you in the sections "Installing Across An NFS Mount," "Installing From A Hard Drive Partition," and "Installing From An HTTP or FTP Server."

If you are unable to find the problem, contact Red Hat technical support if you purchased your CD-ROM directly from them. Also, there is an amazing amount of Linux support online in the form of documents, web pages, and support groups.

Launching The Installer From The CD-ROM

If for some reason the floppy drive is not available to you, you can boot from the CD-ROM if your computer's BIOS supports booting from the CD-ROM. If it does not, you cannot start the installer with this method.

To start the installation program from the CD-ROM, do the following:

1. Boot into MS-DOS.

NOTE: *You cannot do this procedure by running an MS-DOS session within MS Windows. You must be running just MS-DOS.*

2. Change to your CD-ROM drive within MS-DOS. For example, type "cd d:".

3. Change to the CD-ROM's dosutils directory. For example, type "cd \dosutils".

4. Begin the installation process by typing "autoboot.bat".

5. Your computer will reboot, and the installation now proceeds just like an installation that uses a boot disk.

Setting Up A Local Server For An NFS, HTTP, Or FTP Install

Before you can set up any form of network install you first need one of the following:

- A fully installed Linux box with the proper network setup to feed the install data.

- A machine running a different operating system that can handle long filenames on the same LAN as the Linux box you are trying to install on.

If you are going to use a Linux box to feed the install to other Linux boxes, first work through this book for the main Linux box. Then come back to install on the rest.

NOTE: *This injunction includes setting up DHCP or BOOTP servers to handle assigning IP addresses to the machines during the install.*

Assigning IP Addresses For A Private, Local Network

If you are creating an isolated LAN or machine then consider using the sets of IP addresses shown in Table 4.2, which are reserved for just such a purpose.

Table 4.2   IP addresses for private local networks.

IP Class	Address Range
A	10.0.0.0 - 10.255.255.255
B	172.16.0.0 - 172.31.255.255
C	192.168.0.0 - 192.168.255.255

Installing Across An NFS Mount

If you are installing a machine on a LAN and accessing the Red Hat materials from an NFS-mountable drive, then follow through the installation procedure using the bootnet disk until you get to the Installation Method section. Then do the following:

1. Choose NFS image option, then press Enter.

NOTE: *You must make a bootnet disk to do any network install. Follow the same process as you would to make an install boot disk, but choose the \images\bootnet.img file instead of \images\boot.img.*

---

2. If the installer cannot find your network card it will offer a list of drivers and ask which one to use. It then gives you the option of auto-probing the card to see what other options may be necessary, or entering them yourself. Enter the appropriate information if necessary.

3. Choose the method you want to use to assign IP address information to the machine. If you are unsure and the DHCP and BOOTP servers are unfamiliar to you, then choose a Static IP address. Move the cursor to OK and press Enter.

4. What happens now depends on which of the three addressing options you chose:

   • If you chose to fill in a Static IP address, then you will get a dialog box asking for the addressing information. Fill in this information, move the cursor to OK, and press Enter.

   • If you chose BOOTP or DHCP, then fill in the server information so the installer knows where to look for the addressing data, and then continue.

5. Enter the name of the NFS server and the path to the Red Hat install data, then press Enter.

6. Continue with the install as you would for a nonnetwork install.

Installing From A Hard Drive Partition

If your machine does not have a working CD-ROM drive but you have a spare hard drive or partition, do the following:

1. Put the CD-ROM onto this spare space, from the RedHat directory on down.

2. Boot with the standard boot disk.

3. In the Installation Method segment, choose "Hard drive".

4. Enter the partition information necessary for the installer to access the data.

5. Continue with the install as you would for a CD-ROM install.

Installing From An HTTP Or FTP Server

You can install from a local or Internet HTTP (Web) or FTP server, though local is preferred. If you do want to install from a server over the Internet then you will need to have your Linux box connected to a network that is already connected, because dial-up tools are not provided. The speed for installing from a remote server is also rather slow.

NOTE: *You must make a bootnet disk to do any network install. Follow the same process as you would to make an install boot disk, but choose the bootnet.img file instead of boot.img.*

To install from a Web or FTP server, do the following:

1. Boot with the bootnet install disk.

2. When given the choice of installation methods, choose HTTP or FTP.

3. If the installer cannot find your network card it will offer a list of drivers and ask which one to use. It then gives you the option of auto-probing the card to see to see what other options may be necessary, or entering them yourself. Enter the appropriate information if necessary.

4. Choose the method you want to use to assign IP address information to the machine. If you are unsure and the DHCP and BOOTP servers are unfamiliar to you, then choose a Static IP address. Move the cursor to OK and press Enter.

5. What happens now depends on which of the three addressing options you chose:

   • If you chose to fill in a Static IP address, then you will get a dialog box asking for the addressing information. Fill this information in, move the cursor to OK, and press Enter.

   • If you chose BOOTP or DHCP, then fill in the server information so the installer knows where to look for the addressing data, then continue.

6. Fill in the site and path information for the HTTP or FTP server.

7. Continue with the install as you would for a nonnetwork install.

Recovering NT From A Boot Manager Failure

If you lose access to NT from a boot manager failure, do the following to recover from this problem:

1. Boot with your NT Setup Disk 1 in the floppy drive.

2. Insert Disk 2 when instructed to do so.

3. Choose to repair by typing the letter "R".

4. The repair program will do all checked tasks. Uncheck any task you do not want it to perform.

5. Click Continue.

6. Insert Disk 3 when instructed to do so.

7. Insert your Emergency Repair Disk when instructed to do so.

8. Remove the repair disk and press Enter to reboot when instructed.

Choosing Which Components And Packages To Install

When choosing what packages and kernel modules to install for the Custom install class, it is important to give thought to what hardware and services you intend to run on your Linux box. The installer presents hundreds of available packages broken into groups of components. First, you choose which components you want to install; then you can decide whether you want to choose certain packages within the components or just go with everything. How much you customize your machine is entirely up to you.

Keep the following things in mind when choosing what components and packages to install:

- Include drivers for all hardware you intend to use. If it's not installed now but you intend to install it next week, it's worth installing the drivers now.

- Include compilers and libraries for any languages you intend to use. For example, if you plan to do C programming, be sure to install gcc.

- Include networking drivers and software if necessary. Install these even if you won't be setting up your network right away.

- Include servers for the services you intend to run. If this machine will reside on a large enough network, determine which computers will provide which services. Spreading such things as mail servers and Web servers across multiple machines can greatly speed up each individual task.

- Include clients for the services you intend to access. How many clients are necessary on your server machine depends on your plans for its use. If the server is intended to be in a network and serve other machines, you may want to install a few clients for testing purposes. Otherwise, the clients will be more important to install on the end-user machines on your network.

- If you want to use shells other than bash, be sure to include them.

Depending on how much hard drive space you have available to you, you may want to install everything until you understand the system and packages more thoroughly. However, if you want to use the everything option, it requires over 1GB of space just for the packages alone. It is not a good choice unless you have 4GB or so just for Linux itself. You could also do a minimal installation and make notes about what packages you had to add along the way to learn what items you should add during the Custom install process.

Tracking And Debugging Your Install With Virtual Consoles

Once you press the Enter key at the beginning of the install process, there are a number of virtual consoles available that allow you to track the details of what is happening. There are five different virtual consoles. As shown in Table 4.3, each displays specific information regarding how your install is proceeding.

Table 4.3   Red Hat Installer virtual consoles.

Key Combo	Console Name	Console Details
Alt+F1	Main	The Main console is where the installer program asks for the information it needs to do the install through the use of dialog boxes, and provides you with status bars as the install progresses.
Alt+F2	General	The General console offers you a limited bash shell you can interact with as the install continues.
Alt+F3	Expert	The Expert console displays a text-based status listing of how the install is going. This status window is especially useful if the install process hangs somewhere along the line. If this happens, take note of what is on this screen when the install fails. This information is useful to your diagnosis, and to that of Red Hat technical support if you need to talk to them.
Alt+F4	Rescue	The Rescue console displays the behind-the-scenes happenings of the install process. This status window is also helpful in determining the cause behind install hangs. Once again, if you run into install problems, jot down what is on this virtual console before shutting the machine off.

(continued)

Table 4.3   Red Hat Installer virtual consoles (continued).

Key Combo	Console Name	Console Details
Alt+F5	Kickstart	The Kickstart console contains miscellaneous data about the install process, mostly information about where items are stored on the hard drive, and a status display while the installer is making the file system.

Booting Into Linux

To boot into Linux, do the following:

1. Reboot your computer.

TIP: *If you have LILO on a floppy, be sure to have the disk in the floppy drive before rebooting.*

2. LILO activates. If the install hangs at this point (you see L, LI, or LIL instead of the full LILO), see the section "Diagnosing Boot Hang During LILO."

3. Once LILO fully loads, its boot prompt appears as

```
LILO boot:
```

If one of the following cases is true, you don't need to interact with the boot prompt:

- Linux is the only OS on the computer.

- Linux is the OS that LILO was set to boot to by default.

- You are booting into Linux for the first time and have not yet fully set up LILO.

Otherwise, type in the designation for the OS you want to boot into and press Enter.

Diagnosing Boot Hang During LILO

When "LILO" displays on your screen, each letter stands for a part of the boot process. Table 4.4 shows the meaning of each error display within the LILO boot. You will know if you need this table because the boot will stop at one of the stages listed.

Table 4.4   Using LILO to diagnose a boot hang.

LILO Stage	Diagnosis and Suggestions
Blank	LILO did not start to load. It was either not installed, or not installed on an active partition. If you installed LILO on the root Linux partition, be sure that partition was set to be bootable.
L *Error Code*	The first stage of LILO loaded properly, but the second could not. The hex error code is a clue toward the problem at hand. See Table 4.5 for a partial list of error codes and their causes. Often, if the boot fails at this stage, either there is a bad disk (hard or floppy) involved or the disk parameters are not as LILO and the initial Linux kernel expected. See the section "Determine Disk Parameters" for help with this issue.
LI	The first stage of LILO loaded properly, and the second stage was loaded. However, the second stage could not be run. Sometimes this problem is caused by unexpected disk parameters. Otherwise, the file /boot/boot.b (the actual boot loader portion of LILO) may have been moved without rerunning LILO to update the kernel file maps. See the section "Running LILO" for how to take care of this problem.
LIL	The second stage of LILO loaded and started properly, but cannot load the data it needs from the /boot/map kernel file map. Once again, this problem typically happens because of a bad floppy or hard disk, or unexpected disk parameters.
LIL?	The second stage of LILO was loaded at an incorrect address. Usually, this problem results from a slight error in disk parameters, or moving /boot/boot.b without rerunning LILO.
LIL-	The descriptor table was corrupted. This problem can be caused by unexpected disk parameters, or from moving the file /boot/map without rerunning LILO.
LILO	LILO loaded and ran properly.

4. Installing Red Hat

TIP: *Remember that when you are considering moving LILO from floppy to MBR, or vice versa, you can also move LILO onto the root partition of your Linux installation if you change that partition to be bootable (within your partitioning program).*

Table 4.5   LILO disk error codes.

Code	Code Definition	Potential Solutions
0x00	Internal error	Try rerunning LILO to rebuild the map file (see "Running LILO"). This error can result from corrupted data.
0x01	Illegal command	Make sure the drive LILO is installed to is recognized properly by your BIOS. You may have too many physical drives installed. If your BIOS recognizes fewer drives than you have in the computer, consider removable drives and racks so you can swap some of the drives in and out of the machine.
0x02	Address mark not found	This error usually results from a drive problem. Reboot and give it another try. If several reboots later you still get the same error, there may be a physical problem with the floppy or hard disk in question. Boot with your emergency boot disk and try reinstalling LILO.
0x03	Write-protected disk	Double-check the floppy disk containing LILO to ensure you have not moved the write-protect tab.
0x04	Sector not found	LILO encountered unexpected disk parameters. If you used rawrite to create the disk being used to boot, make sure you used a disk with the same density the image was intended for. If the error happens with a hard drive, make sure the kernel has the proper disk parameters set (see "Determining Disk Parameters").
0x06	Change line active	Try rebooting. If doing so several times does not fix the problem, boot with an emergency boot disk and try reinstalling LILO.
0x08	DMA overrun	Try rebooting. If doing so several times does not fix the problem, boot with an emergency boot disk and try reinstalling LILO.
0x09	DMA attempt across 64K boundary	See the section "Editing LILO." Remove the compact option from your LILO configuration and boot with the new LILO settings.
0x0c	Invalid media	This error usually results from a drive problem. Reboot and give it another try. If several reboots later you still get the same error, there may be a physical problem with the floppy or hard disk in question. Boot with your emergency boot disk and try reinstalling LILO.

(continued)

Table 4.5   LILO disk error codes (continued).

Code	Code Definition	Potential Solutions
0x10	CRC error	This error also results from disk problems. First, try rebooting a few times. If that does not fix the problem and you are running LILO from a floppy, consider booting with an emergency boot disk and installing LILO to a new floppy. If you have LILO installed to your hard drive, try reinstalling it. If that still does not fix the problem, consider installing LILO to a floppy instead. There may be damage on the location where you are attempting to install.
0x20	Controller error	This error can result from a drive controller problem. Try rebooting several times. If this does not fix the problem, it may be worth considering installing a new drive controller. Or, move LILO to a floppy if the hard drive is generating the error, or to the hard drive if a floppy is generating the error.
0x40	Seek failure	This error usually results from a drive problem. Reboot and give it another try. If several reboots later you still get the same error, there may be a physical problem with the floppy or hard disk in question. Boot with your emergency boot disk and try reinstalling LILO.
0x80	Disk timeout	For some reason the floppy or hard drive is not ready. Try rebooting. If the error occurs with a floppy, try ejecting it and putting it back into the drive; it may not have been seated properly. If the error occurs with the hard drive, make sure the drive is spinning up correctly by opening the computer and listening to it, or putting a hand against it. You will be able to feel if it is spinning, and if it is spinning steadily or erratically.

(side margin: 4. Installing Red Hat)

Alternatives To Using LILO On Your MBR

There are a number of other methods of booting a Linux machine that do not require LILO to be in your MBR, or even to be in-stalled at all. Two of them are covered here. If you choose to use either of these or any of the others available, then when asked where to install LILO at the end of the installation process, choose the Skip option.

Loadlin

A favorite method some people use to avoid the issue of changing the MBR is installing Loadlin. Using this option requires a DOS partition on your hard drive to contain the program. To install and use Loadlin, do the following:

1. Download Loadlin from **ftp://metalab.unc.edu/pub/Linux/ system/boot/dualboot/**.

2. Unzip and untar the file. The latest versions of WinZip will do this if you have to do this on a Windows machine.

3. Copy the file LOADLIN.EXE into an MS-DOS partition.

4. After installing Linux, copy the file /boot/vmlinuz to the same partition, into the main directory (for example, C:).

5. Now, to boot Linux, type something similar to the following at the MS-DOS partiton's prompt:

```
loadlin c:\vmlinuz root=/dev/hda1 ro
```

Boot Disk

Rather than using LILO or any other boot loader, you can use the custom boot disk created toward the end of the install process to boot every time.

Restoring Your MBR

To restore your MBR, log on as root and type "fdisk /mbr".

TIP: *Don't want to use Fdisk? Programs such as Norton Utilities or North AntiVirus are also capable of helping you restore your MBR.*

Running LILO

To run LILO so it updates itself and its map, log on as root and type "/sbin/lilo".

TIP: *If you get a "No such file or directory error", type "which lilo" and then type the path given in response.*

Editing LILO

To edit LILO's configuration file, log on as root and edit the file /etc/ lilo.conf_ with your preferred text editor. Make the changes you want to make, save and close the file, then rerun LILO (see the section "Running LILO") to activate the changes.

For example, if using the **vi** text editor (see Chapter 5 for more on using **vi**) the steps would be:

1. Log in as **root**.
2. Type "vi /etc/lilo.conf" to edit the file.
3. Use the error keys to move the cursor to where you want to add text.
4. Press "i" to enter vi's Insert mode.
5. Make the desired changes.
6. Press the ESC key to exit Insert mode.
7. Press the colon (:) key to enter Colon mode.
8. Type "wq" and press Enter to save and exit the file.

Configuring LILO To Boot Multiple Operating Systems

To add operating systems aside from LILO to your boot options, do the following:

1. Open the file /etc/lilo.conf.
2. Locate the section similar to

```
image=/boot/vmlinuz
label=linux
root=/dev/hda2
```

TIP: *You can customize the labels that show when LILO offers you a choice of operating systems by changing the label for the section to what you want to use. For example, instead of "label=linux" above, you could change it to "label=Red Hat Linux".*

---

3. Move to the line beneath the image section to add your new material.

4. If you are adding a non-Unix OS, then instead of using the image parameter, you will use the other parameter. For example, let us say that you have an MS Windows partition on hda1 and have just installed Linux to hda2. The new section might begin as follows:

```
other=/dev/hda1
```

If you are adding another Linux partition, you would use the same structure as shown in Step 2.

5. Now, you must tell LILO where on the partition table to find this OS. The next line might be "table=/dev/hda".

6. Finally, add a label for the OS, for example, "label=MS Windows".

7. Save and exit the file.

8. Run LILO to finalize the changes.

Determining Disk Parameters

If at any point you see an error involving disk parameters or geometry, you may have a disk that is set up in a way the kernel was not expecting.

TIP: *Before you go to the trouble of inputting the exact geometry of your disk, first see the section Edit LILO. Add the linear configuration variable or, if you are using command-line configuration, add "-l" to do the same (for example, you could type "-l 24/56/512"). Then reboot and see if that fixes the problem.*

To enter your disk geometry data, do the following:

1. Write down the hex BIOS code for your hard drive. This code is given as part of the error message that led you to this point. It probably said something like one of the following two examples:

```
geo_query_dev HDIO_GETGEO (dev 0x50)
Device 0x50: Got bad geometry 24/48/248
```

TIP: *If the error message comes in the second format, the last three numbers are actually sectors/heads/cylinders. Write these down and skip directly to Step 5.*

---

2. Boot into MS-DOS.

3. Run the following under MS-DOS:

```
DPARAM.COM Hex Error Code
```

For example:

```
DPARAM.COM 0x50
```

4. Write down the results of **DPARAM**.

5. Boot into Linux with an emergency boot disk.

6. Open your LILO settings file (see the section "Editing LILO" for instructions on how to do this).

7. For each hard drive geometry you need to define, you need a disk declaration in the options section. The disk declaration tells LILO what file system device your disk is. For example, if you were defining your first hard drive, which showed in your partitioning program as hda, the disk declaration would be

```
"disk = /dev/hda".
```

8. Within the disk declaration you now define the geometry using the data gathered in Steps 1 and 4. If you need to define more than one drive, start a second disk section after the first with a new disk declaration. However, the primary issue here is to get LILO to boot properly, so focus on the drive where you have LILO stored.

```
bios =
sectors =
heads =
cylinders =
```

If you don't list the number of cylinders, LILO will either get the information it needs from the kernel, or assume the drive has 1,024 cylinders. However, it is best to include this information when possible.

For example, using the numbers obtained in Step 1 you might enter the full statement shown below:

```
disk = /dev/hda
  bios = 0x50
  sectors = 24
  heads = 48
  cylinders = 248
```

9. Save your settings, run LILO (see the section "Running LILO" for assistance), and reboot (see the section "Shutting Down Your System"), seeing if LILO now boots properly. If not, continue to the next step.

10. As part of the disk declaration, you can also declare each partition. Directly after the cylinder listing, begin your partition declaration first by defining which partition you are talking about. For example, the first partition on hda (IDE drive) or sda (SCSI drive) would be

```
partition = /dev/hda1
```

11. The only information remaining is the sector the partition starts on. You can get this data from FDISK or another partitioning program. An example might be

```
start = 2048
```

12. Save your settings, run LILO, and reboot.

Adding A Boot Delay To Allow Time To Select An OS

Add a new line beneath the boot line at the beginning of the /etc/lilo.conf file. The time frame listed is in tenths of a second, so to have a delay of five seconds, you would add the line "delay=50" and then re-run LILO (as discussed in the section "Running LILO").

Setting A Default OS In LILO

Move the image or other section for the OS to be the first among all the image and other settings. If nothing is chosen by the end of the boot delay, LILO boots your computer into whatever OS is listed first. Remember to rerun LILO after making this change or it will not go into effect.

Reinstalling LILO

If you decide you would benefit from a fresh LILO install, first make sure you have emergency boot disks for all of the operating systems on your machine. Then, do the following:

1. Log in as **root**.

2. Delete the current LILO installation per the instructions in the section "Removing LILO."

3. Edit your lilo.conf file to reflect the settings you want, if you feel this is necessary (see the section "Editing LILO" for help).

4. Run LILO to place the information back in your MBR (see the section "Running LILO" for more assistance).

Removing LILO

Removing LILO from your system is as straightforward as logging in as **root** and typing "lilo –u".

Choosing What Services Automatically Start

You could have all installed services automatically start, but that practice creates the following problems:

- Lengthened boot time.
- Lengthened shutdown time.
- Heavy use of RAM.

Ask yourself the following questions when choosing what to start upon bootup:

- Will I use this service at all? For example, it makes no sense to start the lpd service at boot time when you have a Linux box that isn't connected in any way to a printer.
- Will I use this service often enough to warrant paying the prices above?
- Do I understand what the service offers? If not, press F1 for more information about it.

Remember, if you choose not to autostart a service at the beginning, you can change that fact later. If this is purely a practice run, you may want to experiment with starting a bare minimum of services.

Shutting Down Your System

To shut down your system cleanly, use the **shutdown** command. There are a number of variables you can use, depending on what you intend to do. If you want to shut down and shut off the machine, log on as **root** and begin with "shutdown –h".

If you want the machine to reboot when it's finished shutting down, begin with "shutdown –r".

Either of these commands terminates all running processes, including logging out users. However, you must give more information before the shutdown will proceed.

Additional flags and items can be added, depending on what you are doing. If you want to reboot quickly next time, you can shut off file system checking at boot time by adding the **-f** flag. For example, if you wanted to shut down and shut off the machine for some maintenance, you could shut off the next file system check by typing "shutdown –hf".

If you have additional users on your system you may choose to give them some time (in minutes) to tidy up and log out first. In that case, you would add a time remaining count and perhaps a message to the command. For example, to

- Reboot the system.
- Speed up the boot process by turning off file system checking.
- Give users five minutes to clean up and log out.

you would type "shutdown -rft 5 Quick maintenance reboot, back up shortly".

TIP: *If you continually use the -f option, eventually a file system check will be forced by the OS.*

Getting Linux To See More Than One GB Of RAM

Red Hat Linux 6.0 and later by default sees at least 1GB of RAM with no adjustments. If you have more than 1GB—up to 2GB—of RAM, then you can configure Linux to see this extra memory by recompiling the kernel. There is more information on recompiling the kernel in Chapter 17.

Chapter 5

Using Linux

(continued)

In Brief

The Linux programming community has done much to make Linux more GUI-oriented than its earlier versions were. This fact has done much to relieve those who are used to working in a point and click world, and those who like to have flashy colors and backgrounds on their machines. However, you still need to be able to do much of the work in the command-line interface. In fact, it is the capabilities of Linux that shine at the command-line level, giving you control over almost every aspect of what happens on your system. This characteristic is especially true on server machines that function specifically to provide network or Internet services. A GUI only slows these machines down, so knowing how to use command-line tools on them is essential. Fortunately, you have the option of using either aspect, or swapping between the two.

Linux Vs. DOS And NT

Many people find themselves comparing Linux to MS-DOS because of the command-line nature of the operating system. However, this is really a case of comparing apples to oranges. Linux is a multi-tasking network operating system that requires user logins instead of just treating everyone as one person, and the security clearance assigned to the user depends on the settings given to the user when his or her account is created.

DOS, on the other hand, is a uni-tasking system, meaning that it can only do one thing at a time. In addition, it is not developed for networking and cannot handle multiple user accounts; instead, it treats anyone at the console as the same person. Linux is mostly like NT when looking at the Microsoft operating system collection—though Unix has been around for far longer than both.

At a very basic level, one of the primary differences to get used to when moving to Linux is that, in referring to directories, Linux uses forward slashes (/) instead of the back slashes (\) used in DOS and Windows. For example, a valid directory in Linux is /usr/bin. Linux is also very precise in interpreting what you type. The operating system is case sensitive, meaning that typing a capital letter and typing a lowercase letter mean two totally different things. Typing "Vi", for example, is not the same as typing "vi". This is in sharp contrast to the

Windows and DOS world many people come from, because these operating systems are not case-sensitive.

File Permissions And Ownerships

One new thing for the average Macintosh and Windows user to get used to—except for Windows NT users, who are familiar with NT's Access Control List, and those Macintosh users who have set up the file sharing feature—is the concept of files and directories having owners and permissions. Every directory and file has an owner, a group, and a set of permissions. The permissions themselves are broken down into segments that pertain to the owner, the group, and all users.

NOTE: *The Macintosh's file sharing setup is actually structured after the Unix permission setup, so those who are familiar with setting up Mac file security will have an easy time with Linux permissions.*

The permissions for a file are the first item to the left of a long-format (*ls -l*) file listing. These items can be broken down into ten slots.

The Type Bit

The first bit, or character, of the permission set refers to the type of item being referenced, as shown in Figure 5.1. A number of different items can occupy this bit:

- - —Means the object is an ordinary file
- *d*—Means the object is a directory
- *l*—Means the object is a symbolic link (discussed in the section "Creating Links")
- *s*—Means the executable runs as the owner of the file, no matter who invokes it
- *c*—Means the object is a character device driver
- *b*—Means the object is a block device driver

```
drwxrwxrwx
    ↑
Type Bit
```

Figure 5.1   The type bit among the rest of the permission set.

The Triads

The rest of the permission bits are three sets of three, as shown in Figure 5.2. The first three after the type bit are the triad that defines the owner's permissions. The second three are the group's permissions, and the third set of three refers to access for everyone on the system. Already you might see why it is important to set these bits carefully.

Inside The Triad

Reading each triad is an identical process. A triad is made up of three different bits:

- the read (r) bit
- the write (w) bit
- the execution (x) bit

These bits are always displayed in the same order; that is, *rwx*. The way to tell if one of these bits is on or off is whether it shows as a letter or a dash (-). For example, in the permission set *rw-* the read bit is active and the write bit is active, but the execution one is not; therefore, this triad is set to have read and write permissions but no execution permission.

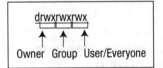

Figure 5.2   The three permission triads: owner, group, and other (the users).

Immediate Solutions

Setting The Date

To set the date, use the **date** command with the format *date -d mm/ dd/yyyy*. For example, type "date -d 01/19/2010".

TIP: *There is far more to the **date** command insofar as formatting options go. Type "man date" for more information.*

Setting The Time

To set the time, use the **date** command with the format *date -s hh:mm:ss*. For example, type "date -s 14:02:00".

TIP: *There is far more to the **time** command insofar as formatting options go. Type "man date" for more information.*

Listing The Contents of Directories

The **ls** command lists the contents of a directory. It is similar in function to the **dir** command in DOS. Figure 5.3 displays the contents of the /root directory obtained with the **ls** command.

```
[root@samurai /root]# ls -s
total 16
    2 figure-5.1.gif    2 lsresults    1 nsmail
   10 figure-5.2.gif    1 mail
[root@samurai /root]#
```

*Figure 5.3   Files in root directory as listed with the **ls** command.*

A number of flags can be used with this command. The most common are shown in Table 5.1. One of the most frequently used flag combinations is *ls -la*, which lists all items within the directory including hidden files. Hidden files are files that begin with a period (.) for their long-format data.

Table 5.1   Flags commonly used with the ls command.

Flag	Purpose
1	Display only one item per line.
a	Include every file, even those normally hidden because they begin with a period (.).
c	Include the last time the file was changed.
l	List the contents in long format, which includes the following data: permissions, number of links for a file or number of files contained in a directory, owner, group, size in bytes, date created, and file name.

TIP: Sometimes there are too many files in a directory to view on a screen. In cases such as /usr/bin, for example, you should use the l more option for ls. Type "ls /usr/bin | more". You will see the screen display the contents of the /usr/bin directory one page at a time.

Changing Directories

To change directories, use the **cd** command. There are two different ways to use **cd**. One involves absolute paths, and the other involves relative paths.

Using **cd** For Absolute Directory Changes

Changing to an absolute directory address is a straightforward process. Use the format *cd /path*. For example, to change to the directory /usr/bin from the directory /var/spool/, type "cd /usr/bin".

TIP: Typing "cd ~" will return you to your home directory. By default the user tom has a home directory of /home/tom. Typing "cd ~" while logged in as tom is the same as typing "cd /home/ tom". Typing the same while logged in as root takes you to /root, which is the root home directory.

Using **cd** For Relative Directory Changes

You can handle relative directory changes in a number of different ways, depending on where you are and where you want to go. If you want to just move up in the directory tree, type "cd ..". For example, this command would move you from /var/spool to /var. To take this one step farther, typing "cd ../.." will take you from /var/spool to the root directory, "/". However, there is no directory above the root directory level, so typing "cd ../../.." from /var/spool takes you to the exact same location as the previous example. The ".." there is self-referential.

If you want to move to a different subdirectory of the same parent directory, say from /etc/rc.d to /etc/skel, you could use the relative path in the format *cd ../skel.*

Finding Out Where You Are

The **pwd** command will tell you the full path of where you are.

Understanding File And Directory Listings

Typing "ls -l" in any directory brings up a long format listing of files and directories. An example line might be:

```
-rw-r--r--  1 linda  user  33191  Aug 15 17:35 text
```

From left to right, you would read this line as:

1. The item is a file and not a directory because the first character is not a *d.*
2. This item is the original and not a link because the first character is not an *l.*
3. The permissions on this file are -rw-r--r--.
4. There is only one version of this file; there are no links.
5. The owner of the file is *linda.*
6. The group the owner is willing to share access with is *user.*
7. This file is 33191 bytes in size.
8. The file was last modified on August the 15th at 5:35 pm.
9. The file's name is *text.*

Changing File And Directory Permissions

There are two different methods used for changing an item's permissions, and they both utilize the **chmod** command in the format **chmod** *perm file.* It's important at this point that you understand how permissions are laid out, so if you are unsure of that, please re-read the discussion of this issue in the beginning of the chapter.

You can change more than one item at a time using wildcards.

Changing By Letters

Changing a file's permissions by using letters may seem straightforward, but it gets complex if the changes are extensive. This method involves a plus (+) or minus (-) to add or subtract permissions to or from the various triads, or all three at once. The triads are *o* for owner, *g* for group, and *u* for user, meaning everyone else.

For example, perhaps the file named "text" starts with full permissions (rwxrwxrwx). This is, in general, a very bad idea. Because this is only a text file, you might first remove the executable permissions by typing "chmod -x text". Now the permissions look like this: rw-rw-rw-. Perhaps you don't want anyone else, either general users or people in your group, to be able to write to it either. Typing "chmod u-w g-w text" changes the permission set to rw-r--r--.

Changing By Numbers

Changing a file's permissions by using numbers may seem complex, but once you understand how to calculate the values it is a relatively simple operation. The values are calculated individually for each triad.

To calculate the numeric value of an item's permissions, do the following:

1. Divide the permission set into its relative triads. For example, a directory named "files" that has full permissions looks like this: drwxrwxrwx. Drop the d to divide the permissions into triads: rwx, rwx, and rwx.

2. Each letter has its own value:
   - An r is a 4.
   - A w is a 2.
   - An x is a 1.

   Use this information to fill in each triad. If the bit is off (a dash), the value is zero. For the example, all of the triads are the same and their values are 421.

3. To get the permission value for the triad, sum the numbers. For example, "4 + 2 + 1 = 7".

4. All three triads are identical, so the permissions for this file are 777.

To change the permissions of an item to a new set, calculate the value for the new set. For example, to change the permissions of the given directory *files* to 644 (rw-r--r--), type "chmod 644 files".

Changing File And Directory Owners

Changing an item's owner is a straightforward process. Use the **chown** command in the format ***chown*** *owner item*. You can change more than one item at a time using wildcards.

Naming Files And Directories

Linux accepts file and directory names up to 256 characters long. The characters, aside from letters and numbers, that can be included in a file name without causing problems are the period (.), the underscore (_), and the dash (-).

Creating Directories

Creating directories is rather straightforward. In DOS, there is the **md** command. Linux's equivalent is the **mkdir** command. To create the directory named "testbed," type "mkdir testbed". You can also utilize absolute and relative paths, as described in the section "Changing Directories."

Creating Links

Linking files is a way of referring to files without making separate copies, so that they appear to be in two places at once. There are two kinds of links: hard and soft (symbolic). Both kinds are created with the **ln** command.

Hard Links

Creating a hard link makes a pointer to the file at the *inode* level. The inode is part of the table that maps file system contents to their descriptors. To create a hard link, use the format *ln source link*. Because hard links point to the same exact location on the file system, deleting the original file does not invalidate the link. The original isn't removed until all of the hard links are deleted.

Symbolic Links

Creating a symbolic link makes a copy of the file at the linked location, with its permissions identical to those of the original. To create a symbolic link, use the format *ln -s source link*. Because symbolic links do not point to the same inode, erasing the original also deactivates all of the links.

TIP: *On the distribution CD-ROMs is an incredibly useful RPM called "symlinks". This program can help you track down all of the dead links—symbolic links that reside on your system but point to programs that no longer exist.*

Removing Directories

There are two different ways to remove directories. One uses the **rmdir** command, which deletes only empty directories. A directory can't contain any files or subdirectories if **rmdir** is to work on it.

A more efficient, but potentially dangerous, command to use—especially as root—is **rm –r**. This command deletes the directory and all of its contents, including any subdirectories. For example, perhaps you created the directory /testbed and filled it with a number of test scripts. The scripts have been modified and those you want to keep have been moved to new locations, while the discards are still there. To remove /testbed plus all of its contents, you would type "rm -r /testbed".

NOTE: *The rm –r command is especially dangerous as root, because you have permissions to remove anything you want. Many a system administrator has wiped out important files at least one time in his or her Linux or Unix career by not using this command carefully enough. This is one reason it is not recommended to work as root unless you absolutely have to.*

Related solution:	Found on page:
Writing A Script	327

5. Using Linux

Copying Files And Directories

Linux uses the **cp** command to copy files. The format used with **cp** is *cp original destination*; or, if you are copying more than one file to the same destination directory, use *cp original1 original2 original3 destination*.

NOTE: *When you copy groups of files, the files' destination must be a directory.*

The **cp** command also accepts the wildcards shown in Table 5.2. For example, the previous command could be shortened to *cp original* destination*.

Table 5.2   Wildcards commonly used with the cp command.

Flag	Purpose
*	Any grouping of unknown characters
[ ]	Any one of the characters or range of characters contained within
?	Any single unknown character

Moving Files And Directories

Moving items is shorthand for copying, then deleting them. This task is accomplished with the **mv** command in the format *mv original destination*. The **mv** command is similar to the **cp** command in that it accepts the wildcards shown in Table 5.2 as well as allowing multiple files to be moved simultaneously into a directory.

TIP: *The **mv** command does not work when transferring files and directories to different partitions. A quick work around is to copy the files and directories, then delete the originals.*

Removing Files

To delete a file, use the **rm** command in the format *rm file*. This command accepts the same wildcards as **mv** and **cp** (shown in Table 5.2) and, also, the -r flag (as discussed in the section "Removing Directories"). The same warnings about doing this as root still apply.

Recognizing Binary Files

Binary files in Linux generally do not have an extension attached to the file name. Typing the command **pico** will run a program with the file name pico. In Windows, typing "notepad" will run a file name called notepad.exe.

One quick way to tell if a file is a binary (program), is if the permissions in the long listing contain an x. The "x" stands for executable, which means a program. Another method involves the **file** command in the format "file *filename*".

Using The **vi** Editor

The **vi** editor is a small but powerful program. Many people consider it awkward at first because of its short, one or two letter commands, but once you're used to using **vi,** editing with it goes very quickly. The reason for this is that the editor is quite a small program, so it has very little memory overhead; also, the commands are brief and are all issued via the keyboard, so there is no need to move between keyboard and mouse.

To edit or create a file with **vi,** type "vi *file name*".

The **vi** editor has three basic modes:

* **Insert mode**—This mode is entered from command mode by pressing the *i* key or using any other command that eventually puts you into this mode, as shown in the list of commands in Table 5.3.

Table 5.3   Common vi commands that bring you to insert mode.

Command	Result
a	Enter insert mode directly after the current cursor position.
A	Enter insert mode at the end of the current line.
i	Enter insert mode directly in front of the cursor position.
I	Enter insert mode at the beginning of the line.
o	Create a new line below the cursor and move to it, entering insert mode.
O	Create a new line above the cursor and move to it, entering insert mode.

- **Command mode**—This is where you enter the one-keystroke commands. Pressing **Esc** moves you into command mode from the other modes.

- **Colon mode**—This mode is entered from the command mode by typing a colon (:). This is where you enter more complex commands, generally involving file manipulation. A list of possible colon mode commands is shown in Table 5.4.

Hand in hand with editing and inserting comes deleting text, as shown in Table 5.5.

There is far more to **vi** than what is covered in this book, which is why there are a number of books on the specific subject of using the **vi** editor. If you want to learn more about it, visit the following Web pages:

- **www.vim.org**
- **www.roxanne.org/faqs/vi_editor/index.html**
- **www.genome.washington.edu/uwgc/unix/howtousevi.htm**
- **www.fisica.uson.mx/UnixDocs/unix4.vi.8-1-94.html**
- **http://physics.ucsc.edu/tutor/vi.html**

Table 5.4   Common vi commands used while in colon mode.

Command	Result
wq	Save and exit the file.
w	Save without exiting.
q	Exit without saving.
q!	Exit without saving changes made.

Table 5.5   Common vi commands used to delete text.

Command	Result
dd	Delete the entire current line.
#dd	Delete the number of lines entered, beginning with the current line.
D	Delete the rest of the line after the cursor.
dw	Delete the current word.

Using The **pico** Editor

The **pico** editor offers an easy-to-use interface and is similar to the DOS **edit** command. Figure 5.4 shows the **pico** interface.

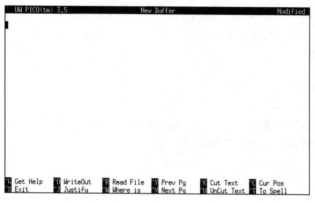

Figure 5.4   The **pico** *text editor.*

To edit or create a file with **pico**, type "pico *file name*". This program offers a menu along the bottom of the screen that lists what choices you have in editing functions. These options are defined in Table 5.6.

Table 5.6   Commonly used functions available in the pico text editor.

Key Combination	Result
Ctrl+c	Displays data about the cursor's current position within the file.
Ctrl+g	Utilizes the help system.
Ctrl+j	Justifies text, or displays it so that it spreads from left to right margin.
Ctrl+k	Cuts selected text and saves it into the buffer.
Ctrl+o	Saves to file.
Ctrl+r	Opens file.
Ctrl+t	Runs a spell-check.
Ctrl+u	Pastes text out of the buffer and onto the current cursor location.
Ctrl+w	Initiates a text search.
Ctrl+x	Exits the pico text editor.

5. Using Linux

Linux is not short on text editors to choose from. Here is a small list of text-based editors for you to experiment with:

- **joe**
- **jed**
- **jpico**
- **elvis**
- **vim**
- **ed**
- **cjoe**

This list does not include the GUI-based text editors, which may be more to your preference. Some of these are:

- **xemacs**
- **cooledit**
- **asedit**
- **aswedit**
- **nedit**
- **xedit**
- **kedit**
- **gedit**
- **gnotepad+**
- **gxedit**
- **xjed**

Some of the text- and GUI-based editors are available with the distributions themselves.

Viewing Text Files Without An Editor

Using a text editor is useful, if not essential, to editing the contents of text files. However, using a text editor only to view the contents of text files is not necessary.

More Or Less

Two useful and almost identical content-viewing programs are **more** and **less**. To view a file with one of these commands, type "more *file* *name*" or "less *file name*". The advantage of using one of these programs to view text files is that if they are longer than one screen, the text pauses in place until you press the appropriate key, and then it continues to scroll.

There are minor differences between the **more** and **less** commands. The **more** command is the more primitive of the two, although it is quite enough for most people. The commands used while utilizing **more** to read text files are displayed in Table 5.7. An advantage to using either of these two commands is that they need not read in the entire text file to display it, so they work equally quickly on any file size.

The **less** command allows for more options when it comes to moving backwards through a file. The commands utilized while using **less** to read a text file are shown in Table 5.8. Some of these are identical to those in **more**, and some are radically different.

The **cat** Command

The **cat** command in its simplest form does in Linux what the **type** command does in DOS. Typing "cat *file name*" dumps the text of the file to the screen. Although this is useful for short files, longer files are better viewed with **more** or **less**.

Table 5.7   Common commands used while reading text files with more.

Key	Result
b	Backs up one line of text.
Enter or f	Advances one line of text.
h	Displays help information.
Spacebar	Advances to the next page of text.
q	Exits the more viewer.

Table 5.8   Common commands used while reading text files with less.

Key	Result
b	Backs up one page of text.
Enter	Advances one line of text.
f	Advances one screenlength of text.
h	Displays help information.
Spacebar	Advances to the next page's worth of text.
q	Exits the less viewer.
y	Scrolls back one line.

5. Using Linux

Outputting Command Results To Text Files

Some Linux commands output screens and screens of data. At such times, it's useful to send the output to a file so that you can read through it at a more reasonable pace, and refer back to it later. This process is called *redirection.*

To redirect the output of a command into a file, use the greater than symbol (>) in the format *command > file*. For example, **ls** > listing.

Creating Aliases

After a while it becomes clear that you type certain complex commands a lot, or tend to almost always use the same flags for a particular command. To reduce the amount of typing you do, you can create *aliases*, or shortcuts that incorporate these specifics into a single short command. To create aliases, edit the .bash_profile file located in your home directory. Regardless of the account you're logged into, you can type "vi ~/.bash_profile".

NOTE: These instructions apply to the bash shell, which is the default shell used in Linux.

Go to the bottom of the file and build your alias statements. They're done in the format *alias name='command'*. For example, to add an alias that changes the **ls** command to be by default "ls -la", the code added would be

```
alias ls='ls -la'
```

To utilize the new aliases, log out of the account and then back in.

TIP: If you want to get really fancy and have a color monitor, try typing: alias 'ls -laF -colorize=yes'.

Locating Files With **find**

The **find** tool is powerful and sometimes a bit confusing. The basic syntax is *find startingpoint flags file name*. The most common version of the command used is *find / -name file*, which starts looking for the file or directory name that contains *file*, beginning with the root directory.

This command is complex and deserves more research over time. Table 5.9 lays out a number of the more commonly used flags and how they are used.

TIP: *An especially useful method of utilizing the* **find** *command is to combine it with the xargs command. The* **xargs** *command allows you to pass the files that find digs up as input to another program. An example of the use of this combination is find /home/bob -name 'Notes' I vi, which will open any files with the text 'Notes' in their names within the* **vi** *editor.*

Table 5.9   Common options used with the **find** *command.*

Flag	Description	Format	Example
atime	Look for files based on the time last accessed. The plus (+) refers to "more than", the minus (-) stands for "less than", and neither refers to "exactly".	find *start* -atime +*days file_name*, find *start* -atime -*days file_name*, or find *start* -atime *days file_name*	find /etc/rc.d -atime -5
ctime	Look for files whose directory listing values changed in the specified time period. The plus (+) refers to "more than", the minus (-) stands for "less than", and neither refers to "exactly".	find *start* -ctime +*days file_name*, find *start* -ctime -*days file_name*, or find *start* -ctime *days file_name*	find / -ctime 2
exec	Look for the files that match the criteria, and then run the given command on them. The { } (note the space between the brackets) denotes where to include the file name found, and the \; is necessary to end the statement.	find *start criteria* -exec *command* { } \;	find /var/log -ctime -4 -exec grep 'http' { }\;
group	Look for files belonging to the group listed.	find *start* -group *groupname*	find / -group staff
iname	Look for files containing the name listed, ignoring case.	find *start* -iname *file_name*	find /home -iname data

(continued)

Table 5.9   Common options used with the find command (continued).

Flag	Description	Format	Example
mtime	Look for files whose contents last changed within the specified time period. The plus (+) refers to "more than", the minus (-) stands for "less than", and neither refers to "exactly".	find *start* -mtime +*days file_name*, find *start* -mtime -*days file_name*, or find *start* -mtime *days file_name*	find /var/log -mtime -10
name	Look for files containing the name listed.	find *start* -name *file name*	find /mnt/cdrom -name '*.rpm'
print	Output the contents of the files and directories which match the find criteria.	find *start criteria* -print	find /home/bob -name 'Notes' -print	more
user	Look for files belonging to the user listed.	find *start* -user *username*	find / -user joy

Finding Files By Searching The Locate Database

The **locate** command is not as powerful as **find**, because it searches a database that contains the contents of the file system at a specific time, not during the actual life of the file system. However, it's faster than **find** and is a great tool if you're searching for a file that isn't newer than the last database update.

The format to use this command is *locate file*.

TIP: *To update the database, type "updatedb". This database is often automatically updated as part of a standard cron job.*

Related solution:	Found on page:
Setting Backups To Run At Specific Times	368

Finding Files Within Your Path Statement

The **whereis** tool is the quickest for a limited set of tasks. This program is used in the format *whereis file*.

The limitation of the **whereis** program is that it only looks in your existing path statement. If the file is not within that path, it won't be found. To see the existing path, type "echo $PATH".

Adding To Your Path Statement

To extend the path statement in the bash shell (the default Linux shell), do the following:

1. Edit the file ~/.bash_profile with a command such as "vi ~/.bash_profile".
2. Locate the line beginning with PATH.
3. Add a colon (:) to the end and add the new path segment.
4. Log out and back in for the new changes to take effect, or re-run the account's profile. For example, if you're using the bash shell, you'd type "source ~/.bash_profile".

Finding Text Within Files

The **grep** tool is used to search for information inside text files. The format for this command is *grep flags expression files*. Some of the possible flags are shown in Table 5.10; *expression* is the text you want to find, and *files* is what to search within.

For example, **grep** might be used to search the file ~/test for the non-case-sensitive text *red*. This command would be typed "grep -i red ~/test".

Table 5.10   Common options used with the grep command.

Flag	Description
-i	Ignore case.
-n	Include the line number along with the line the text is found in.
-v	Print every line that does not match the expression.
-C	Print two lines above and below the text match.

Finding Help

Many of the commands in Linux come with extensive documentation. The quickest way to get assistance is with the **man** (short for manual) command. This will bring up the manual page for the command, if there is one. To open a man page, type "man *command*"; to exit it, press the *q* key.

If the beginning of the man page says that the documentation is no longer maintained and should be viewed with the **texinfo** program instead, use the format **info command** to read the file.

Running Commands In The Background

To run a command without allowing it to take over your login session, use the ampersand (&) in the format *command &*.

Identifying Currently Running Commands

There are two subtly different methods of seeing what's currently running on a machine. One lists the commands currently being run, and the other lists the processes.

Finding Out What Commands You Are Running

To see what commands are running in the background, use the **jobs** feature. Typing this lists any commands you may have in the background, if any. The most important piece of information in this listing is often the job number, which is the number to the far left.

Finding Out What Processes You Are Running

To see what processes you are currently running, use the **ps** command. This listing only reflects what you are doing in the specific virtual terminal it's typed within. Once again, the most important piece of information is the number at the far left, or the Process ID (PID).

Moving Commands To The Background

To move a command you have running on the screen to the back-ground in order to free up that terminal for other uses, use the **bg** (background) command. To move a program into the background, do the following:

1. Type "jobs" to get the job number for the command.

2. Use the key combination Alt+FX, where X is the number of a function key that corresponds to a free terminal.

3. Log into the same account you're using in the other terminal window.

4. Type "bg *job*" to move the job into the background.

TIP: *Often a shortcut for accomplishing this task is to press the key combination Ctrl+Z while in the terminal that is tied up while showing the process results.*

Moving Backgrounded Commands To The Foreground

To move a command you have running in the background to the screen so you can work with it, first obtain the job number, as described in the section "Identifying Currently Running Commands," and then use the **fg** (foreground) program in the format *fg job*.

Canceling Commands In Progress

You can cancel commands within Linux in more than one way. The fast way to cancel a program that's currently running is to press Ctrl+C. This method only works, however, if you have access to the program itself in a virtual terminal.

Another way to stop an errant program is by killing its process. To accomplish this, do the following:

1. Get the process ID by typing "ps", either as the person who ran the program or as **root**. If you're on as **root**, type "ps -aux" to see every process that's running regardless of who owns it.

5. Using Linux

2. Look through the listing and locate the errant process. Usually you can spot it because the program's name is to the far right of the listing.

3. Look to the left of the process line in the **ps** output to get its ID number.

4. Type "kill *ID*" to try to gently stop the process.

5. Use the **ps** command to see if the process is still running.

6. If it isn't running, you're done. If it is running, type "kill -9 *ID*". This command should take care of it, but it tends to be brutal because the process is not cleanly shut down, so it should be avoided when not necessary.

Clearing The Screen

To clear the screen, use the **clear** command.

Running Multiple Commands At Once

You can string multiple commands together by separating them with a semicolon (;). For example, to send the output of the command *ls -la /etc/rc.d/init.d* to the file *systeminits* and then view the file with **more**, use the following:

```
ls -la /etc/rc.d/init.d > systeminits ; more systeminits
```

Another way to group a number of commands together is with a shell script. Shell scripting is discussed in detail in Chapter 18.

Logging Out

To log out of an account, use the **logout** command.

Rebooting The Machine

To reboot a Linux box, type either "reboot" or the more standard "shut-down -r now". If the machine locks up and will not accept typing on the keyboard, sometimes the key combination Ctrl+Alt+Del will work, but most avoid this whenever possible because it may not shut down your system cleanly. However, taking a look in /etc/inittab may show that your Ctrl+Alt+Del is aliased to "shutdown -h now". If this is so, then it can be used safely to shut down the machine and power it off.

Shutting Down The Machine

To shut your machine down so you can turn the power off, use the **halt** command or the more standard *shutdown -h now.*

Chapter 6

X Configuration

In Brief

The base for the GUI in Linux is the X Window System, or often just X. On top of this run a number of window manager programs (covered in detail in Chapter 7), but first it is important to get the basics set up properly. The installation programs for both Red Hat and Caldera allow you to test the GUI configuration before continuing with the install, but sometimes you may decide afterwards that you are unhappy with the results, or you may have changed hardware and need to change the X setup to reflect this. Remember, it is important that with anything involving X you have the exact information for your video card and monitor available to work with when at all possible. If you do not, err on the side of caution.

Configuring X

Setting up X is easier than it used to be, with tools like XF86Setup and Xconfigurator at your disposal. However, this fact does not eliminate the need to potentially have to edit the raw data files themselves.

The following devices must be configured in order for your X sessions to run properly:

- Mouse
- Keyboard
- Monitor
- Video Card
- Color and Graphics Modes

There are three different methods available for configuring X after the installation process is completed: XF86Config, Xconfigurator, and manually.

XF86Config

The XF86Config utility comes with the X server itself and is available with both the Caldera and Red Hat distributions. It is semi-graphical and user-friendly mainly to those who fully understand the hardware and drivers. However, it does contain hardware listings, which save you much time because you don't have to look up specific hardware data.

Xconfigurator

The program Xconfigurator is specifically a Red Hat distribution tool. This is the same routine used during the installation process when configuring X, so it should already be familiar to you.

Manually

Unless you are extremely familiar with the hardware in your machine and especially video and graphics issues, you will probably not want to configure X manually. However, if the other programs fail to give you good results, you might find that fiddling with the files manually will repair the problems.

6. X Configuration

Immediate Solutions

Preparing To Configure X In Caldera

To configure your X settings within Caldera, do the following:

1. Log in as **root**.

2. Type "init 3" to close the GUI and go to command-line only mode if you are currently in the GUI.

3. Log in as **root** once again in one of the virtual terminals.

4. Type "XF86Setup" to run the setup program, which brings you to the screen shown in Figure 6.1.

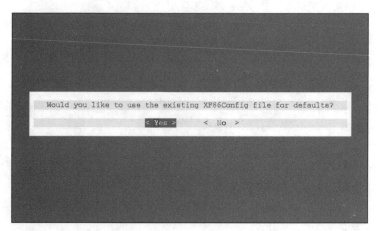

Would you like to use the existing XF86Config file for defaults?

< Yes >   < No >

Figure 6.1   The XF86Setup initial screen.

5. If many of the X settings are already correct, choose Yes to using the current file for the default settings. If you want to make significant changes, choose No. Use the Tab key to move between the options. Press Enter once you have made your selection. This brings you to the next screen, shown in Figure 6.2.

6. Press Enter to go into graphics mode. This mode involves a simple GUI with a basic configuration that will not damage your monitor, as shown in Figure 6.3.

7. Once you are in this mode, you can configure the various X settings. Each of these is covered in its own individual section.

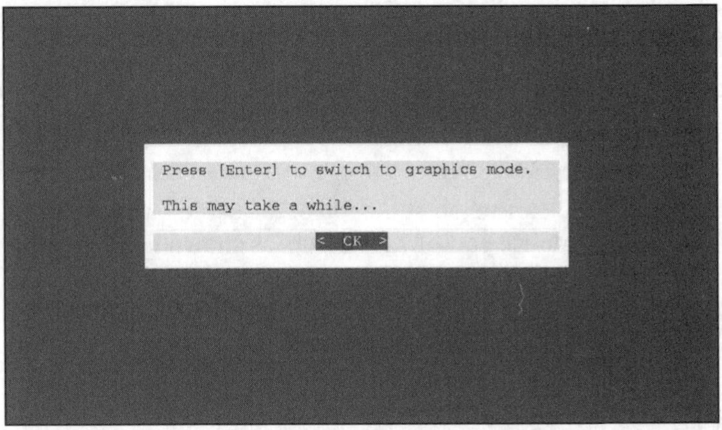

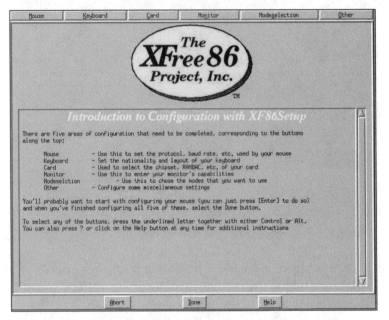

Figure 6.2   The XF86Setup second screen.

Figure 6.3   The XF86Setup program itself.

6. X Configuration

NOTE: *In fact, the XF86Setup program is available in Red Hat Linux as well. If you would rather use it instead of Xconfigurator, that isn't a problem.*

Configuring The Mouse In Caldera

To configure the mouse to work within X in Caldera, do the following:

1. Enter XF86Setup, as described in the section "Preparing To Configure X In Caldera".

2. Click on the Mouse tab at the top of the screen, which brings you to the Mouse part of XF86Setup, as shown in Figure 6.4.

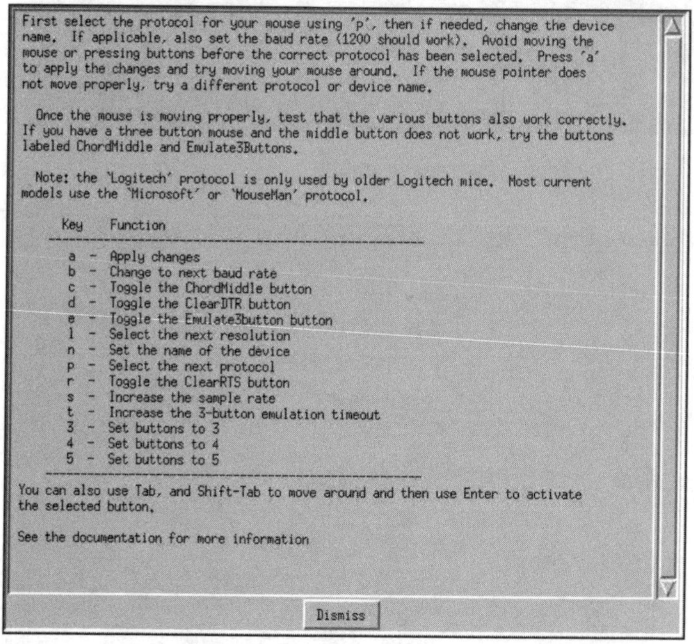

```
First select the protocol for your mouse using 'p', then if needed, change the device
name.  If applicable, also set the baud rate (1200 should work).  Avoid moving the
mouse or pressing buttons before the correct protocol has been selected.  Press 'a'
to apply the changes and try moving your mouse around.  If the mouse pointer does
not move properly, try a different protocol or device name.

Once the mouse is moving properly, test that the various buttons also work correctly.
If you have a three button mouse and the middle button does not work, try the buttons
labeled ChordMiddle and Emulate3Buttons.

Note: the 'Logitech' protocol is only used by older Logitech mice.  Most current
models use the 'Microsoft' or 'MouseMan' protocol.

Key    Function
----------------------------------------------------
  a  -  Apply changes
  b  -  Change to next baud rate
  c  -  Toggle the ChordMiddle button
  d  -  Toggle the ClearDTR button
  e  -  Toggle the Emulate3button button
  l  -  Select the next resolution
  n  -  Set the name of the device
  p  -  Select the next protocol
  r  -  Toggle the ClearRTS button
  s  -  Increase the sample rate
  t  -  Increase the 3-button emulation timeout
  3  -  Set buttons to 3
  4  -  Set buttons to 4
  5  -  Set buttons to 5
----------------------------------------------------
You can also use Tab, and Shift-Tab to move around and then use Enter to activate
the selected button.

See the documentation for more information
```

Dismiss

Figure 6.4   The XF86Setup Mouse help screen.

3. Thoroughly read the instructions that open, then click the Dismiss button to get them out of the way and to get into the Mouse setup part of the tool, as shown in Figure 6.5. After doing this, immediately let go of the mouse and do not touch it until the instructions say it is all right.

TIP: Typing a question mark (?) returns you to this instruction dialog box at any time while in XF86Setup.

---

4. If you are unsure of what device to configure your mouse for, try the default; if that fails, try ttyS1. To move the cursor to the device menu, press the n key. If you don't need to set the device, then proceed to Step 6.

6. X Configuration

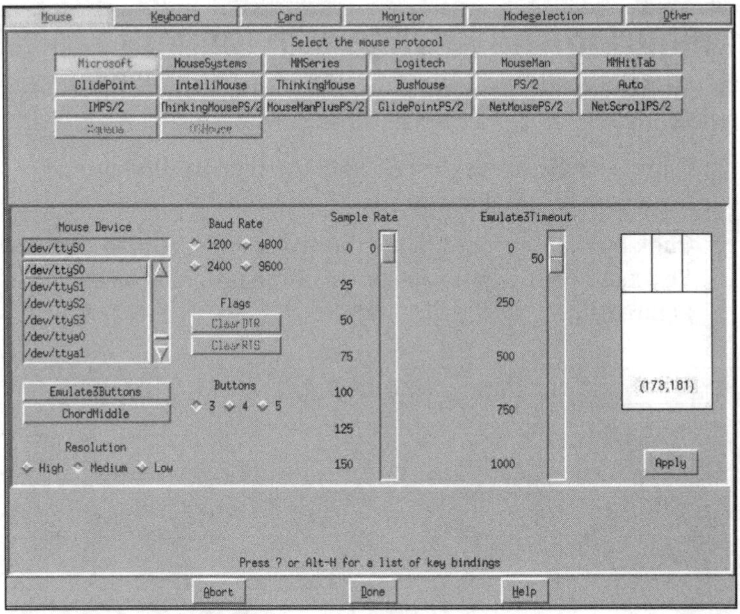

Figure 6.5   The XF86Setup Mouse setup screen.

5. Use the up and down arrow keys to move through the device menu. Stop on the item you want to choose and press Enter.

6. If you need to set the mouse type, press the p key to declare that you want to set the mouse protocol.

7. Use the arrow keys to move between the mouse protocol options at the top of the screen. If you want to try one, press Enter while the black border is on the protocol to select it. Then press the a key to apply the protocol.

8. Move the mouse and test that it is working correctly. If it isn't, return to Step 6 and try another protocol.

9. If there are other items you want to configure, utilize the help screen (type "?" to reach it).

10. Click Done when you are finished if you want to save the changes, or Abort if you don't want to save them.

11. If you have further changes to make, do not click the OK button in the middle of the screen! Instead, proceed to the section for the next set of changes you want to make. If you are finished, click OK to test the configuration.

6. X Configuration

Configuring The Keyboard In Caldera

To configure the keyboard to work within X in Caldera, do the following:

1. Enter XF86Setup, as described in the section "Preparing To Configure X In Caldera."

2. Click on the Keyboard tab at the top of the screen to open the Keyboard configuration segment of the program, as shown in Figure 6.6.

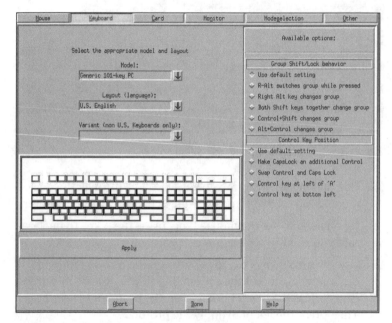

Figure 6.6   The XF86Setup Keyboard setup screen.

3. To set the keyboard model type, click the arrow next to the Model setting.

4. To set the layout for another language, click the arrow next to the Layout setting.

5. To set defaults for special keys and combinations, click on the options on the right. The button that is indented and a light blue is the option that's selected.

6. Click the Apply button underneath the keyboard to activate the changes.

7. Click Done when you are finished if you want to save the changes, or Abort if you don't want to save them.

8. If you have further changes to make, do not click the OK button in the middle of the screen! Instead, proceed to the section for the next set of changes you want to make. If you are finished, click OK to test the configuration.

Configuring The Video Card In Caldera

To configure the video card to work within X in Caldera, do the following:

1. Enter XF86Setup, as described in the section "Preparing To Configure X In Caldera."

2. Click on the Card tab at the top of the screen to get to the Card setup part of the program, as shown in Figure 6.7.

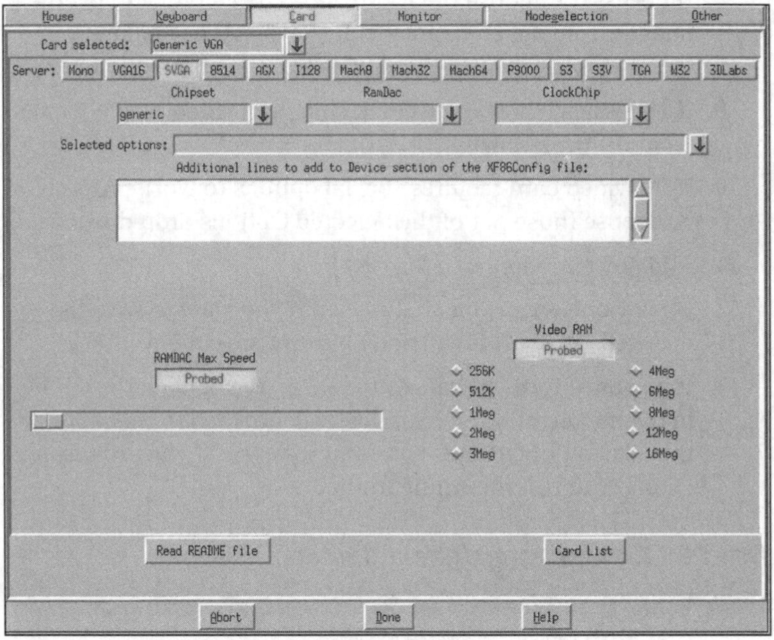

Figure 6.7   The XF86Setup Card setup screen.

3. Drag the slider bar through the list of cards and choose the video card in your machine. It is important to make an accurate choice. If you can't find the card in the list anywhere, choose "Unsupported VGA Compatible."

6. X Configuration

4. Click the Read README file button and read through the details listed in the dialog box that comes up. When finished, click the Dismiss button.

5. If you ran into problems with the video card settings from the initial install, check the Detailed Setup button. If not, skip to Step 12.

6. If necessary, choose the X server you want to use. The options are detailed in Table 6.1.

7. If necessary, choose the chipset your video card is made with from the drop-down list. To determine what type of chipset is on the video card, look in the manuals, in the manufacturer's Web site, or at the card itself.

TIP: *All hardware items that are not explicitly set up by hand will be probed automatically.*

---

8. If necessary, choose the RAMDAC—the chip that converts images from digital to analog, RAM Digital to Analog Converter—your video card contains from the drop-down list.

9. If necessary, choose the clock chip your video card contains from the drop-down list.

10. If the video card requires special options to work properly with X, choose those out of the Selected Options drop-down list box.

11. Add any extra items to the text box.

12. Click Done when you are finished if you want to save the changes, or Abort if you don't want to save them.

13. If you have further changes to make, do not click the OK button in the middle of the screen! Instead, proceed to the section for the next set of changes you want to make. If you are finished, click OK to test the configuration.

Table 6.1   The X servers available in XF86Setup.

Server	Purpose
Mono	Black and white.
VGA16	16 colors, or 4 bit color.
VGA32	32 colors, or 5 bit color.
SVGA, 8514, AGX, I128, Mach8, Mach32, Mach64, P9000, S3, S3V, TGA, W32, 3DLabs	All accelerated video cards.

(sidebar) 6. X Configuration

Configuring The Monitor In Caldera

To configure the monitor to work within X in Caldera, do the following:

1. Enter XF86Setup, as described in the section "Preparing To Configure X In Caldera."

2. Click on the Monitor tab at the top of the screen to enter the Monitor configuration part of the program, as shown in Figure 6.8.

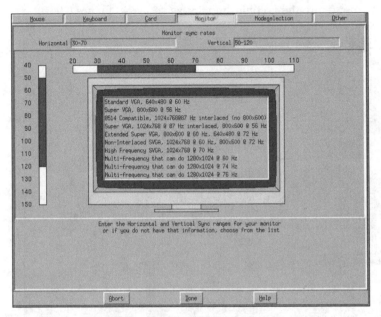

Figure 6.8   The XF86Setup Monitor setup screen.

3. Either enter the vertical and horizontal sync rate ranges by hand, or click on the setting that falls within the proper range.

4. Click Done when you are finished if you want to save the changes, or Abort if you don't want to save them.

5. If you have further changes to make, do not click the OK button in the middle of the screen! Instead, proceed to the section for the next set of changes you want to make. If you are finished, click OK to test the configuration.

Configuring The Graphics Mode And Color Settings In Caldera

To configure the graphics mode and colors settings within X in Caldera, do the following:

1. Enter XF86Setup, as described in the section "Preparing To Configure X In Caldera."

2. Click on the Modeselection tab at the top of the screen to configure the graphics modes, as shown in Figure 6.9.

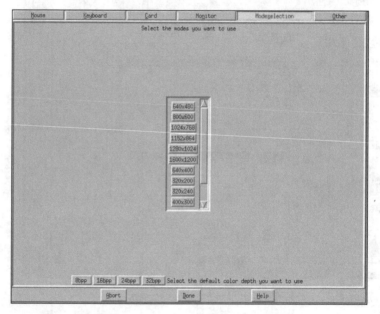

Figure 6.9   The XF86Setup Mode selection setup screen.

3. Click the graphics mode you want to use, keeping the capabilities of your monitor and video card in mind.

4. Click the number of bits per pixel you want to use:

    • The 8bbp setting is 256 colors.

    • The 16bbp setting is approximately 65,000 colors.

    • The 24bbp setting is approximately 17 million colors.

    • The 32bbp setting is approximately 4.2 billion colors.

5. Click Done when you are finished if you want to save the changes, or Abort if you don't want to save them.

6. If you have further changes to make, do not click the OK button in the middle of the screen! Instead, proceed to the section for the next set of changes you want to make. If you are finished, click OK to test the configuration.

Configuring The X Server Itself In Caldera

To tweak X server settings in Caldera, do the following:

1. Enter XF86Setup, as described in the section "Preparing To Configure X In Caldera."

2. Click on the Other tab at the top of the screen to configure the server itself, as shown in Figure 6.10.

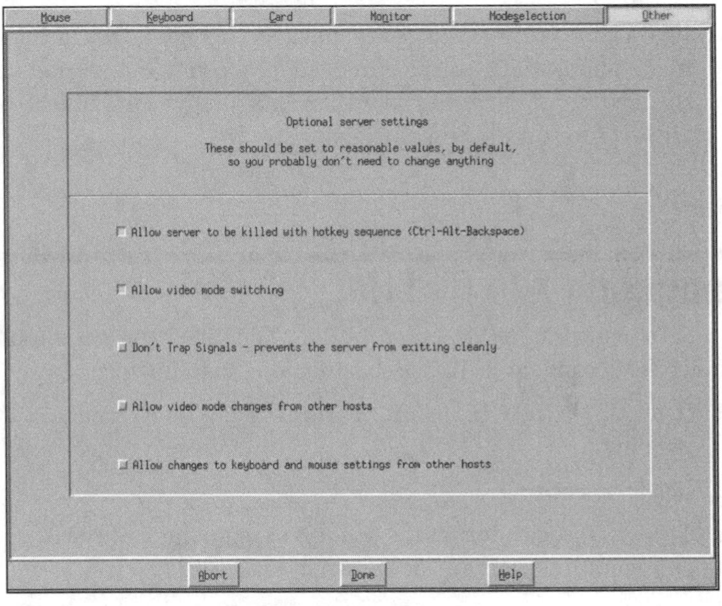

Figure 6.10   The XF86Setup Other setup screen.

3. If you don't want to allow the server to be killed by typing the key combination Ctrl+Alt+Backspace, then deselect this option. However, this action is not recommended. Doing so removes the possibility that you could get out without using the power switch on the machine if the X server crashes.

4. If you don't want to allow video mode switching, deselect this option. Doing so prevents using key combinations to change screen resolution.

5. If you want to avoid trapping signals, select this option. When this setting is turned on, it prevents X from hiding its error signals from you. Most of the time you probably don't want to see them.

6. If you want to allow video mode changes from other hosts, select this option. Doing so allows users to change video modes on remote machines. Sometimes this feature can be useful if you are using a multiple-monitor X session, but in general it is not necessary.

7. If you want to allow mouse and keyboard setting changes from other hosts, select this option. This item is useful for fixing problems remotely with a machine's X settings, but in general it is not necessary.

8. Click Done when you are finished if you want to save the changes, or Abort if you don't want to save them.

9. If you have further changes to make, do not click the OK button in the middle of the screen! Instead, proceed to the section for the next set of changes you want to make. If you are finished, click OK to test the configuration.

Configuring X In Red Hat

If you're using the Red Hat distribution, Xconfigurator is the tool of choice for setting up X. To use this tool, do the following:

1. If you are in the GUI, exit it by typing "init 3" in a terminal window.

2. Log in as **root**.

3. Type "Xconfigurator" at the prompt to open the Red Hat X configuration program, as shown in Figure 6.11

4. Read the initial screen, then press Enter to proceed to the video card selection screen, as shown in Figure 6.12.

5. Choose your video card from those listed. If yours isn't included, go to the bottom of the list and choose the "Unsupported VGA Compatible" option. You will have to fill in the card's statistics manually, so have them available. Press Enter when you are ready to proceed to the monitor selection screen, as shown in Figure 6.13.

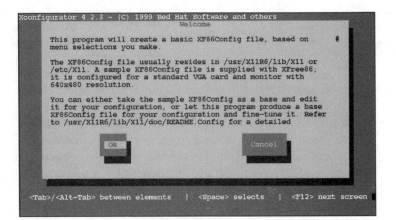

Figure 6.11   The Xconfigurator initial screen.

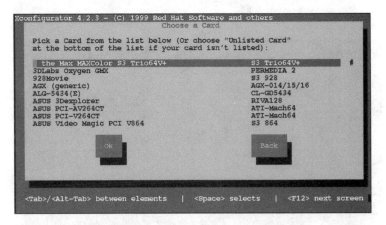

Figure 6.12   The Xconfigurator video card selection screen.

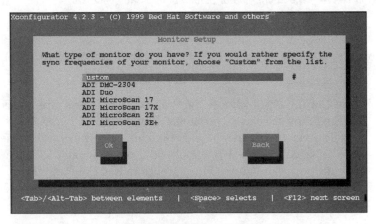

Figure 6.13   The Xconfigurator monitor selection screen.

TIP: *Type the first letter of the manufacturer's name to jump down to the correct alphabetical segment of the card list. For example, if your card is made by Trident, type "T" and you will be in the Ts.*

6. Choose your monitor from those listed. If yours isn't included, go to the top of the list and choose the "Custom" option. You will have to fill in the monitor's statistics manually, so have them ready. It is important not to guess too high, or damage to your equipment can result. Press Enter when you are ready to continue, then refer to the section "Setting Up A Custom Monitor In Red Hat." When you have finished the custom configuration, return here to Step 7.

   If your monitor is included in the list, choose it and press Enter to go to the graphics configuration probe query screen, as shown in Figure 6.14.

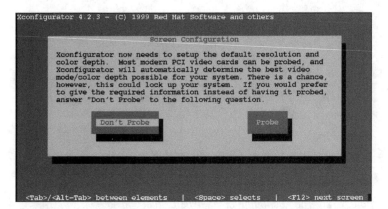

Figure 6.14   The Xconfigurator Screen Configuration screen.

TIP: *Type the first letter of the manufacturer's name to jump down to the correct alphabetical segment of the monitor list. For example, if your monitor is made by Sony, type "S" and you will be in the Ss.*

7. Use the Tab key to choose the Probe option, unless probing the video hardware caused problems during the initial install or while previously trying to run Xconfigurator. If you don't choose to probe, you will have to choose your options manually—see the section "Configuring Video Modes In Red Hat," and then return here to Step 10. After choosing Probe, press Enter to get to the confirmation screen, as shown in Figure 6.15.

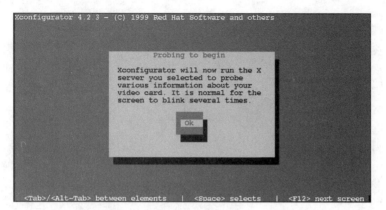

Figure 6.15   The Xconfigurator probe confirmation screen.

8. When you're ready to allow the probe to begin, press Enter. The screen will flicker and flash as the hardware is tested. If you're using any form of monitor switchbox, don't switch away from the Red Hat machine at this stage. When the probe is complete, it will offer you a chance to select a set of default graphics settings, as shown in Figure 6.16.

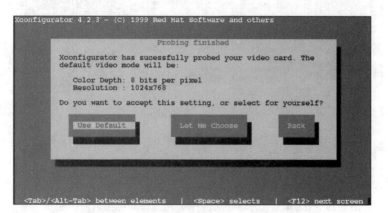

Figure 6.16   The Xconfigurator default graphics query screen.

9. Choose the Default setting when offered if you want to do so, then press Enter. If you would rather choose which mode(s) you want to use, Tab to "Let Me Choose" and press Enter to go to the mode selection screen, shown in Figure 6.17.

To select one or more of the video modes, all of which will be available when you are in the GUI, do the following:

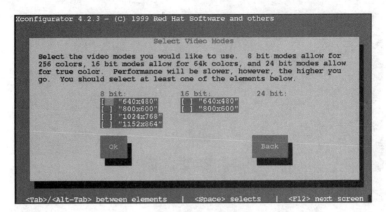

Figure 6.17   The Xconfigurator mode selection screen.

- Use the up and down arrow keys to move between the modes.
- Press the Tab key to move from bit setting to bit setting.
- Tab to the OK button when finished and press Enter to go to the test confirmation screen, shown in Figure 6.18.

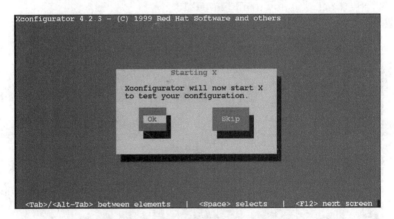

Figure 6.18   The Xconfigurator X server test confirmation screen.

10. When ready to test the X server, press Enter.

11. The machine changes to X mode and displays a dialog box saying that if you can read the text within it, click OK. Do so.

12. If you want Red Hat to automatically boot into the GUI, click OK in the next dialog box. If not, click No.

13. Read any subsequent dialog boxes. Click OK. The program exits and returns you to the command line.

Setting Up A Custom Monitor In Red Hat

If during the X server setup in Red Hat you don't find your monitor in the listing, you have to choose the "Custom" option from the list. To configure a custom monitor, do the following:

1. Read carefully the instructions in the initial custom configuration screen shown in Figure 6.19, then press Enter to reach the custom monitor horizontal sync range screen shown in Figure 6.20.

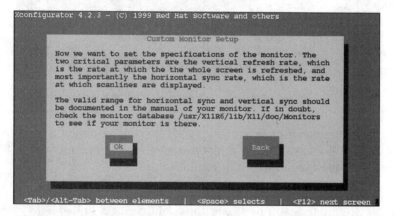

Figure 6.19   The Xconfigurator custom monitor configuration initial screen.

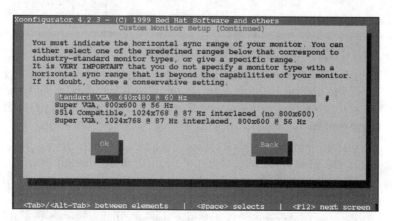

Figure 6.20   The Xconfigurator custom monitor horizontal sync screen.

2. Determine the horizontal sync range for your monitor. It is incredibly important that this value be, if not accurate, guessed on the low side. Physical damage to your equipment is possible if you place it too high.

3. Select the appropriate range, then press Enter to go to the vertical sync configuration screen shown in Figure 6.21.

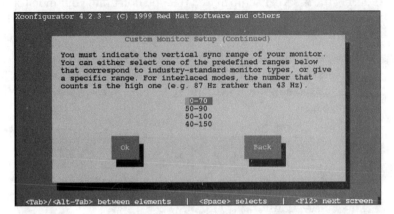

Figure 6.21   The Xconfigurator custom monitor vertical sync screen.

4. Determine the vertical sync range for your monitor. Once again, it is better to guess low if you are not sure, in order to avoid physical damage to your equipment.

5. Select the appropriate range, then press Enter.

6. Return to Step 7 of the section "Configuring X In Red Hat."

Configuring Video Modes In Red Hat

If during the X server setup in Red Hat you chose not to probe because the autoprobe hung your machine, or if you don't want to use the autoprobe feature for some other reason, you will need to set the video modes manually. To set these modes, do the following:

1. Determine how much RAM is on the video card in your machine. This value may be in the manual, on the manufacturer's Web site, or on the invoice from when you purchased the machine if you purchased more than the default value.

2. Choose the amount in the Video Memory dialog box shown in Figure 6.22, then press Enter to go to the Clockchip configuration screen shown in Figure 6.23.

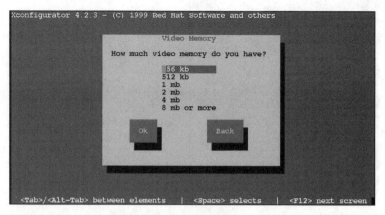

Figure 6.22   The Xconfigurator VRAM screen.

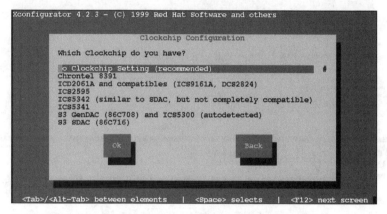

Figure 6.23   The Xconfigurator Clockchip configuration screen.

3. Determine which clock chip is on the video card. This chip may be listed in the manual or on the manufacturer's Web site. If the autodetection feature already found a clock chip, "(auto-detected)" will appear after the particular entry. One way to test whether this is the item that locked up your system during the X server test—if this is what happened to cause you to want to configure the modes manually—is to choose a different chip, or choose "No Clockchip Setting," and see if the X server is able to test properly afterwards.

4. Choose the chip you believe is there, then press Enter to go to the video modes screen shown in Figure 6.24.

5. Select one or more of the video modes presented. Use the up and down arrow keys to move between the modes within each bit setting. Press the Tab key to move from bit setting to bit

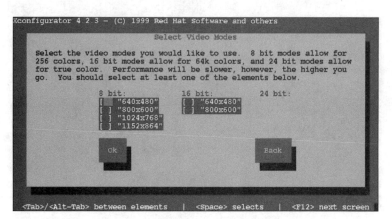

Figure 6.24   The Xconfigurator video modes screen.

setting. All of the modes you choose will be available to you while you are in the GUI.

6. Tab to the OK button and press Enter.

7. Return to Step 10 of the section "Configuring Red Hat."

Adjusting X Manually

You may need to adjust X settings manually rather than relying on any of the tools provided. If this is the case, do the following:

1. The file you need to edit is *XF86Config*. To find this file, type "locate XF86Config". If the locate database is not built for some reason, you can also use *find / -name 'XF86Config'*. This command will just take longer because it's searching the live file system.

2. Open the file with a command such as "vi *path*/XF86Config".

3. This file is heavily commented—comments are lines or ends of lines that begin with the hash mark (#). Because it is most likely that what you need to edit is either the video card or monitor settings, search down through the file until you find sections with one of the following headers:

    • Monitor refers to the display itself.

    • Graphics Device refers to the video card.

    • Screen refers to the graphics modes and color depths.

4. See the section "Configuring The Monitor Manually," "Configuring The Video Card Manually," or "Configuring The Graphics Modes Manually" for details on how to understand the
sections and how to safely edit them.

Related solution:	Found on page:
Using The **vi** Editor	91

Configuring The Monitor Manually

To configure or tweak your monitor settings manually, first follow
the instructions in the section "Adjusting X Manually" and then do
the following:

1. Search for the text:

```
#  ************************************************************
#  Monitor section
#  ************************************************************
```

To do this search within **vi,** type "/Monitor section" and then
press Enter.

2. The section that contains the monitor labels is:

```
Identifier    "MAG DX700T"
VendorName    "Unknown"
ModelName     "Unknown"
```

These three items can be changed safely in the following ways,
so long as you are sure not to erase the quotes:

- To assign a new label to the monitor itself, change the text in
the Identifier tag.

- To set the name of the manufacturer, change the text in the
VendorName tag.

- To set the model of your monitor, change the text for the
ModelName tag.

3. To change the horizontal sync range for your monitor, change
the value of HorizSync. This value can either be a range of
numbers out to one decimal place (for example, "40.5-85.3") or
a series of numbers out to one decimal place (for example,

6. X Configuration

"40.5, 50.5, 60.5, 70"). In this case, there are no quotes in the code, so it might look like:

```
HorizSync 40.5-85.3
```

WARNING!   *Be careful to use the exact range listed in your monitor manual or manufacturer's Web site, or guess on the low side. You can damage your equipment if you place the value too high for it to handle.*

4. To change the vertical refresh rate for your monitor, change the value of VertRefresh. This value is in the same format as HorizSynch, and the same warnings apply.

5. To define how the monitor will behave in particular graphics modes, set the Mode or ModeLine sections. These two variables define exactly the same terms, but are formatted differently. A Mode statement looks like:

```
Mode "1024x768i"
  DotClock 45
  HTimings 1024 1048 1208 1264
  VTimings 768 776 784 817
  Flags "Interlace"
EndMode
```

The values in this statement are:

- The value associated with Mode itself is the name of the mode. This name is usually the resolution of the monitor setting being assigned in the format *(horizontal pixels)×(vertical pixels)*, with an i added on the end if the monitor is interlaced. An interlaced monitor draws the entire screen picture in two passes; non-interlaced is preferred because it draws the screen in one pass.

- The DotClock item is a value in MHz that expresses how fast a single pixel can be displayed on the monitor. To calculate this value approximately, use this formula: (horizontal pixels)×1.28x(horizontal refresh rate).

- The HTimings term consists of four different values. The first is the number of pixels displayed horizontally (in the example above, 1024). The second is the location of the exact dot where the horizontal image begins, and the third is where it ends. The last value is the total number of horizontal pixels in existence. These values are often documented in the monitor manuals.

- The VTimings term is laid out the same way as the horizontal timings, except that it refers to the vertical statistics for the monitor.

- The Flags term calls for any flags necessary to tell the X server specific things about your display. Interlace is the one most commonly used.

A ModeLine statement, however, has all this information on a single line of text. So the data given in the previous Mode statement translates to the following ModeLine statement:

```
ModeLine "1024x768i" 45 1024 1048 1208 1264 768 776 784 817
Interlace
```

There is usually a long series of these statements, each defining behavior for a particular mode type.

6. Save and exit the file.

7. Type "startx" to test the new configuration.

Configuring The Video Card Manually

To configure or tweak your video card settings manually, first follow the instructions in the section "Adjusting X Manually" and then do the following:

1. Search for the text:

```
# *********************************************************
# Graphics device section
# *********************************************************
```

To do this search within **vi,** type "/Graphics device section" and then press Enter.

2. The section that contains the card's labels is:

```
Section "Device"
   Identifier "Generic VGA"
   VendorName "Unknown"
   BoardName "Unknown"
   Chipset "generic"
   VideoRam 1024
EndSection
```

These three items can be changed safely, so long as you are sure not to erase the quotes:

- To assign a new label to the card itself, change the text in the Identifier tag.
- To set the name of the manufacturer, change the text in the VendorName tag.
- To set an additional name that may be used for the particular graphics card, change the text in the BoardName tag.
- To set the types of chips used in the graphics card, change the text in the Chipset tag.
- To set the amount of RAM you have on your video card, change the text next to VideoRam.

3. Save and close the file.

4. Type "startx" to test the new configuration.

Configuring The Graphics Modes Manually

To configure or tweak your graphics modes manually, first follow the instructions in the section "Adjusting X Manually" and then do the following:

1. Search for the text:

```
# ************************************************************
# Screen sections
# ************************************************************
```

To do this search within **vi,** type "/Screen sections" and then press Enter.

2. There is often more than one screen definition in the X configuration file. The general format for each section is:

```
Section "Screen"
  settings
EndSection
```

To begin with, choose one section.

3. The section that contains the screen setting labels looks like this:

```
Driver "svga"
Device "My Video Card"
Monitor "MAG DX700T"
```

These three items can be changed safely, so long as you are sure not to erase the quotes:

- The Driver data should be kept to very specific entries. Options available are Accel (Accelerated video), Mono, SVGA, VGA2, and VGA16.
- To change the label for the device itself, change the text in the Device tag.
- To change the listing for your monitor brand and model, change the information in the Monitor tag.

4. Within the Screen sections are specific subsections that define the colors and resolution for the specific video modes being configured to use with the driver. These sections look like this:

```
Subsection "Display"
    Depth 8
    Modes "1024x768" "1152x864"
    ViewPort 0 0
EndSubsection
```

TIP: *Notice a trend here. Each Screen section is for a specific level of driver. Each subsection is for a specific color depth available in that driver, and the modes available at that color depth.*

Locate or create a subsection to work with.

5. The color depth is the critical component, because your card and monitor together can only support particular graphics modes with particular color depths. Determine how much video RAM (VRAM) is on the graphics card, and look in the manual to see what it supports with that amount of VRAM. Then look in the monitor manual and determine what color depths it supports for what graphics modes.

6. Set the color depth to what you've chosen.

7. In the Modes line, list in quotes the modes you want to use at that color depth.

8. The ViewPort setting determines where in the virtual desktop the X session starts. It is often good to leave it at the default of 0 0.

9. Edit the other subsections.

6. X Configuration

10. Edit the other sections.

11. Save and exit the file.

12. Type "startx" to test the GUI.

Entering the GUI

Type "startX" to enter the GUI. If you're using Caldera, they also have a **KDE** command that does the same thing.

Chapter 7

Window Managers And Desktop Environments

In Brief

Those who prefer a colorful, point-and-click environment will like this chapter. While the X server provides the engine, so to speak, for graphical utilities to run on top of, the window managers provide the environment's look, feel, and functionality. This chapter takes you on a tour through which window managers are available and covers some basics on how to use them.

The Window Managers

Window managers provide you with interfaces in navigating the X environment. These window managers have their own tool boxes, their own way of handling the mouse to execute and access commands, their own program menus, and their own unique layouts and flavors.

You can run GUI- and non-GUI-based programs within a window manager, so there is no right or wrong choice. Choosing a manager is mostly an issue of what style you prefer and how much stability you require, because some of them are more robust than others.

Here is a partial list of the many window managers out there:

- fvwm
- fvwm2
- fvwm95
- mwm
- twm
- ctwm
- qvwm
- afterstep
- enlightenment
- blackbox

The list continues to grow; see the section "Finding Window Managers" for where to find those listed and, also, some desktop themes.

Desktop Environments

Desktop environments complete the full Linux GUI picture. While the X server provides the background engine for building and running the GUI and the window managers provide the environment for handling the windows themselves (such as title and scroll bars), the desktop environment has a set of tools and applications. Many of these tools and programs enable you to control the settings of your environment (screensavers, fonts, icons, window sizes, and so on) as well as manage your machine (e.g., GUI-based mount, Zip, archive, and network management tools). The larger this set of tools and the more complex the desktop environment, the more RAM is needed, so keep this in mind when you choose between them. The two most talked-about desktop environments for X are KDE and Gnome.

Both KDE and Gnome have matured into reliable, stable desktop environments that have large suites of custom applications.

The KDE Environment

KDE is the default desktop environment in Caldera and is included with Red Hat as well. This is a commercial environment that has been around for some time, long enough to reach a point of stability and maturity that attracts a lot of its fans. However, those who want to develop software for this environment have to purchase the professional version of the libraries. Once you are in the GUI in Caldera, the desktop environment looks like what is shown in Figure 7.1.

The reason KDE has now been included on the Red Hat CD-ROMs is that KDE has made the free libraries—those that are available to the public—open source. For more on this environment, see the KDE home page at **www.kde.org**.

The Gnome Environment

Gnome is the default desktop environment in Red Hat. It is a free environment in that it is covered by the GNU Public License (GPL) and is open source. The libraries are freely available for developers. However, this environment is slightly less mature than KDE, so it is not yet as stable. Once you are in Gnome's desktop environment in Red Hat Linux, the default screen looks like what is displayed in Figure 7.2.

For more on this environment, visit the Gnome home page at **www.gnome.org**.

7. Window Managers And Desktop Environments

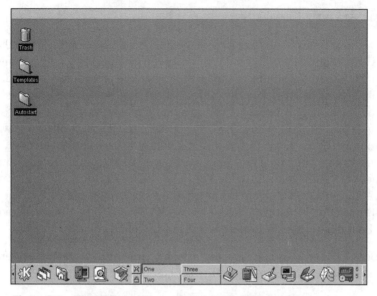

Figure 7.1   The KDE desktop environment in Caldera Linux.

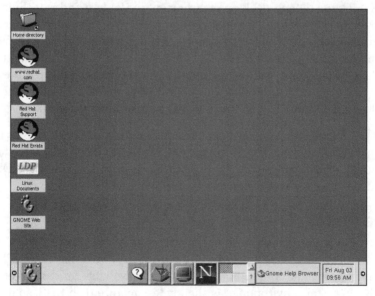

Figure 7.2   The Gnome desktop environment in Red Hat Linux.

Immediate Solutions

Finding Window Managers

Check out the Web site **www.themes.org** for a great selection of window managers and desktop themes.

Accessing Programs In Gnome

To pull up the list of programs Gnome offers, left-click on the big foot in the lower left-hand corner. Doing so will display something similar to Figure 7.3.

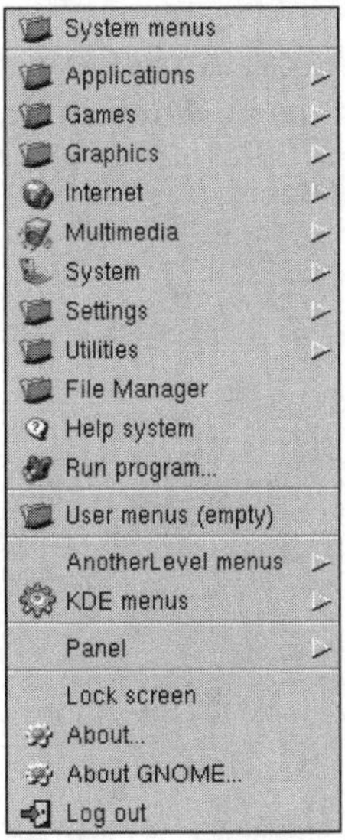

Figure 7.3   Pulling up Gnome's program menu.

This program menu contains a number of tools and utilities, which are outlined in Table 7.1.

Table 7.1   GNOME's program menus.

Menu	Contains
Applications	Spreadsheet, calendar, text editors
Games	Games designed for GNOME
Graphics	Image viewers and editors
Internet	Web browsers, FTP clients, IRC clients
Multimedia	Mp3, CD-ROM, wav players, music mixers, volume settings
System	Disk management, control panel
Settings	Tools to configure GNOME's layout
Utilities	Terminals, system information, disk and file utilities
AnotherLevel Menus	Menu of programs and utilities used by the fvwm95 window manager
KDE Menus	Menu of programs and utilities used by the KDE desktop manager

To open one of the programs, do the following:

1. Click the menu item corresponding to the program. For example, click Games to open the Games submenu shown in Figure 7.4.

Figure 7.4   The Gnome Games submenu in Red Hat Linux.

NOTE: The contents of the submenus will depend on what packages you installed.

2. Click the submenu program you want to run, or the next submenu item, if there is one.

3. Continue until you get to the program you want to run.

Related solution:	Found on page:
Entering The GUI	132

Retracting The Task Bar In Gnome

To get the task bar out of the way so you can use your entire screen, click the left-facing arrow to the left side of the task bar. The task bar will slide off the screen to the left and the screen will only display the arrow, as shown in Figure 7.5. Click this arrow to pull the task bar back out.

Figure 7.5   The Gnome task bar slider retrieval tab in Red Hat Linux.

Using The Gnome Help System

The Gnome Help system is a Web-like browser that allows you to move through the sum total of Help items installed on your Linux box. To use this system, do the following:

1. Click the Help icon on the task bar, as shown in Figure 7.6.

Figure 7.6   The Gnome Help icon in Red Hat Linux.

The Gnome Help browser opens, as shown in Figure 7.7.

2. Click on one of the following options at the bottom:

- **GNOME User's Guide**—For an outline of the Help options for how to use the desktop environment.

- **Man Pages**—For the sum total of the manual pages available on your system.

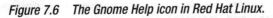

TIP: These are the same man pages you access by typing "man command" at the command prompt.

7. Window Managers And Desktop Environments

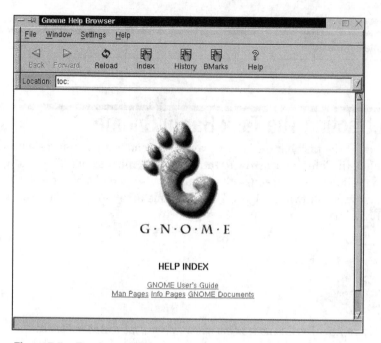

Figure 7.7   The Gnome Help browser in Red Hat Linux.

- **Info Pages**—For the *texinfo* manual pages available on your system. This is the format that the rest of the man page system is migrating to.

  - **GNOME Documents**—For instructions on using Gnome-specific applications.

3. When finished, click File in the menu bar, then Exit in the File menu, to close the browser.

Using The Gnome Control Panel

Gnome also includes a Control Panel that has icons that open a number of useful configuration tools. To open the Control Panel, do the following:

1. Click the foot icon—the picture of the foot—on the task bar to open the menus.

2. Click the System submenu menu.

3. Click Control Panel in the System submenu. The Gnome Control Panel opens, as shown in Figure 7.8.

Figure 7.8   The Gnome Control Panel in Red Hat Linux.

4. Click one of the icons in the Control Panel to open the tool you want to use. Icons for the following services are included, listed in order from top to bottom:

   • A runlevel editor, which allows you to graphically edit which daemons are started and stopped while entering and exiting runlevels.

   • A time and date editor that lets you set the system clock.

   • The printer configuration tool.

   • The network configuration tool.

   • The modem configuration tool, which helps you set up to connect to the Internet.

   • A kernel daemon configuration tool, which allows you to reconfigure the kernel within a certain extent, loading and unloading modules.

   • A Help search tool.

   • The Linuxconf tool, which is shown in Figure 7.9. This is an incredibly useful tool that allows you to graphically manage many of your system's settings and, also, user settings.

7. Window Managers And Desktop Environments

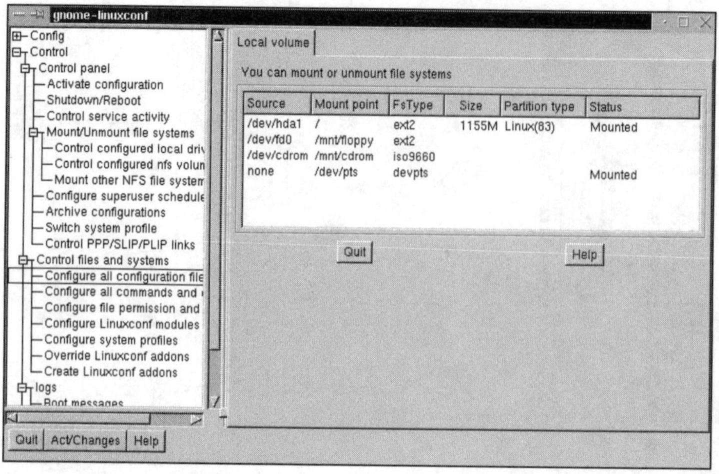

Figure 7.9   The Linuxconf Gnome tool in Red Hat Linux.

Accessing Programs in KDE

To access the programs available in KDE, click the K button in the lower left corner. Clicking this K button brings up a menu similar to the one shown in Figure 7.10.

Figure 7.10   The KDE program menu in Caldera Linux.

KDE's program menu contains a number of tools and utilities, which are outlined in Table 7.2.

Table 7.2   The KDE program menu in Caldera Linux.

Menu	Contains
Applications	Text editors and organizer
Games	Games designed for KDE
Graphics	Various viewers, image editors, and capture programs
Internet	Network utilities, ppp setup tools, news and irc clients
Multimedia	Midi, CD, media players, and mixers
Settings	Desktop, device, sound, and window configurations as well as system information
System	File, task, font, and user managing tools
Utilities	Address book, calculator, terminals, clipboard, menu editor
Disk Navigator	Shortcuts to commonly accessed directories
Panel	Options to configure the KDE layout

To open one of the programs, do the following:

1. Click the menu item corresponding to the program. For example, click Games to open the Games submenu shown in Figure 7.11.

*Figure 7.11   The KDE **Games** submenu in Caldera Linux.*

NOTE: *The contents of the submenus depends on what installation combination you chose.*

7. Window Managers And Desktop Environments

2. Click the submenu program you want to run, or the next submenu item, if there is one.

3. Continue until you get to the program you want to run.

Related solution:	Found on page:
Entering The GUI	132

Retracting The Task Bar In KDE

To get the task bar out of the way so you can use your entire screen, click the arrow to the left side or right side of the bottom task bar. The task bar will slide off the screen to the left or right, depending on which side you clicked, and the screen will only display the arrow on the side the task bar slid to, as shown in Figure 7.12. Click this arrow to pull the task bar back out.

Figure 7.12   The KDE task bar slider retrieval tab in Caldera Linux, after clicking the left side of the task bar.

Using The KDE Help System

The KDE Help system is a Web-like browser that allows you to move through the sum total of Help items installed on your Linux box. To use this system, do the following:

1. Click the Help icon on the task bar, as shown in Figure 7.13.

Figure 7.13   The KDE Help icon in Caldera Linux.

The KDE Help browser opens, as shown in Figure 7.14.

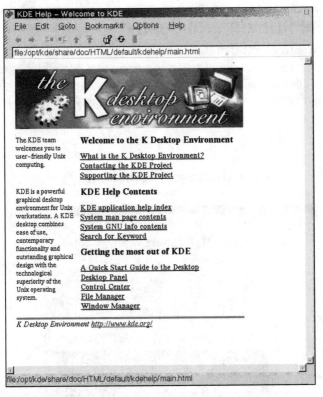

The KDE team welcomes you to user–friendly Unix computing.

Welcome to the K Desktop Environment

What is the K Desktop Environment?
Contacting the KDE Project
Supporting the KDE Project

KDE is a powerful graphical desktop environment for Unix workstations. A KDE desktop combines ease of use, contemporary functionality and outstanding graphical design with the technological superiority of the Unix operating system.

KDE Help Contents

KDE application help index
System man page contents
System GNU info contents
Search for Keyword

Getting the most out of KDE

A Quick Start Guide to the Desktop
Desktop Panel
Control Center
File Manager
Window Manager

K Desktop Environment http://www.kde.org/

Figure 7.14   The KDE Help browser in Caldera Linux.

2. The KDE Help system is divided into three separate main components:

- **Welcome to the K Desktop Environment**—Contains background behind the environment and contact information for the people behind it.

- **KDE Help Contents**—Contains the meat of the Help system so far as using your Linux system is concerned.

TIP: *The man pages listed in this section are the same man pages you access by typing "man command" at the command prompt.*

- **Getting the most out of KDE**—A guide to using the environment itself.

Click on the menu item you want to follow and continue navigating until you find the information you're looking for.

3. When finished, click File in the menu bar, then Exit in the File menu, to close the browser.

Using The KDE Control Center

The KDE Control Center in Caldera is a graphical manager for both your desktop environment and, to a certain extent, for your system. To open it, click the KDE Control Center button, as shown in Figure 7.15, to display the Control Center shown in Figure 7.16.

Figure 7.15   The KDE Control Center icon in Caldera Linux.

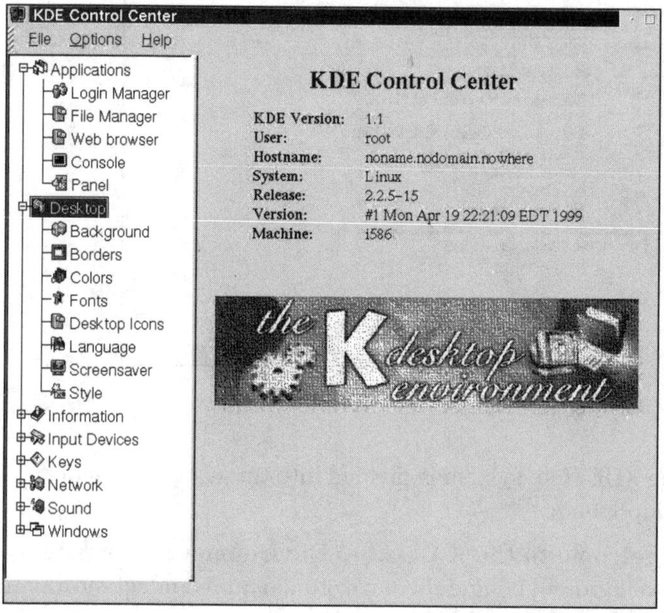

Figure 7.16   The KDE Control Center in Caldera Linux.

Using COAS In KDE

To configure your system using graphical tools, use the Caldera Open Administration System (COAS) tool. To utilize this tool, do the following:

1. Click the COAS icon, as shown in Figure 7.17, to get the COAS menu.

Figure 7.17   The KDE COAS icon in Caldera Linux.

2. Choose a menu option:

    • Choose the Network menu to configure TCP/IP services—such as NIS networking or DNS, Ethernet interfaces, or mail.

    • Choose the Peripherals menu to configure the keyboard, mouse, or printer(s).

    • Choose the System menu to configure system accounts, daemons, the file system, or the system's name, to view how the resources are allocated, or to change the date and time.

    • Choose the Kernel menu item to configure the kernel.

    • Choose the Software menu item to configure what software you want installed on the system.

3. Choose submenus, if necessary, until you find what you want to configure.

Installing A New Window Manager

If you want to use a different window manager than the default, do the following:

1. Exit the GUI if necessary.

2. Log into the account you want to change the window manager for.

3. Install the window manager on your machine. It may be on the CD-ROM, or you may need to download it from the Internet.

4. Type "vi ~/.xinitrc" to open the file you need to create.

5. Type the name of the window manager—for example, "fvwm".

6. Type ":wq" to save and exit the file.

7. Test by typing "startx". This should bring you into an X session with the new window manager.

Related solution:	Found on page:
Using The **vi** Editor	91

Creating User Accounts

In Brief

Regardless of whether your Linux box is meant to service many users over a network or to be a personal desktop machine, it is wise to create separate user accounts. The primary reason for this is that the **root** account is a very powerful tool, but it's just that, a tool. Everyone makes the occasional mistake. Making a mistake as a user can be a minor hassle. Making a big mistake as **root** can bring you to wish you had kept better backups.

TIP: *Here are some things you should know about **root** and the Internet: A number of Internet services also have special considerations for handling root. For example, by default you cannot Telnet into a Linux box as root. It is considered a significant security hole to make that available, because a person need only figure out your root password to gain access to your entire system. It is much better to require at least breaking into a user account first, which makes the process longer and more involved, and gives you a better chance of detecting it.*

Going onto IRC as root will get you kicked or banned from many channels. Root access allows you to run a number of attack features on a Unix machine, and many IRC channels are not willing to find out the hard way whether that is your intent or not.

*Sending email or posting to newsgroups as **root** tends to be frowned upon as well, unless you are speaking as an administrative function. In this case, it is considered more a matter of unnecessarily showing off, and not understanding your system well enough to realize you are using **root** needlessly.*

System security is covered in more detail in Chapter 21, but a brief discussion of passwords follows here.

Passwords

The account password is an important barrier between your system and those who might like to steal information and resources from it, or just wreak havoc. If your Linux box is accessible on the Internet or by modem, you must choose your passwords carefully. This is especially true for administrative passwords, such as the one for **root**, and for your Internet services.

TIP: *A good password is not made up of a dictionary word. It includes mixed-case letters, numbers, and allowable symbols. A secure password is also longer than eight characters.*

Although you cannot entirely control what passwords users choose, you can do your best to educate them. You also can occasionally use tools to seek out poorly chosen passwords (see the following Tip). Then, you can notify individual users that they need to change their passwords, sending them instructions on how to choose more secure ones.

TIP: *A bad password is made up of dictionary words, all lowercase letters, or shorter than eight characters. Another type of bad password is something that is easily identifiable by anyone who knows the person, such as birthdays, pets' names, or names of significant others.*

Whether you run password checks or not depends on how vulnerable your system is (see the section "Determining System Vulnerability," later in this chapter), how well it is known, and how security conscious you feel the need to be. Whenever you assign someone a new password (temporary or otherwise) or a user changes his or her own password, the passwd program does point out any glaringly bad choices. However, if the user is persistent he or she can ignore the warnings and use the bad password anyway. Remember, though, that using bad passwords easily caught by the passwd program compromises system security.

TIP: *There are user management tools available both at the command-line level and in the GUI. Which tools you use is mostly a matter of preference. Linuxconf is often the tool of choice. Although this chapter focuses on command-line tools, instructions for how to do tasks within Linuxconf are also sprinkled throughout.*

Shadow Passwords

The passwords stored in the /etc/passwd file are encrypted, so not as vulnerable as raw text. This means that you can't just see someone's password by looking in the file, which is a good first step in security. However, the encryption is not strong. It is not difficult to decode the passwords once they are taken from the file.

The reason to worry is that your /etc/passwd file is readable by everyone. All an intruder needs to do is break into any user account—by running a password cracker that runs through a set of dictionary words, or knowing what kinds of passwords that user tends to choose, or a number of other methods discussed in Chapter 21—and then he can easily make a copy of your /etc/passwd file and then decrypt the data. It might seem a simple thing to fix by changing the permissions on the file, but this does not work. Your /etc/passwd file contains vital items, such as user information, group information, and shell information—and too many programs need to access it for you to be able to painlessly make it readable only by **root**.

A commonly used method of dealing with this problem is installing the Shadow password suite. This suite moves all the passwords into a file that only **root** can read, thus eliminating the damage someone can do by simply stealing the /etc/passwd file. As you can likely imagine, moving all passwords to a new file has the potential to cause problems with some programs and services that require access to that file. If you have access to the source code (see the section "Modifying Source To Work With The Shadow Suite"), or the program has settings that let you tell it you are using the Shadow Suite, then this is not an issue. However, there are some cases where you cannot use the suite:

• The Linux machine is on a LAN using NIS to exchange usernames and passwords with other machines on the network.

• The Linux machine is used by terminal servers to verify users via NFS, NIS, or another method.

• There is software you must use that has a need to validate users, and you don't have access either to a version built specifically for the Shadow Suite or to the source code.

To set up your machine to use the Shadow Suite, see the section "Converting Your System To Use Shadow Passwords." Instructions are also included on how to remove the suite (in the section "Converting Your System To No Longer Use Shadow Passwords"), in case you find that it gets in the way of other things you need to do.

Custom User Addition Scripts

Many system administrators find that they develop a familiar routine when creating users. In an effort to save themselves work down the road, many choose to create a shell script to automate the list of tasks into one smooth process.

As you add each user, make notes of what tasks you must do. The more complex your setup, the more involved this process can be. For example, you might need to create a Web directory or FTP directory for them or to alter their PATH statement to include file paths they commonly need to access.

Once you have this data compiled, you can begin building your script. A detailed discussion on writing shell scripts is given in Chapter 18.

Immediate Solutions

Adding A New User

There are two different commands available with which you can add a user: **adduser** and **useradd**. Both commands work the same way. To add a new user, type "adduser username".

TIP: *You may find that the default values assigned to a new user are not what you want to use. See the section "Viewing New User Defaults" to see if this is the case.*

For example, to add the new user account *mary*, type "useradd mary".

You must then create a password for the user. See the section "Add Or Change A Password" for how to do this.

TIP: *To create users, you must be logged in as **root**.*

Adding Or Changing A Password

The **root** account has the permissions to add and change passwords for any user. The same command is used for either function, **passwd username**.

TIP: *You can also change passwords within Linuxconf. See the section "Modifying Existing User Information With Linuxconf." Once you click on the user you want to modify, you can then click the Passwd button to change that user's password.*

For example, to change the password for the user *birdy*, type "passwd birdy".

TIP: *The **passwd** command also works for changing the password for the non-**root** account you're currently logged into. You use it without needing to include the username. You would just type "passwd".*

---

8. Creating User Accounts

Adding A New User In Linuxconf

To add a user within Linuxconf, do the following:

1. Open Linuxconf (for instructions on how to do this, see the section "Open Linuxconf").

2. Navigate through the directory tree to the Users Accounts, Normal submenu.

3. Click the Users accounts option. The Users Accounts option opens, as shown in Figure 8.1).

4. Click the Add button. The User account creation option opens to the Base Info tab, as shown in Figure 8.2.

5. Enter the relevant information into the textboxes. The only item that you absolutely must fill in is the account name. If you want, click the Privileges tab and choose the options there that are appropriate.

6. Click the Accept button. The Changing password option opens, as shown in Figure 8.3.

7. Enter the user's password.

8. Click the Accept button. If the password checker objects to the password you've assigned, you will get a dialog box saying you have chosen a bad password. Click OK.

9. Enter the password again when prompted. If you wish to use the same password the checker did not like earlier, type it again. However, if the system will at some point be connected

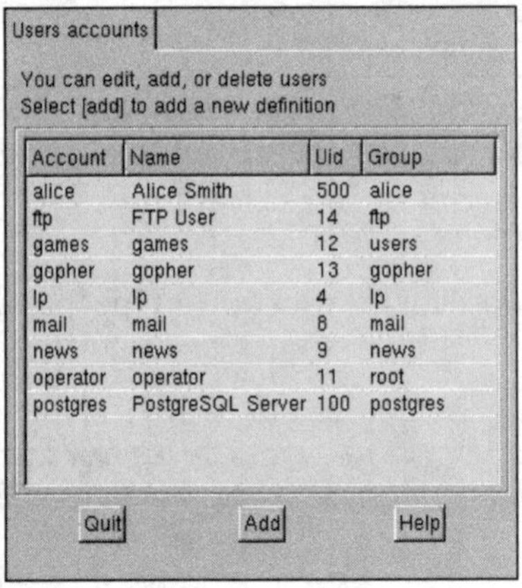

Figure 8.1   The Linuxconf Users Accounts option.

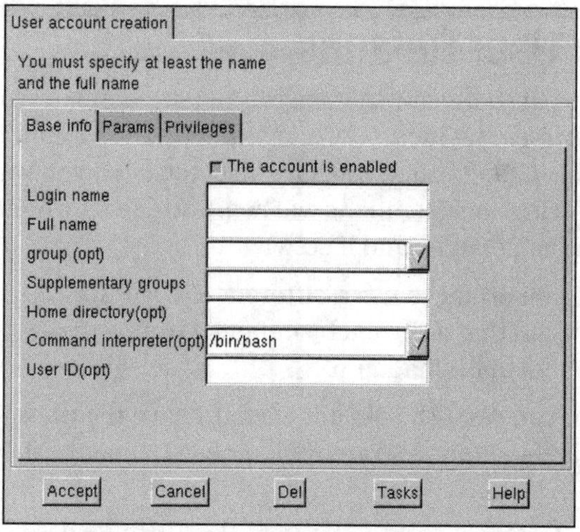

Figure 8.2   The Linuxconf User Account Creation option.

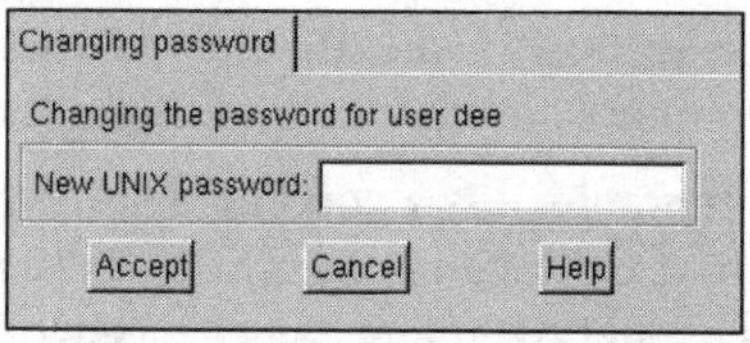

Figure 8.3   The Linuxconf Changing Password option.

to the Internet, it would be wise to return and change the password to something more secure.

10. Click the Accept button. You are returned to the Users Accounts option.

Viewing New User Defaults

To view the default settings assigned to new users, use the -D flag for either **adduser** or **useradd**, such as

```
useradd -D
```

8. Creating User Accounts

Choosing New User Defaults

You will likely find that you want to change the user defaults with **useradd** or **adduser** (see the section "Changing New User Defaults" for how to change the defaults once you have selected what you want to change). The following considerations will help you decide whether you want to change the defaults, and if so what to:

- You may find that you prefer to use a different GROUP for the average new user than that assigned by default. Groups are discussed in more detail in Chapter 5.

- If for some reason you want the default users to have their home directories outside the /home hierarchy, you need to change the HOME setting.

- If you want to render user accounts inactive if they don't change an expired password, change the INACTIVE setting. Enter the number of days you want your system to wait after the password expires before it shuts down the account. Using the default value of 0 says that you don't want accounts automatically deactivated.

- If your system is sufficiently vulnerable, it is a good idea to have passwords expire on a regular basis. Changing the EXPIRE setting to a number tells your system how many days a password is valid before it forces the user to change it.

- The default SHELL is usually /bin/bash. If you want to change this, you will need to enter the full path for the new default shell.

- Many savvy system administrators customize new user directories by taking advantage of the skeleton directory. This directory contains the files placed in the directory of every new account you create. If you want to set up the skeleton directory in a location other than the default (often /etc/skel) change the SKEL setting to the full path of the new skeleton directory.

Changing New User Defaults

To change the defaults used when creating new user accounts, use the command **adduser** or **useradd** with its appropriate flags. Table 8.1 shows the flags used to change each of the default user settings (see the section "Choosing New User Defaults" for a more detailed discussion of the settings).

Table 8.1   Flags used to change generic user defaults with useradd/adduser.

User Setting	Flag	Value Format
GROUP	-g	Group number from the file /etc/group
HOME	-d	Full path to the account's parent home directory (e.g. /home)
INACTIVE	-f	Days
EXPIRE	-e	Days
SHELL	-s	Full path to the shell
SKEL	-k	Full path to the skeleton file

For example, if you wanted to do the following:

- Set passwords to expire in 90 days.

- Automatically deactivate the account if the expired password is not changed within 30 days.

- Change the default shell to /bin/ksh.

you would use the **adduser -e90 -f30 -s/bin/ksh** command.

Modifying Existing User Information

You change information for specific existing users with the command **usermod**. Flags are used to signal which information you want to change. What flags to use are shown in Table 8.2.

WARNING!   If you use the G flag, then any groups not listed with it or g will be removed from the user's group definitions.

Table 8.2   Flags used to change user info with usermod.

Flag	Name	Comments
c	Comment Information	Comment Information used in your finger file. This field is better to alter using the **chfn** command.
d	Home Directory	Enter a new home directory location for this user, which is automatically created. If you include the m flag after the d flag, the contents of the user's current home directory are moved into the new one.
e	Expire Date	If you want the user account to expire on a specific date, use this flag and enter the date in the format MM/DD/YY.

(continued)

Table 8.2   Flags used to change user info with usermod (continued).

Flag	Name	Comments
f	Inactive Days	The number of days after a password expires to wait before disabling the account. This option is only activated if the user does not change the password. To not use this option, enter the value -1 (the default).
g	Initial Group	The group name or number you want to assign to the user. This group must already exist.
G	Group	You can add additional groups to the user with this flag. To add more than one, separate them with a comma but no spaces. For example, if you wanted to add groups wheel, root, and admin to the user, you would enter "wheel,root,admin".
l	Login Name	Use this flag to change the user's login name. The home directory is not automatically changed when you do this. You cannot change a user's login name while the user is logged in.
s	Shell	If a user requests a different login shell, change it with this flag. Use the name of the shell.
u	UID	Change a user's numeric userid. Not recommended unless you understand the ramifications of doing so and the range of IDs available on your system.

For example, if the user *chris* requested that his login name be changed to *c.adams*, you would log in as **root** and type "usermod -d /home/ c.adams -m -l c.adams chris".

Modifying Existing User Information With Linuxconf

To change settings for existing users with Linuxconf, do the following:

1. Open Linuxconf (see the section "Open Linuxconf" for details).

2. Navigate through the directory tree to the Users Accounts, Normal submenu.

3. Click the Users Accounts option. The Users Accounts option opens (see Figure 8.1).

4. Navigate through the user list until you see the account you want to modify.

8. Creating User Accounts

5. Click the item you want to modify. The User information option opens, as shown in Figure 8.4.

6. Change the information you want to modify.

7. Click the Accept button.

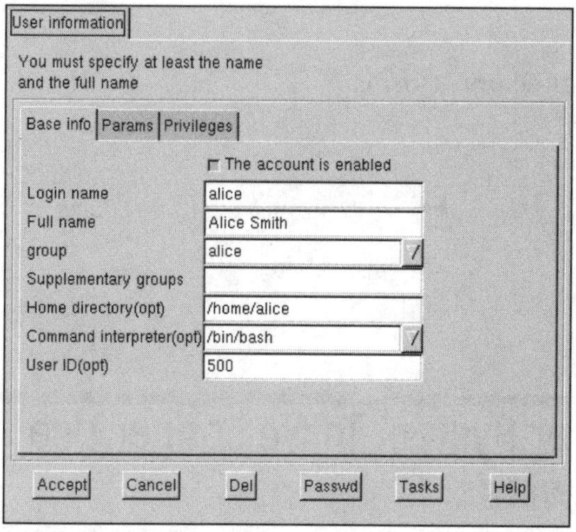

Figure 8.4   The Linuxconf User Information option.

Installing The Shadow Password Package

To change your system to use shadow passwords, you first must install the shadow utilities if they were not installed on your system already. If you're using Red Hat Linux, you'll find them on the Red Hat CD-ROM in the package shadow-utils within the /RedHat/RPMS. The package shadow-misc is on Caldera's CD-ROM in /Packages/RPMS. See Chapter 15 for a detailed discussion on how to install RPM packages.

NOTE: *Shadow passwords are installed by default in both Red Hat and Caldera. However, in the custom installs it is possible to shut them off during the install process.*

Related solutions:	Found on page:
Installing An RPM Package	295
Determining What Files Are In An RPM Package	296
Entering The GUI	132
Mounting Onto The File System	168

Converting Your System To Use Shadow Passwords

To set up your system to use shadow passwords if it is not already configured to do so, do the following:

1. Log in as **root**.

2. Change to the directory /usr/sbin.

3. Type "pwconv".

NOTE: If the command is not in that directory, see the section "Installing The Shadow Password Package".

Converting Your System To No Longer Use Shadow Passwords

To remove password shadowing from your system, do the following:

1. Log in as **root**.

2. Change to the directory /usr/sbin.

3. Type "pwunconv".

4. Then, remove the shadow utilities. The package names for Red Hat and Caldera respectively are listed in the section "Installing The Shadow Password Package".

Locating The Default User Profile

The generic user profile is found in /etc/profile. The shell assigned to /etc/profile determines what format the changes you make are done in. The bash shell is assigned to all users by default, so it is often safe to assume that is what your users will use. If they choose to change shells, they can customize their own profile (profile).

TIP: You can use a series of if/then statements to offer customization for other shells. See Chapter 18 for more information on writing shell scripts.

Looking For Bad Passwords

Two commonly used programs for checking all passwords on a system are:

- John the Ripper at **www.false.com/security/john/index.html**
- Crack at **ftp://info.cert.org/pub/tools/crack/**

Disabling A User

To disable a user's account without removing it, do the following:

WARNING! *Do not disable the root account!*

1. Log in as **root**.
2. Edit your password file:
   - If you are not using the Shadow suite, edit /etc/passwd.
   - If you are using the Shadow suite, edit /etc/shadow.
3. Locate the account within the file.
4. Replace the account's password entry with an asterisk (*). The password is the second field of a user's entry.

TIP: *Each user in /etc/shadow and /etc/passwd has his or her account information on a single line. The information is divided into entries with colons (:). So the first entry is the first piece of information on the line, the second entry is after the first colon, and so on.*

---

5. Save and exit the file.

Disabling A User In Linuxconf

To disable a user within Linuxconf, do the following:

1. Open Linuxconf (as discussed in the section "Open Linuxconf").
2. Open the User Information option in Linuxconf (see the section "Modify Existing User Information With Linuxconf" for more details).
3. Click the "The account is enabled" checkbox to de-select it.
4. Click the Accept button.

Deleting A User

To delete a user along with his or her home directory, use the **userdel -r username** command.

For example, to fully remove the account belonging to *paula*, you would type "userdel -r paula".

TIP: *If you have reason to want to remove an account but leave the user's home directory intact, use userdel without the -r option.*

Deleting A User In Linuxconf

To delete a user in Linuxconf:

1. Open Linuxconf (as discussed in the section "Open Linuxconf").

2. Open the User Information option in Linuxconf (see the section "Modify Existing User Information With Linuxconf" for more details).

3. Click the Delete button.

4. Choose one of the three options of how to deal with the account's data.

5. Click the Accept button.

Determining System Vulnerability

System vulnerability depends on a number of factors. Answering "Yes" to any of the following raises the need to keep a tight watch on passwords (the more Yeses, the tighter the watch):

• Is the computer or network connected to the Internet on a constant basis?

• Is the computer or network physically accessible by a large number of people?

• Do you host any high-profile Internet services? For example, do any of your users host a popular Web site without having their own domain name?

• Do you get a lot of complaints about any of your users, due to their participation in Internet forums?

Modifying Source To Work With The Shadow Suite

If a package handles user authentication but does not come with a version that handles the Shadow suite, you have two alternatives:

- If you have access to the program's source files, alter them so they work with the Shadow Suite.

- If you need the package and there is no way to fix the problem, convert back to not using the Shadow Suite (see the section "Convert Your System To No Longer Use Shadow Passwords").

The ins and outs of doing this modification are more thoroughly addressed by consulting the appropriate programming references. However, there are some general things to keep in mind:

- /etc/shadow is only accessible by **root**. Therefore, any program that uses the file to authenticate users must run **SUID root** (see Chapter 5 for more information) or **SUID shadow**.

- Allowing any program to run **SUID root** is a security hole. This program must be written carefully if you intend to do this.

- The header files, if you are dealing with C code, are available in /usr/include/shadow.

- The library is in /usr/lib/libshadowa.

Opening Linuxconf

To open Linuxconf, do the following:

1. Log in as **root**.
2. Enter the Linux Graphic User Interface (GUI) if necessary.

TIP: To enter the GUI by hand, type "startx" at the command line. X, or XWindow, is the general term for the Linux (and Unix) GUI.

3. Drag the slider bar in the Control Panel until you see the System Configuration button, as shown in Figure 8.5.
4. Click the System Configuration button. If this is the first time you have done this, you will get a dialog box. Click OK to clear it.
5. The Linuxconf window now opens, as shown in Figure 8.6.

Figure 8.5   The fvwm Control Panel System Configuration button.

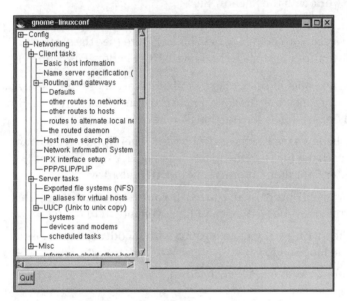

Figure 8.6   The Linuxconf window.

The Linux File System

In Brief

In Linux there is a lot of talk about the *file system*. A file system is the collection of all partitions, directories, storage devices, and files that make up Linux and all its components. Rather than seeing floppy disks, CD-ROMs, tapes, and other storage media as outside components, these devices have to be added to the file system itself and then released from it when you are finished working with them. Even hardware devices, such as monitors and printers, are seen to some extent as part of the file system. The device drivers themselves determine how the operating system talks to each item.

File System Basics

The main file system is that which is permanently a part of the file and directory structure on your machine. It is the structure in which you can change directories (**cd**) without needing to add anything new. The items in the primary file system are automatically mounted at boot time through the file /etc/fstab.

When you want to access something on a removable media, such as a floppy disk or CD-ROM, you have to add that item temporarily to the file system. Doing this requires first that you create a spot called a *mount point* for the disk to exist within the file system. Think of the mount point as a kind of docking station, a place where the disk docks and makes its files accessible to the rest of the file system. Once you create this mount point, you can then mount (dock) the disk's contents onto this point and browse the files, copy, delete, or do whatever is necessary. When you are finished, you then have to unmount the disk before removing it from the system, so that no data is lost.

The specifics of mounting and unmounting disks are covered in the "Immediate Solutions" section of this chapter.

Linux File System Format

As you are likely already aware, each operating system uses its own file system format. You can't use an MS-DOS formatted floppy in a Macintosh, or vice versa, without special conversion software. Linux also has its own file system, called *ext2*, the Linux Second Extended File System.

> **NOTE:** In Linux storage, media is not "formatted" as the term is used in Windows. Instead, you make a file system in Linux. Both terms refer to preparing the floppy, hard drive, or other storage media so that it can read the particular operating system's file storage setups.

Immediate Solutions

Making A File System

Linux has the ability to make several file systems with the **mkfs** command. The most useful of these are the Linux file system ext2 and the MS-DOS file system. This feature makes it much simpler for you to transfer data between different operating systems.

To make a Linux file system on a device, do the following:

1. Determine what device you want to make the file system on. Is it a floppy disk? In that case, is it in the first floppy drive? If so, the device is likely /dev/fd0.

2. Determine if you want to check for bad blocks—physical defects—during the formatting process. If so, you will need to include the -c flag.

TIP: Another frequently used flag is -v, for verbose. In the examples below you would use-cv instead of -c.

---

3. Determine which type of file system you want to make: Linux's ext2 or MS-DOS.

4. Build the command in one of the following formats:

   - For a Linux floppy use the **mke2fs** command, in the format *mke2fs flags device*. For example, type "mke2fs -c /dev/fd0".

   - For an MS-DOS floppy, use the **mkdosfs** command in the format *mkdosfs flags device*. For example, type "mkdosfs -c / dev/fd0".

TIP: You may need to install the mkdosfs package as an RPM off the distribution CD-ROM.

Mounting Onto The File System

To mount a partition or disk onto the file system, use the **mount** command. Build the command with its options, as follows:

1. Determine what device you want to mount onto the file system. Is it a floppy disk? The device in that case is likely /dev/fd0.

2. What type of formatting does the device have? Table 9.1 lists the commonly used formatting types.

WARNING! If you're creating files under Linux via the Linux vfat format, which are intended to be moved to the Microsoft vfat format, be careful to use the eight character naming convention required.

3. Where do you want to mount the device onto the file system? As a standard, temporary devices tend to be added under the /mnt hierarchy. It helps to give the mount point a meaningful name, in case you have more than one device mounted at a time.

4. Change to the /mnt directory by typing the command "cd /mnt".

5. List the contents of the directory with the **ls** command.

6. If the mount point does not already exist—some are created by the distributions by default—create the directory for it. For example, type "mkdir /mnt/floppy".

7. Build the command in the format *mount -t type /dev/device / mnt/mountpoint*. Examples for the four file system types listed in the table are:

   • To mount a Linux floppy, type "mount /dev/fd0 /mnt/floppy".

   • To mount a CD-ROM, both distributions create a link from the CD-ROM device driver to a driver called *cdrom*. Type "mount -t iso9660 /dev/cdrom /mnt/cdrom".

   • To mount an MS-DOS floppy, type "mount -t msdos /dev/fd0 / mnt/floppy".

   • To mount a Windows partition on the first SCSI hard drive, third partition, type "mount -t vfat /dev/sda3 /mnt/win".

Table 9.1   File system formats often encountered while mounting devices.

Format	Description
ext2	Linux format. This is the default.
iso9660	CD-ROM format.
msdos	MS-DOS format.
vfat	This term means different things, depending on whether you are referring to it from the Microsoft viewpoint or the Linux viewpoint. The Linux version encompasses both the Windows 3.x and 9x format. Windows 9x actually uses vfat32 from the Microsoft viewpoint, but the vfat Linux file system type covers both.

9. The Linux File System

169

Unmounting Off Of The File System

To remove a device from the file system, use the **umount** command in one of the following two formats:

- umount /dev/*device*
- umount /mnt/*mountpoint*

NOTE: Notice that the command to unmount is **umount**. This difference causes a lot of confusion.

Shortening Common Mount Commands

You can shorten common mount commands by adding references to them in the file /etc/fstab. To accomplish this task, do the following:

1. Log in as **root**.

2. Open the file /etc/fstab with a command such as *vi /etc/fstab*.

3. Look to see if a line pertaining to what you want to add already exists. For example, /mnt/cdrom and /mnt/floppy often already exist in this file because they are commonly used. The second column contains the names of the mount points. If your idea already exists in the file, exit by typing ":q", then pressing Enter.

4. If using **vi**, type "G" to go to the end of the file, then "o" to open a new line.

5. Entries for /etc/fstab follow the following format:

```
/dev/device  /mnt/mountpoint  type  rules  dumpable  order
```

Because this is a device that will not be automatically mounted at boot time, this format can be reduced to:

```
/dev/device  /mnt/mountpoint  type  noauto  0  0
```

6. Determine the device you want to mount.

7. Create the mount point at which you want to mount this device at. Keep in mind that this needs to be something easy to remember. If, for example, you are specifically creating a short mount command to mount MS-DOS floppies, then consider a mount point such as /mnt/dosfloppy.

8. Choose the appropriate file system type. For the /mnt/dosfloppy example, this type is *msdos*.

9. Fill out the statement. In the case of the MS-DOS floppy example, it would be:

```
/dev/fd0   /mnt/dosfloppy  msdos  noauto  0  0
```

10. Save and exit the file by pressing the ESC key, then typing ":wq", then pressing Enter.

Mounting A Prepared Device Type

Once the instructions in "Shortening Common Mount Commands" are followed, you can mount the device by first placing it in the drive (for example, an MS-DOS floppy) and then typing "mount /mnt/ *mountpoint*" (for example, *mount /mnt/dosfloppy*).

Automatically Mounting A Device At Boot Time

Setting a device to automount onto the file system involves inserting it into /etc/fstab. To accomplish this task, do the following:

1. Log in as **root**.
2. Open the file /etc/fstab with a command such as *vi /etc/fstab*.
3. If you are using **vi**, type "G" to go to the end of the file, then "o" to open a new line.
4. Entries for /etc/fstab follow the following format:

```
/dev/device  mountpoint  type  rules  0  order
```

5. Determine the device you want to mount. For example, perhaps you added a second IDE hard drive and allocated its second partition for Linux use. The device then would be /dev/hdb2.
6. Create the mount point where you want to mount this device. It is important to make sure this junction is carefully considered, because you are making it a part of the permanent file system. Typically the /mnt hierarchy is for temporary additions, so this time the new partition should be added somewhere else. This decision is a matter of taste, the File System Standard

9. The Linux File System

(FSSTND), and what function the new partition serves. For example, if the new partition is meant to be a shared place for users to work on projects together, then perhaps a good mount point would be */home/projects*.

7. Choose the appropriate file system type. For the Linux partition in question, it would be ext2.

8. Choose the rules to apply to the mounted device. The more commonly used rules are shown in Table 9.2. To get a full listing, type "man mount".

   Because the partition being mounted for the example is meant for all users to share project data, the *defaults* option covers everything necessary.

9. The final field specifies the device's mount order. If the device is not one you have set to automount, then give this a value of zero (0). The root (/) partition always has a value of one (1). From then on, the items are numbered in order of when they should be mounted, with integers from two (2) and up.

10. Enter all of the values at the end of the /etc/fstab file. Following the example, you would have:

```
/dev/hdb2  /home/projects  ext2  defaults  0  2
```

The partition will not automatically mount until the system is rebooted. For now it can be mounted manually with the command

```
mount /dev/hdb2 /home/projects.
```

Table 9.2   Often used rules for mounting devices automatically through /etc/fstab.

Rule	Purpose
auto	Mount the defined device automatically at boot time.
defaults	Mount the defined device with the defaults used for most permanent file system additions, such as automounting and read-write access.
noauto	Do not mount the defined device automatically at boot time.
nouser	Don't allow anyone who does not have superuser access to mount this device.
ro	Mount the defined device with read-only access.
rw	Mount the defined device with read-write access.
user	Any user is allowed to mount the device.

Related solution:	*Found on page:*
Choosing Where To Install New Software	304

Moving An Existing Directory To A New Partition

Perhaps you have just added a new hard drive and want to move a directory onto it and into its own partition. To accomplish this task, do the following:

1. Install the new hard drive into the machine.

TIP: *This task is best to do when there are no users, other than yourself as root, using the machine.*

2. Partition it as necessary with your favorite partitioning tool. See Chapter 2 for details about disk partitioning.

3. Rename the existing directory with a temporary name to assist with the shuffle. For example, to move the /home directory onto its own partition, change it with *mv /home /hometmp*.

TIP: *Another, and in some ways safer because **tar** has better protection against data loss, method of handling this task is with the **tar** command in the format: mkdir /newdir; cd /dir; tar cf - . | (cd /newdir; tar xf -).*

4. Add the new partition to /etc/fstab. See the section "Automatically Mounting A Device At Boot Time" for explicit instructions. For example, if the /home directory is moving onto the second SCSI drive's first partition, then the entry might be:

```
/dev/sdb1  /home ext2  defaults  0  2
```

5. Either reboot the machine to automatically mount the partition, or mount it by hand with a command such as *mount /dev/sdb1 /home*.

6. Copy the entire contents, including all subdirectories, of the segment you're moving onto the partition. For example, with the /home directory, you would type "cp -R /hometmp /home". See the Tip for Step 3 for another way to accomplish this task.

9. The Linux File System

7. Wait a short while to make sure everything is working properly for the users, and then delete the contents of the old directory and the directory itself with the **rm** command in a format such as *rm -dr /hometmp*. The d flag tells **rm** that you are removing a directory, and the r flag signals that every file and subdirectory within that subdirectory needs to be deleted.

WARNING!   *Be very careful with the -dr flags with rm. Because you have to be logged in as root, careless use of rm -dr can wipe out a good portion of the file system.*

Related solution:	Found on page:
Working With **tar** archives	298

Chapter 10

Compiling The Kernel

In Brief

The kernel is the Linux operating system itself. While the command interface—the shell—does not tend to change often, the Linux kernel is constantly being worked on by people all over the world. The temptation is to upgrade immediately each time a new version of something is released. However, this is not necessary with Linux, nor is it recommended.

Why To Compile

Many experienced Linux users install their systems, and then immediately turn around and recompile their kernels. The reason they do this is that, even though Red Hat and Caldera both provide more optimized kernels from the beginning than they used to, the only way to fully optimize the kernel is to compile it yourself.

Here are some reasons for you to consider recompiling the kernel:

- There is a program you want to run, but the operating system keeps telling you the kernel doesn't support a feature it needs.
- There is a kernel feature you need, such as having between 1GB and 2GB of RAM in your machine that can only be activated by compiling the kernel with modifications.
- You want to optimize the kernel so that it runs its best on the machine in question and also takes up less RAM.

Why Not To Compile

If you only want to add a small amount of functionality to your kernel, you may not need to compile at all. By default, Red Hat and Caldera kernels are modular; this means that there is a small base kernel, and specific modules are loaded and removed as needed. Using modular kernels can free up a significant amount of RAM, depending on how large the kernel would be otherwise.

NOTE: *A non-modular kernel, where everything is compiled directly into it, is called a monolithic kernel.*

Sometimes adding a new feature is as simple as loading a new kernel module.

> **TIP:** *When Caldera provides an upgraded kernel on its site, the kernel comes as a binary RPM, which is simple to install—no compiling necessary.*

Kernel Upgrade Issues

Another reason to compile a kernel is to upgrade to a new version. Because the kernel changes so rapidly, it is important not to upgrade every time a new version comes out, especially on a production machine that requires stability. Instead, many users only upgrade when necessary, or when a major kernel version becomes available. Reasons to upgrade include:

- You need access to specific device drivers and/or support added to the new kernel version.

- Bugs listed as fixed in the new kernel version are adversely affecting your machine's performance.

- Software you want or need to install needs a newer kernel than you are using.

- It has been a long time since you upgraded and the machine is not critically important, so you want to upgrade now while you have the time to fix anything that breaks in the process.

- New features have been added to the new versions of the kernel that you want to access.

- A security problem has been found and fixed in the new version of the kernel.

> **NOTE:** *A flip-side issue is that once you upgrade your kernel, you will likely have to upgrade software packages you've been using fine up until that point. This issue is one reason to try to wait to do kernel upgrades until you have time to deal with all the side issues involved.*

Which Kernels To Use

It is important to pay attention to kernel numbers when determining which one to use. There are two different streams of kernel development. One of these paths is highly experimental and only recommended for use by those who can afford to be running a beta kernel on their machine. Generally, the kernel path you want to choose from is the production kernel, because it is well tested and ready to be used on a machine that cannot afford operating system bugs and downtime.

However, if there are features that would greatly benefit your system and are available only in the latest experimental version, sometimes it is worth attempting. Be sure to keep a copy of a LILO instance for the kernel that already works for you, so that you can easily move back to it if the experimental kernel causes too many problems. See the section "Adding A LILO Option For The New Kernel" for more information.

Kernel Configuration Options

Once you reach the point in the kernel replacement process where you have to configure what it supports, you're faced with the difficulty of understanding the options presented to you. Things to eliminate from the kernel are:

- Drivers for hardware you don't have and don't intend to install.

- Math emulation in a machine that has a math coprocessor chip. Almost every machine that's a 486DX and above has such a chip built in.

- Anything labeled "Experimental" unless you absolutely need it.

- Networking capabilities you have no use for.

You can refer to the file Documentation/Configure.help in the /usr/src/linux directory for a breakdown of the individual options.

Immediate Solutions

Determining Which Kernel You Are Running

To tell which kernel version you are currently running, type "uname -r".

Determining Whether A Kernel Is Experimental Or Production

To determine which stream a kernel is in, do the following:

1. Ignore the first number, the one in front of the period (.).
2. Look at the second number, the one directly after the period.

   • In an experimental kernel, the first number after the first period (.) is an odd number.

   • In a production kernel, the first number after the first period (.) is an even number.

For example, kernel version 2.2.5-15 is part of the production stream, and version 2.3.4-12 is part of the experimental stream.

Preparing To Update A Kernel Through The Distributor

Both Red Hat and Caldera provide kernel binary updates through their Web sites when these updates fix security problems in the latest release of their distribution. These problems are generally inherent to the kernel itself, not caused by the distributor.

To see if an update is available and then get it, do the following:

1. See which kernel you're currently running (see the section "Determine Which Kernel You Are Running" for how to accomplish this).
2. Go to the Red Hat or Caldera Web site, depending on which distribution you're using:

- The Red Hat updates and errata page is at **www.redhat.com/ corp/support/errata/**.

- The Caldera updates page is available through **www.caldera-systems.com/support/resources.html**.

3. If necessary, navigate further through the site until you reach the updates for the specific version you have.

4. Look through the listing of updates to see if there is a kernel update available. There may not be. If no kernel update is available, stop here. If you still intend to install a newer kernel version, see the section "Upgrading A Kernel."

5. It is rare that you can get away with only upgrading the kernel, but this is sometimes possible if the jump between versions is small. Read the documents associated with the errata item and make sure nothing else is needed. Download any recommended additional packages.

6. Once you have the appropriate packages downloaded, go to the section "Updating A Kernel Through Caldera" or "Updating A Kernel Through Red Hat" for further instructions.

Places To Look For Kernel Source

Some good places to go for kernel source, or help with kernel issues, are:

- **http://kernelnotes.org/**
- **www.linuxhq.com**
- **www.kernel.org**

Adding A LILO Option For The New Kernel

In order to tell your system how to boot with the new kernel, you have to insert the necessary information into LILO's configuration file. To set this up, do the following:

1. Log in as **root**.

2. Edit the file /etc/lilo.conf by typing, for example, "vi /etc/ lilo.conf".

3. The new section should be identical to the one for the older kernel you are currently running, except with updated values. For example, you might already have:

```
image=/boot/vmlinuz-2.2.5-15
   label=linux
   root=/dev/hda1
   initrd=/boot/initrd-2.2.5
```

4. Move the cursor to the line that begins with the text "image".

5. Type "4yy" to copy the four lines into the buffer.

6. Press G to go to the end of the file.

7. Press the O key to add a new line at the end.

8. Press the ESC key to return to command mode.

9. Press the P key to paste the copied text to the end of /etc/lilo.conf.

10. Change the values necessary in the new statement. For example, change 2.2.5-15 to 2.2.5-25. The initrd reference might or might not need to change, depending on how large the version jump was.

11. Go back to the original entry and change its label to something like *linuxold*, so you can discriminate between the two.

12. Save and exit the file by typing ":wq".

13. Run LILO to place all the pertinent data correctly by typing "/sbin/lilo -v".

Testing A Kernel Install

Once you have your new kernel configured and installed and have an instance in LILO that allows you to boot into it, it is time to test the kernel. To accomplish this, do the following:

1. Log in as **root**.

WARNING! Things can go wrong at this stage. You might not be able to boot the machine because of something wrong in LILO or in the kernel, or some other unpredictable problem. Be sure that you have a boot disk available just in case.

2. Reboot the machine with the **shutdown** command.

3. When you reach the LILO prompt, press the Tab key. This action brings up the LILO menu.

4. Type the menu option for the new kernel, then press Enter.

5. Watch the machine work through the boot process. Much of this information will scroll past too quickly for you to catch, but sometimes watching the process allows you to catch errors that you weren't aware existed even before the new kernel was installed. Also, if the boot fails, you will see the succession of messages that lead to this.

6. There are basically two outcomes for this process:

   • If the boot succeeded, then log in and enjoy. At your leisure you can remove the old kernel and its menu option.

   • If the boot failed, reboot the machine, choosing the old kernel's menu option in LILO, and investigate the problem.

Related solutions:	Found on page:
Making A Custom Linux Boot Disk	39
Shutting Down Your System	47

Updating A Kernel Through Caldera

Once you have downloaded the kernel package(s), as provided on Caldera's Web update site (see the section "Preparing To Update A Kernel Through The Distributor" for how to get the package), follow this procedure:

1. Log on as **root**.

2. Using the **cd** command, change to the directory where the package is stored.

WARNING! *Be sure you have a boot disk on hand just in case something goes wrong with the new kernel.*

3. Type "rpm -Uvh *packagename*" to update the kernel binary.

4. Rerun LILO by typing the command "/sbin/lilo /-v" to update the kernel references in the MBR.

5. Now, reboot the machine by typing the command "shutdown -r" so the new kernel will take effect.

NOTE: *If there are instructions on Caldera's Web site that contradict these instructions, use the ones on Caldera's Web site.*

Related solutions:	Found on page:
Making A Custom Linux Boot Disk	39
Installing An RPM Package	295

Updating A Kernel Through Red Hat

Once you have the kernel update package—and potentially other packages recommended to go along with it—from Red Hat (see the section "Preparing To Update A Kernel Through The Distributor" for how to do this), do the following:

1. Log in as **root**.

2. Upgrade the non-kernel files you downloaded with the **rpm** command by typing "rpm -Uvh *packagename*".

WARNING!   Be sure you have a boot disk on hand just in case something goes wrong.

3. It is important not to erase the old version of a kernel before you test the new one. Install the kernel files themselves by typing "rpm -ivh *packagename*", because upgrading will erase the old kernel.

4. Look in the /boot directory to see what the current kernel is called. It is likely /boot/vmlinuz-*version-ext*, where *version-ext* is the version of the current kernel you're using (see the section "Determine Which Kernel You Are Running"), with the final part on the end (for example, *version* is 2.2.5 and *version-ext* is 2.2.5-15).

5. To build the RAM disk that's loaded during the boot process and then removed from your machine's memory, type "mkinitrd /boot/initrd-*version*.img *version-ext*".

6. See the section "Adding A LILO Option For The New Kernel" for instructions on how to add a boot option that calls on the kernel you just installed.

7. See the section "Testing A Kernel Install" for instructions on how to make sure things are working properly.

NOTE: If there are instructions on Red Hat's Web site that contradict these instructions, use the ones on Red Hat's Web site.

Related solutions:	Found on page:
Making A Custom Linux Boot Disk	39
Installing An RPM Package	295
Editing LILO	44, 71
Running LILO	43, 70
Using The **vi** Editor	91

Compiling A Kernel

Part of installing a new kernel involves compiling the source into the binary that is your system's kernel. One way to approach this process is:

1. Obtain the source for the kernel you want to install. If you are approaching this process by applying patches to source that already exists, see the section "Applying A Kernel Source Patch."

2. Unpack this source into the directory /usr/src/linux-*version-ext* by using the **gunzip** and **tar** commands.

3. Change to this directory with the **cd** command.

4. Choose which kernel configuration program you want to use:

   • The least graphical, but most tedious, version is **config**. See the section "Using config" for how to use this program.

   • A graphical, but X graphical, version is called **menuconfig**. See the section "Using menuconfig" for how to use this program.

   • The X tool for kernel configuration is often the most popular; it is called **xconfig**. See the section "Using xconfig" for how to use this program.

   After saving and exiting the configuration program, you have the settings necessary to configure the kernel itself.

5. Type "make dep" to build the dependency list, which defines which files have to be changed if each specific file involved in the kernel's source is changed.

6. Type "make clean" to get rid of the stack of temporary files generated during the install process.

7. Type "make bzImage" to complete the creation of your new kernel.

8. Type "make modules" to compile the kernel modules and put them in place. These are the modules that will be loaded and unloaded on the fly, plus those that are permanently loaded.

9. Now the kernel is fully compiled, but it still needs to be installed. See the section "Installing The Kernel" for more information.

Related solutions:	Found on page:
Ungzipping A File	300
Untarring A File	298

Upgrading A Kernel

Upgrading your system's kernel can be an involved process. The general steps involved in doing this are as follows:

1. See which kernel you're currently running (see the section "Determine Which Kernel You Are Running" for how to accomplish this).

2. Download the kernel version you want to apply. This version may be from Red Hat or Caldera itself (in which case, see the section "Updating A Kernel Through Red Hat" or "Updating A Kernel Through Caldera" for the rest of the process) or from a trusted download site. Either download the entire kernel if you are going for a major version change, or the collection of patches necessary to bring the main version's source up to the version you want to use.

3. If you need to apply patches, see the section "Applying A Kernel Source Patch" for instructions on how to do this. Otherwise, continue.

4. Read the README file that comes with the kernel source. This file lists where to look to find out what other software needs to be upgraded in order to move to the new kernel.

5. Upgrade the packages that need to be upgraded before you can compile the kernel.

6. See the section "Compiling A Kernel" for instructions on how to compile the new kernel.

7. See the section "Installing A Kernel" for instructions on how to put the kernel into place once it is compiled.

8. See the section "Adding A LILO Option For The New Kernel" for instructions on how to add this new kernel to the boot menu.

9. See the section "Testing A Kernel Install" for instructions on how to make sure things are working properly.

Applying A Kernel Source Patch

Kernels tend to be updated in small increments. Each increment fixes a specific bug, adds a new driver or features, or accomplishes some other task. After deciding which exact version you want, do the following:

1. Download the major version's source and then the source for each patch that leads up to that version.

TIP: *If the major version you want to use is the same major version as the kernel you currently have, and the version you want to upgrade to is higher than what you already have, then you can start with the source on the distribution CD-ROM and patch it up from there.*

2. Using the **cd** command, change to the directory /usr/src.

3. Use **ls** to list what is in the directory. If there is a /usr/src/linux-*version-ext* directory already there, this is the source for the kernel you're already running.

4. Create a new source directory by typing the command "mkdir linux-*newversion-ext*".

5. Copy the source and patches you downloaded into the new directory.

6. Unpackage the source with the **tar** and **gunzip** commands.

7. Each patch should be handled individually and in order. Unpackage the first patch with the **tar** and **gunzip** commands.

8. Utilize the **patch** command to apply the patch to the source by typing "patch -p0 *original* < *patchname*".

9. Repeat Steps 9 and 10 for each patch you need to apply, then continue to the section "Compiling A Kernel."

TIP: *Applying a long series of patches is a good application for a shell script! In fact, a script called kernel-patch is sometimes included with the source.*

Related solutions:	Found on page:
Ungzipping A File	300
Untarring A File	298
Writing A Script	327

Refining The Default Kernel

Refining the kernel that comes with the distribution is almost identical to installing a new kernel. The process to follow is:

1. Log in as **root**.

2. Mount the Red Hat or Caldera CD-ROM onto the file system with the **mount** command.

3. Change to the directory that contains the RPM packages (assuming /mnt/cdrom as the mount point):

   • On the Red Hat CD-ROM this directory is /mnt/cdrom/ RedHat/RPMS.

   • On the Caldera CD-ROM this directory is /mnt/cdrom/ Packages/RPMS.

4. Locate and install the kernel source package and any other packages you may need—RPM will tell you if you need to update a different package while trying to install the source:

   • In Red Hat you can find the file with the text "kernel-source*". You will likely need to install the kernel-header* package first.

   • In Caldera you can find the file with the text "linux-source-common". You should install linux-source-i386* as well.

5. Unmount the CD-ROM with the **umount** command.

6. Put the source CD-ROM that came with the distribution into the CD-ROM drive.

7. Mount the source CD-ROM with the **mount** command.

8. Change to the directory that contains the SRPM packages (RPM packages that contain source code):

    - On the Red Hat CD-ROM, this directory is /mnt/cdrom/ SRPMS.

    - On the Caldera CD-ROM, this directory is /mnt/cdrom/ Packages/SRPMS.

9. Installing a source RPM (SRPM) is the same as installing a program RPM. The package you need to install is:

    - On Caldera's source CD-ROM, look for the text "linux-*version**".

    - On Red Hat's source CD-ROM, look for the text "kernel-*version**".

TIP: *You can distinguish an SRPM from an RPM not from the end extension (they both end in .rpm), but because the SRPM ends in .src.rpm.*

---

10. Now it is time to compile the kernel. See the section "Compiling A Kernel."

11. After you've compiled the kernel, it's time to install it. See the section "Installing A Kernel."

12. Once the kernel is installed, see the section "Adding A LILO Option For The New Kernel" in order to prepare to reboot the machine and test the kernel.

13. Finally, see the section "Testing A Kernel Install" for how to make sure the kernel works properly.

Related solutions:	Found on page:
Mounting Onto The File System	168
Unmounting Off Of The File System	170
Installing An RPM Package	295

Installing A Kernel

Once you have a kernel compiled (see the section "Compiling A Kernel" for how to accomplish this), you need to install it. To install a kernel, do the following:

1. List the contents of the /boot directory with the **ls** command.

2. If a file called vmlinuz already exists there, use the **mv** command to rename it to vmlinuz-*version-ext* (of the kernel version you're currently running).

3. Using the **cp** command, copy the bzImage file you created during the compilation process to /boot. This file is likely found in /usr/src/linux/arch/i386/boot/. If it's not there, then use the **find** command to track it down. Remember that **locate** will not work, because the **locate** database hasn't been updated.

4. Rename the bzImage file in /boot to "vmlinuz".

5. Copy the file /usr/src/linux/System.map to /boot.

6. Change back to the /usr/src/linux directory.

7. Type "make modules_install" to move your kernel modules into place.

8. If your system is booting from a SCSI hard drive, type "mkinitrd /boot/initrd-*version-ext version-ext*" to ensure that the SCSI-handling module is loaded early enough in the boot process. For example, type "mkinitrd /boot/initrd-2.2.5-22 2.2.5-22". Otherwise, skip this step.

9. Proceed to the section "Adding A LILO Option For The New Kernel."

Loading A Kernel Module

Most system administrators these days use modular kernels. These kernels are on average smaller than their monolithic cousins, which have to hold every possible necessary set of code within them at all times. Use the following procedure to locate and install a kernel module:

1. Log in as **root**.

2. Using the **cd** command, change to the /lib/modules directory.

3. List the contents of this directory with the **ls** command. There should be one subdirectory for each version of the kernel you have installed. Change into the directory for the kernel you're currently running (see the section "Determining Which Kernel You Are Running" for instructions on how to get this information).

4. Use the **insmod** command to load a kernel module in the format "insmod *modulename*".

Unloading A Kernel Module

To unload a kernel module that is not in use, do the following:

1. Log in as **root**.

2. Type "lsmod" to get a list of what modules you currently have running.

3. To remove a module from those currently loaded—which will only work if the module is idle and not being used—use **rmmod** in the format "rmmod *modname*". If you get a warning that other modules are dependent on this one and if you want to remove these as well (and you may not want to remove them if you need them), use the format "rmmod -r *modname*".

Using **config**

The **config** kernel configuration tool is the least graphical and most time-consuming to use if you don't want to consider every small detail of your system. However, it does force you to consider each detail, so it does have its place among the kernel configuration tools. To use **config**, do the following:

1. When you have reached the point in the kernel replacement process where it is time to configure the settings, type "make config" to start the **config** tool, shown in Figure 10.1.

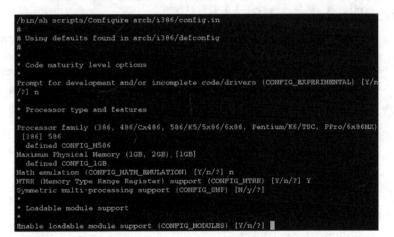

```
/bin/sh scripts/Configure arch/i386/config.in
#
# Using defaults found in arch/i386/defconfig
#
*
* Code maturity level options
*
Prompt for development and/or incomplete code/drivers (CONFIG_EXPERIMENTAL) [Y/n
/?] n
*
* Processor type and features
*
Processor family (386, 486/Cx486, 586/K5/5x86/6x86, Pentium/K6/TSC, PPro/6x86MX)
[386] 586
  defined CONFIG_M586
Maximum Physical Memory (1GB, 2GB) [1GB]
  defined CONFIG_1GB
Math emulation (CONFIG_MATH_EMULATION) [Y/n/?] n
MTRR (Memory Type Range Register) support (CONFIG_MTRR) [Y/n/?] Y
Symmetric multi-processing support (CONFIG_SMP) [N/y/?]
*
* Loadable module support
*
Enable loadable module support (CONFIG_MODULES) [Y/n/?] ▮
```

*Figure 10.1   The **config** tool for configuring the Linux kernel.*

2. Answer the questions this tool asks you. The questionnaire is adaptive, so each answer you give determines whether it will continue along its current topic or move to another.

TIP: *You are told the valid answers for each question. One of these answers begins with a capital letter. If you just press Enter without typing anything, config assumes you want the capitalized answer.*

The options given for each question tend to be yes, no, or modular.

3. When you are finished, the answers you chose are all written to the configuration file the compiler will read when you tell it to compile the new kernel.

Using **menuconfig**

The **menuconfig** kernel configuration tool is a cross between a graphical kernel configuration tool and text only. It is a good option to choose on a machine where you don't have a GUI installed, because it only has specific server functions. To use **menuconfig**, do the following:

1. When you have reached the point in the kernel replacement process where it is time to configure the settings, type "make menuconfig" to start the configuration tool shown in Figure 10.2.

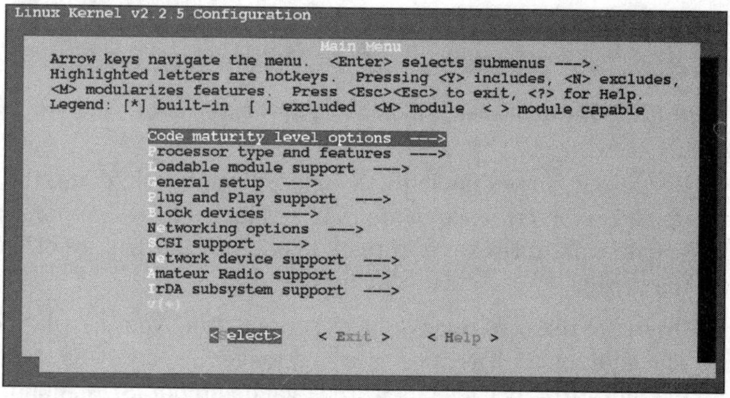

Figure 10.2   The menuconfig tool for configuring the Linux kernel.

2. This tool groups the kernel configuration options under a series of menus. To navigate throughout the main menu, use the up or

down arrow key. The right and left arrow keys move you through the options along the bottom row:

- *Select* opens the menu item.

- *Exit* closes the **menuconfig** tool.

- *Help* gives overall help on using the **menuconfig** tool.

For example, if your LAN and Internet connections in no way involve ISDN lines, you do not need ISDN support in your kernel, even as a module. Use the down arrow to go to the ISDN Subsystem menu option.

3. Use the left or right arrow key if the Select option on the bottom is not already highlighted.

4. Press Enter to see the ISDN Subsystem dialog box, shown in Figure 10.3.

```
Linux Kernel v2.2.5 Configuration

  Arrow keys navigate the menu.  <Enter> selects submenus --->.
  Highlighted letters are hotkeys.  Pressing <Y> includes, <N> excludes,
  <M> modularizes features.  Press <Esc><Esc> to exit, <?> for Help.
  Legend: [*] built-in  [ ] excluded  <M> module  < > module capable

        <M> ISDN support
        [*]   upport synchronous PPP
        [*]   se VJ-compression with synchronous PPP
        [*]   upport generic MP (RFC 1717)
        [ ]   upport dynamic timeout-rules
        [ ]   upport budget-accounting
        [*]   upport audio via ISDN
        [*]   .25 PLP on top of ISDN (EXPERIMENTAL)
        <M>   CN 2B and 4B support
        <M>   sdnloop support
        V(+)

             <Select>    < Exit >    < Help >
```

*Figure 10.3   The **menuconfig** ISDN Subsystem dialog box.*

5. Because in this example ISDN support is not desired, use the up and down arrows to go to the line labeled ISDN Support. If you do want ISDN support then do not shut this feature off in the kernel!

6. Press the N key to remove ISDN support from your new kernel. The additional ISDN options are no longer displayed, as shown in Figure 10.4, because they aren't valid without ISDN support.

7. Press the Esc key twice to back up to the main menu.

8. Continue this process, choosing which section of the kernel you want to configure.

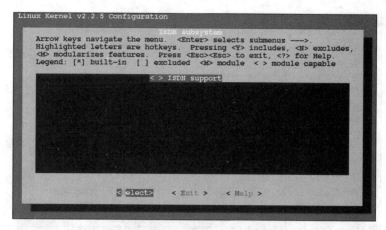

*Figure 10.4   The **menuconfig** ISDN Subsystem dialog box, with ISDN support deselected (as evidenced by there being no options beneath the label).*

9. When you're finished configuring your custom kernel, use the left or right arrow key to select the Exit item at the bottom of the screen.

10. Save your changes if you want to keep them.

11. If you saved the changes, you are ready to compile the new kernel.

Using **xconfig**

The **xconfig** kernel configuration tool is a graphical kernel configuration tool. Many people feel this is the best option available to them, especially those who remember the days of only having access to **config**. To use **xconfig**, do the following:

1. When you have reached the point in the kernel replacement process where it is time to configure the settings, type "make xconfig" to start the configuration tool, shown in Figure 10.5.

2. This tool groups each of the kernel configuration options under a clearly -labeled button. To configure a specific segment, say the Old CD-ROM drivers, click the button corresponding to it. The Old CD-ROM drivers configuration dialog box is shown in Figure 10.6.

3. Unless you specifically have a CD-ROM drive that is not SCSI, IDE, or ATAPI, there is no reason to even have these modules

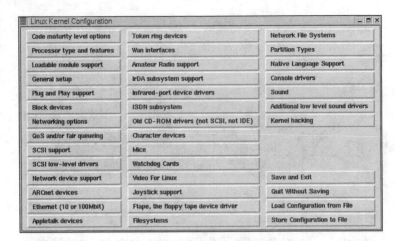

*Figure 10.5   The **xconfig** tool for configuring the Linux kernel.*

			Old CD-ROM drivers (not SCSI, not IDE)	
◆ y	◇ -	◇ n	Support non-SCSI/IDE/ATAPI CDROM drives	Help
◇ y	◆ m	◇ n	Aztech/Orchid/Okano/Wearnes/TXC/CyDROM CDROM support	Help
◇ y	◆ m	◇ n	Goldstar R420 CDROM support	Help
◇ y	◆ m	◇ n	Matsushita/Panasonic/Creative, Longshine, TEAC CDROM support	Help
◇ y	◇ -	◇ n	Matsushita/Panasonic, ... second CDROM controller support	Help
◇ y	◇ -	◇ n	Matsushita/Panasonic, ... third CDROM controller support	Help
◇ y	◇ -	◇ n	Matsushita/Panasonic, ... fourth CDROM controller support	Help
◇ y	◆ m	◇ n	Mitsumi (standard) [no XA/Multisession] CDROM support	Help
11			MCD IRQ	Help
300			MCD I/O base	Help
◇ y	◆ m	◇ n	Mitsumi [XA/MultiSession] CDROM support	Help
◇ y	◆ m	◇ n	Optics Storage DOLPHIN 8000AT CDROM support	Help
◇ y	◆ m	◇ n	Philips/LMS CM206 CDROM support	Help
◇ y	◆ m	◇ n	Sanyo CDR-H94A CDROM support	Help
◇ y	◆ m	◇ n	ISP16/MAD16/Mozart soft configurable cdrom interface support	Help
◇ y	◆ m	◇ n	Sony CDU31A/CDU33A CDROM support	Help
◇ y	◆ m	◇ n	Sony CDU535 CDROM support	Help
	Main Menu		Next	Prev

*Figure 10.6   The **xconfig** Old CD-ROM drivers configuration dialog box.*

available for loading. On the first line, "Support non-SCSI/IDE/ATAPI CD-ROM drives", click the "n" diamond to remove support for this subsystem from the kernel. Every option below the first line now grays out and becomes unavailable, as shown in Figure 10.7, because they are all dependent on having the support active.

			Old CD-ROM drivers (not SCSI, not IDE)		
y	-	● n	Support non-SCSI/IDE/ATAPI CDROM drives	Help	
y	m	n	Aztech/Orchid/Okano/Wearnes/TXC/CyDROM CDROM support	Help	
y	m	n	Goldstar R420 CDROM support	Help	
y	m	n	Matsushita/Panasonic/Creative, Longshine, TEAC CDROM support	Help	
y	-	n	Matsushita/Panasonic, ... second CDROM controller support	Help	
y	-	n	Matsushita/Panasonic, ... third CDROM controller support	Help	
y	-	n	Matsushita/Panasonic, ... fourth CDROM controller support	Help	
y	m	n	Mitsumi (standard) [no XA/Multisession] CDROM support	Help	
11			MCD IRQ	Help	
300			MCD I/O base	Help	
y	m	n	Mitsumi [XA/MultiSession] CDROM support	Help	
y	m	n	Optics Storage DOLPHIN 8000AT CDROM support	Help	
y	m	n	Philips/LMS CM206 CDROM support	Help	
y	m	n	Sanyo CDR-H94A CDROM support	Help	
y	m	n	ISP16/MAD16/Mozart soft configurable cdrom interface support	Help	
y	m	n	Sony CDU31A/CDU33A CDROM support	Help	
y	m	n	Sony CDU535 CDROM support	Help	

Main Menu   Next   Prev

Figure 10.7   The xconfig Old CD-ROM drivers configuration dialog box, deselected.

4. Click the Main Menu button to return to the main dialog box.

5. Continue this process, choosing which section of the kernel you want to configure.

6. When you've finished configuring your custom kernel, click one of the two following buttons:

   • Click Save and Exit to save the configuration and close **xconfig**.

   • Click Quit without Saving to close **xconfig** without saving your changes.

7. If you saved the changes, you are ready to compile the new kernel.

Configuring A LAN

In Brief

Many key aspects of Local Area Network (LAN) configuration are addressed during the install process. However, these values can change as you decide you want to use another machine name here, or alter the IP structure of your network there. This chapter covers the steps used to change those items after the install process is completed, as well as configuration issues not covered during the install.

Planning A LAN

Setting up a LAN goes best if thought and planning are put into it. This analysis needs to be done for both the hardware and the software. Some initial issues to consider are:

- What combination of Operating Systems (OS) does the LAN need to support?

- What network services need to be provided? Which OS should they be provided in?

- How much data will be transmitted? How fast a connection between machines will be required?

- How many machines are involved in the network?

TIP: *There are entire books available on the various aspects of networking. Helpful hints are provided in this chapter.*

Once these questions have been addressed you will be better prepared to continue with your LAN.

If you intend to hook up your LAN to the Internet, it is best to choose TCP/IP as the communications protocol used between machines, and this book assumes you are choosing TCP/IP as your network protocol. This choice prevents the need for adding translators if you do eventually decide to hook up to the Internet, and it allows you to use Internet tools within your own intranet if you so choose.

TIP: *While there was an opportunity to configure the machine to work within the LAN during the installation process, these individual procedures are still discussed in this chapter.*

Networking Hardware

The type of cabling and network connections you choose determine the route through which data flows in your network, and how quickly it moves. The most commonly chosen options are Ethernet and Token Ring.

Ethernet

An Ethernet network is comprised of a long chain of machines with terminators on both ends to close the connections, as shown in Figure 11.1. Data is instantaneously broadcast to every machine on the network. If the Ethernet card on the machine detects that the data is meant for its unique address, the machine receives the information. If the data is not meant for its address, the machine ignores it.

The speeds available in an Ethernet network depend on the cabling solution you choose, as shown in Table 11.1.

NOTE: *Twisted-Pair cables look like standard telephone cables. 100baseTX Ethernet is also called Fast Ethernet. Performance is best on a network that is inconsistently loaded.*

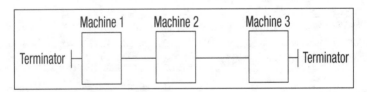

Figure 11.1   Ethernet network.

Table 11.1   Comparison of Ethernet hardware standards.

Standard	Cable	Speed(s) in Mbps	Maximum Cable Length in Feet
10base5	Thick Coaxial	1, 5, 10, 20	1500
10base2	Thin Coaxial	10	600
10baseT	Twisted-Pair	10	300
100baseTX	Twisted-Pair	100	328

11. Configuring A LAN

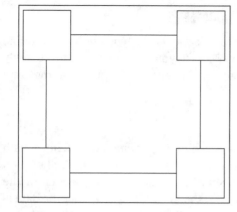

Figure 11.2   Token Ring network.

Token Ring

A Token Ring network is, as its name implies, a ring-shaped network, as shown in Figure 11.2. Data travels in one direction around the ring at 4 or 16Mbps, with each machine looking to see if the data is meant for it. If the data is not meant for that particular machine, the data continues around the ring until it finds its destination.

NOTE: *Network performance remains consistent regardless of network size, with a maximum of 260 nodes on the network. It is possible to find bridging solutions that allow you to use Token Ring on a Fast Ethernet 100Mbps network.*

Services

If you are running a single Linux machine at home, then which services to run and on which machine are not complex issues. However, the heavier the load your servers can expect and the larger the network they reside on, the more complicated this decision becomes.

The services, or servers, are also known as *daemons*. You can often spot them easily in a list of processes because they generally end in the letter "d" (for example, "httpd"). Exceptions are programs such as "sendmail", which do not end in "d" but run in a fashion similar to daemons.

TIP: *Many services, Internet or otherwise, are broken down into two components: clients and servers. Clients are what the end user accesses the service with (for example, a Web browser). Servers are the programs that wait to provide the information the client requests.*

Spreading Out Services

The heavier the load your network needs to support, the more it benefits you to spread services across multiple machines. Which services need to reside where is entirely dependent on which will have the heaviest loads. Servers that commonly benefit from having dedicated or mostly dedicated computers while under heavy load are:

- Email
- Web
- FTP
- Database
- News

Not only do the services benefit from being split onto other machines alone or in groups, but other processes benefit as well. When a server on a machine is under a heavy load, everything else happening on that computer is slowed down. If the load is heavy enough, the machine can become unusable.

TIP: *If you cannot split services off to other machines, then increasing the overloaded computer's RAM and/or processor speed can help greatly.*

Determining If You Need Dynamic Routing

If your network or subnet requires a router, as shown in Figure 11.3, you can configure one of the Linux machines to perform this task. Whether this box has another job as well is up to you, but in general since it's the only machine directly connected to the network or Internet, it's good to make it a single-task machine or to place your Internet servers directly on it instead of behind the router.

Not all networks need an explicit router; in some cases the modem itself can act as a router. If your modem does not do routing for you, then an explicit router is necessary if you have one or more of the following conditions:

- Only one IP address for the Internet is available for your network, even though the network has multiple machines.
- You want to connect on one or more machines from a different network (one with a different block of IP addresses) to the current network.

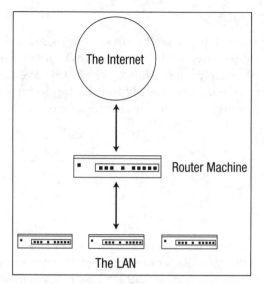

Figure 11.3   Using a router to pass data between a network and another network or the Internet.

- You want to create a separate subnet to function alongside the main LAN, with them connected together.
- Only one machine on your LAN is connected directly to the Internet, and there are enough IP addresses available for all.

Immediate Solutions

Checking Your Current Network Settings

To check your current network settings, first log in as **root**. Then type "netstat -nr". The *n* flag tells netstat to display addresses as raw IP numbers rather than looking up the full domain information, and the *r* flag tells netstat to only display information for items using TCP/IP.

TIP: *A quick way to determine if DNS is working is to try "netstat -nr" and then "netstat", or try pinging a machine at its IP address and then with its name.*

Setting The IP Address

To set your machine's IP address—if not already set during the install—do the following:

1. Log in as **root**.

2. Edit the file /etc/hosts.

3. Add a new line for your current host. Leave the loopback line (127.0.0.1) intact. This should look similar to:

```
127.0.0.1      localhost      localhost.localdomain
```

The new line should be in at least two parts: the IP address, then the machine's full name (including domain). You can also add aliases if you choose. For example, if you are configuring the computer "blue" on the domain "colors.org" to have the IP address 185.36.20.3, the line you might add beneath the loopback line is:

```
185.36.20.3    blue.colors.org      blue
```

4. Save and exit the file. Any login sessions and programs that use the domain name need to be restarted at this point. Sometimes it is simplest to reboot the machine.

Setting The IP Address In The GUI

The tools provided with the Red Hat and Caldera GUIs are different, so each is covered separately. It is possible that you already set IP information during the installation process.

Related solutions:	Found on page:
Launching The Installer From A Boot Disk	59
Launching The Installer From The CD-ROM	60
Launching The Installer From Floppy Disks	38

Setting The IP Address In Red Hat

To set your IP address in Linuxconf, do the following:

1. Log in as **root**.

2. Start Gnome if necessary.

3. Click the Network Configuration button in the Control Panel, as shown Figure 11.4.

   The Network Configurator window opens, as shown in Figure 11.5.

4. Click the Hosts tab if necessary.

5. If the machine already has a name (see the sections "Naming The Machine" or "Naming The Machine In The GUI" for more information), double-click the name entry in the list. Otherwise, click the Add button to add the machine. Regardless, the Edit /etc/hosts dialog box opens, as shown in Figure 11.6.

6. Type the machine's IP address in the IP textbox.

7. Click the Done button to close the dialog box.

8. Click the Save button to save the changes to your network configuration.

9. Click the Quit button to close the Network Configurator. Any programs that have a need to know your current IP addresses should be restarted. The simplest fix for this issue is a quick reboot of the system.

Figure 11.4   The Network Configurator Control Panel button.

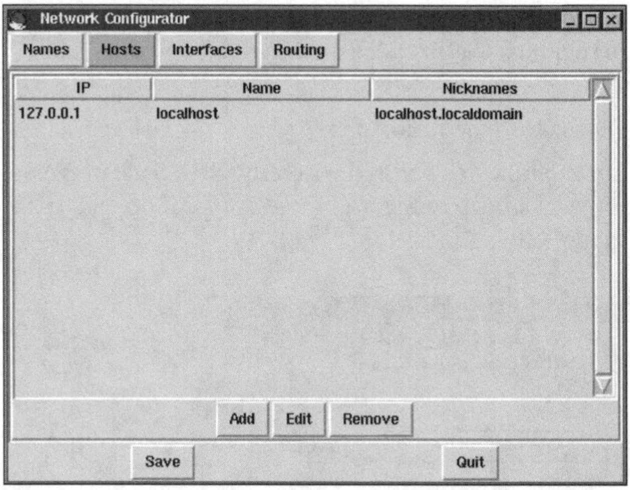

IP	Name	Nicknames
127.0.0.1	localhost	localhost.localdomain

Network Configurator

Names | Hosts | Interfaces | Routing

Add   Edit   Remove

Save   Quit

Figure 11.5   The Network Configurator window with Hosts tab displayed.

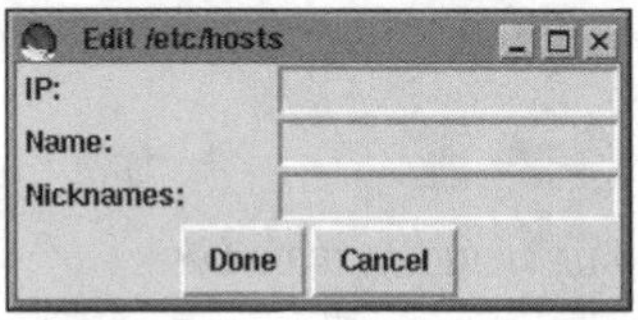

Edit /etc/hosts

IP:
Name:
Nicknames:

Done   Cancel

Figure 11.6   The Edit /etc/hosts dialog box.

Setting The IP Address In Caldera

To set your IP address in COAS, do the following:

1. Click the Caldera Open Administration System (COAS) icon to open the COAS menu, as shown in Figure 11.7.

Figure 11.7   The COAS icon.

205

2. Click the Network menu option to open the COAS Network menu.

3. Click the TCP/IP menu option to open the COAS TCP/IP Networking menu.

4. Click the Ethernet option to open the Ethernet Interface Configuration dialog box as shown in Figure 11.8.

5. Enter the machine's IP address in the Interface address text box.

6. Be sure to adjust the Broadcast address and Netmask if necessary.

7. Click OK to close the dialog box.

8. If the information was entered correctly, click Save in the Save dialog box, as shown in Figure 11.9. If not, or if no changes were made, click Discard.

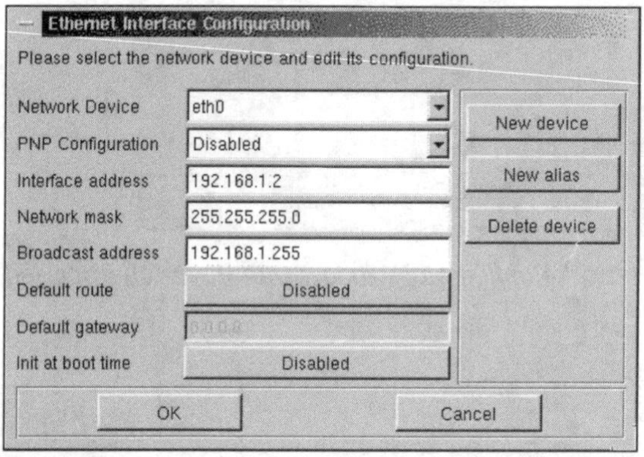

Figure 11.8   The COAS Ethernet Interface Configuration dialog box.

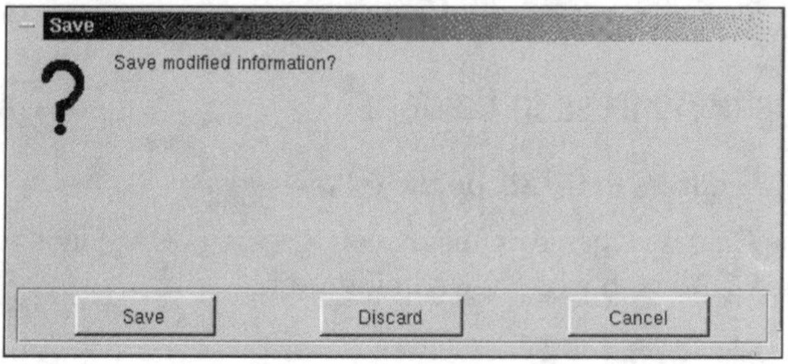

Figure 11.9   The COAS dialog box determining whether to save or discard changed data.

Naming The Machine

To assign a name to the specific machine you are configuring, do the following:

1. Log in as **root**.

2. Edit the file /etc/sysconfig/network.

3. Locate the line.

```
HOSTNAME=localhost.localdomain
```

TIP: *This line may look slightly different if you have already assigned a host or domain. The HOSTNAME component is the key to look for.*

---

4. Change the word "localhost" to the name of the machine. For example, to assign the machine name "blue" you could change the line to:

```
HOSTNAME=blue.localdomain
```

5. Save and close the file. The new hostname will be reflected by exiting any login sessions and logging back in, and stopping then restarting any programs that need the hostname information. In many ways, the easiest method of handling all of this is a quick reboot.

TIP: *You can change the name of a machine at any time using this method. However, if the machine is listed in users' bookmarks then services it runs will be broken until users find its new location. Changing the machine's listing in your DNS tables is imperative.*

Naming The Machine In The GUI

Red Hat and Caldera GUIs each handle network configuration within their GUIs differently, so each is covered separately.

Naming The Machine In Red Hat

To assign a name to the specific machine you are configuring within Linuxconf, do the following:

1. Log in as **root**.
2. Start Gnome if necessary.
3. Click the Footprint box to open the system menu.
4. Click System to open the System submenu.
5. Click Control Panel to open the system Control Panel.
6. Click the Network Configuration button in the Control Panel, as shown in Figure 11.4. The Network Configurator window opens, as shown in Figure 11.10.

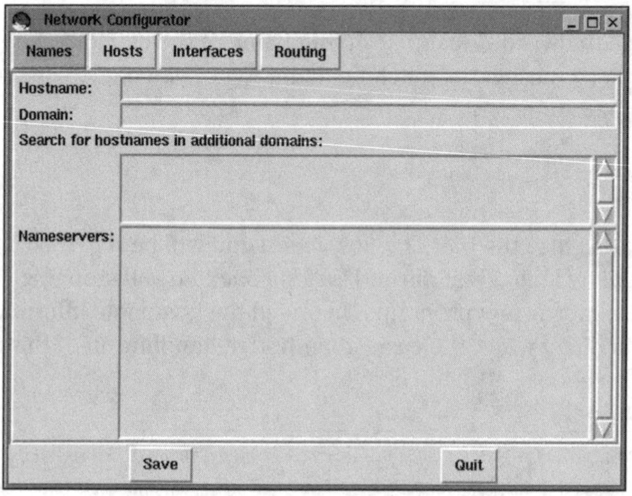

Figure 11.10   The Network Configurator window with Names tab displayed.

7. Click the Names tab if necessary.
8. In the Hostname textbox, change "localhost" to the name you want your machine to have.
9. Click the Save button.
10. Click the Quit button to close the Network Configurator. The new hostname will be reflected by exiting any login sessions and logging back in, and stopping then restarting any programs that need the hostname information. In many ways, the easiest method of handling all of this is a quick reboot.

TIP: *You can change the name of a machine at any time using this method. However, if the machine is listed in users' bookmarks then services it runs will be broken until users find its new location. Changing the machine's listing in your DNS tables is imperative.*

Naming The Machine In Caldera

To assign a name to a machine in COAS, do the following:

1. Click the COAS icon (see Figure 11.7) to open the COAS menu.
2. Click the System menu option to open the COAS System menu.
3. Click the Hostname menu option to open the COAS System Hostname dialog box, as shown in Figure 11.11.

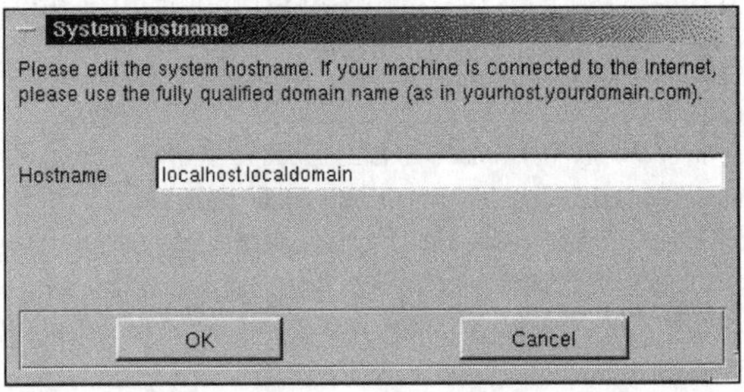

Figure 11.11   The COAS System Hostname dialog box.

4. In the text box, enter the machine's hostname. If the computer is part of a named network then be sure to change only the host portion of the name.
5. Click OK to close the dialog box.
6. Read the Warning dialog box and choose the appropriate option. If you definitely want the name change but are unsure of whether you are ready to reboot or not, click Postpone.

Naming The Domain

To assign the name of the domain your machine resides on, do the following:

1. Log in as **root**.
2. Edit the file /etc/sysconfig/network.
3. Locate the line

```
HOSTNAME=localhost.localdomain
```

TIP: *This line may look slightly different if you have already assigned a host or domain. The HOSTNAME component is the key to look for.*

---

4. Change the word "localdomain" to the name of the domain the machine resides on. For example, to assign the domain name "colors.org" you could change the line to

```
HOSTNAME=localhost.colors.org
```

If the machine already has a name, then use its name instead of the word "localhost".

5. Save and close the file. Any login sessions and programs that use the domain name need to be restarted at this point. Sometimes it is simplest to reboot the machine.

TIP: *You can change the name of the domain a machine is assigned to at any time using this method. However, if the domain is on the Internet people can reach it by name because it is listed in the Internet-wide DNS tables. Changing the domain name—which first must be owned by and registered to you—will make it impossible for anyone to reach the system via Internet until they locate the machine's new name. It is imperative as well to be sure to change your DNS tables to reflect the new information.*

Naming The Domain In The GUI

The Red Hat and Caldera GUIs handle network configuration differently, so each is covered separately.

Naming The Domain In Red Hat

To tell the machine you are configuring what domain it resides on within Red Hat Linux, do the following:

1. Log in as **root**.

2. Start Gnome if necessary.

3. Click the Footprint box to open the system menu.

4. Click System to open the System submenu.

5. Click Control Panel to open the system Control Panel.

6. Click the Network Configuration button (see Figure 11.4) in the Control Panel. The Network Configurator window opens (see Figure 11.10).

7. Click the Names tab if necessary.

8. In the Domain textbox, change "localdomain" to the name you want your machine to have.

9. Click the Save button.

10. Click the Quit button to close the Network Configurator. Any login sessions and programs that use the domain name need to be restarted at this point. Sometimes it is simplest to reboot the machine.

11. Configuring A LAN

TIP: *You can change the name of the domain a machine is assigned to at any time using this method. However, if the domain is on the Internet people can reach it by name because it is listed in the Internet-wide DNS tables. Changing the domain name—which first must be owned by and registered to you—will make it impossible for anyone to reach the system via Internet until they locate the machine's new name. It is imperative as well to be sure to change your DNS tables to reflect the new information.*

Naming The Domain In Caldera

To assign a domain name to a machine in COAS, do the following:

1. Click the COAS icon to open the COAS menu, as shown in Figure 11.7.

2. Click the System menu option to open the COAS System menu.

3. Click the Hostname menu option to open the COAS System Hostname dialog box, as shown in Figure 11.11.

4. In the textbox, enter the machine's full domain name. Be sure to include a name for the individual machine as well.

5. Click OK to close the dialog box.

6. Read the Warning dialog box and choose the appropriate option. If you definitely want the name change but are unsure of whether you are ready to reboot or not, click Postpone.

Setting Up Dynamic Routing

Configuring dynamic routing entails setting up the services IP forwarding and IP masquerading. Fortunately, both Caldera and Red Hat support these features without requiring compilations of the kernel. Do the following to set this up:

1. Log in as **root**.

2. Assign each machine behind the router its number if it does not already have one. These should not be actual Internet addresses if you are using the router to connect them to the Internet. Instead, they should use the address blocks reserved for internal networks. These blocks are as follows:

   • Class A 10.0.0.0 - 10.255.255.255

   • Class B 172.16.0.0 - 172.31.255.255

   • Class C 192.168.0.0 - 192.168.255.255

   However, this statement is somewhat misleading. The first address is reserved as the Network address (for example, the Class B Network address is 172.16.0.0) and the Broadcast address is also reserved, which is the last component of one of the blocks (for example, the Class A Broadcast address is 10.0.0.255, B is 172.16.0.255, and C is 192.168.0.255).

   Typically, the second address (ending in .1) is used for the router itself.

3. Create the file /etc/rc.d/rc.masq, which will contain the script (more on writing shell scripts in Chapter 18) that sets up routing for you.

4. Add the following to the beginning of the script:

```
#!/bin/sh
# Tell the kernel to load necessary modules automatically, as
# described in man depmod.
/sbin/depmod -a
```

5. Enable IP forwarding by adding the line:

```
echo "1 > /proc/sys/net/ipv4/ip_forward
```

TIP: *The Linux IP Masquerade mini HOWTO also suggests that Red Hat users edit the file /etc/ sysconfig/network and change the statement FORWARD_IPV4=false to FORWARD_IPV4=true.*

---

6. Enable timeouts for IP masquerading with the format:

```
/sbin/ipchains -M -S TCPtimeout FINtimeout UDPtimeout
```

   The timeout assignments are listed in seconds and each applies to specific aspects of TCP/IP traffic:

- The TCPtimeout option sets how long the router will wait before severing a connection if there has been no traffic across a TCP/IP client/server connection. For example, if a user has connected to an FTP server and allows the connection to sit idly for hours, or even forgets and leaves it sitting overnight, this is a waste of resources. This option is usually set for a matter of hours, to avoid cutting things off prematurely. Remember, however, to list the hours as seconds.

- The FINtimeout option sets how long the router will wait after completing the initial TCP/IP connection (receiving the "FIN" packet) before severing the connection. This option is usually set for a number of seconds, from perhaps ten to thirty, since usually the connection is initiated so data transfer can begin so should not be immediately silent.

- The UDPtimeout option sets how long the router will wait before severing a connection if there has been no traffic across a UDP client/server data stream. As UDP does not keep a steady connection open as TCP/IP does, the wait times are much shorter, typically a matter of a few minutes.

7. To turn on the actual forwarding add these two lines of code:

```
/sbin/ipchains -P forward DENY
/sbin/ipchains -A forward -s network/subnetmask -j MASQ
```

The network item is the network number used in your system, and the subnet mask is the last portion of that mask, the number after the last period.

8. Now, you must load modules for each service that requires masquerading to access the Internet from behind the router. Table 11.2 lists which modules need to be loaded for which services.

9. Save and exit the file.

10. Change the file's mode to 700.

11. Open the file /etc/rc.d/rc.local.

12. Add the following line to load your script:

```
/etc/rc.d/rc.masq
```

13. Save and exit the file.

NOTE: *Be sure to go to the other machines on the LAN and set the router as their Gateway.*

Table 11.2   Modules necessary to forward and masquerade specific services.

Service	Module Loading Code
CuSeeme	/sbin/modprobe ip_masq_cuseeme
FTP	/sbin/modprobe ip_masq_ftp
IRC DCCtransfer	/sbin/modprobe ip_masq_irc
Quake I/II/III/World	/sbin/modprobe ip_masq_quake
UDP RealAudio	/sbin/modprobe ip_masq_raudio
VDO Live	/sbin/modprobe_ip_masq_vdolive

Related solutions:	Found on page:
Changing File And Directory Permissions	86
Writing A Script	327

Setting Up Static Routing In Red Hat

There is no specific routing utility provided in COAS, so what is covered here is Linuxconf's routing dialog box. To set up a machine's routing table within Linuxconf, do the following:

1. Log in as **root**.

2. Start Gnome if necessary.

3. Click the Footprint box to open the system menu.

4. Click System to open the System submenu.

5. Click Control Panel to open the system Control Panel.

6. Click the Network Configuration button (see Figure 11.4) in the Control Panel. The Network Configurator window opens, as shown in Figure 11.12.

7. Click the Routing tab if necessary.

8. Click Add to add a new static route, or Edit to edit an existing one.

9. Enter the information in the dialog box as it applies to your system. Some of this information is already there, depending on what else you've already configured; just fill in the blanks as necessary.

10. Click Done when finished adding or editing the entry.

11. Click Save when finished with configuring routing.

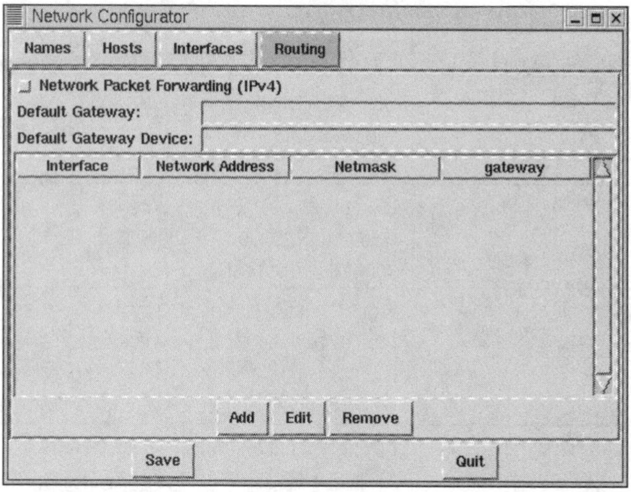

Figure 11.12 The Network Configurator Routing dialog box.

Configuring Name Resolution For The Machine

To configure Domain Name Service (DNS) within your LAN, you may need to edit multiple files. First you must tell your system what DNS services to use. It also needs to know what order to use these services in, and what options you want set. The defaults set during the initial install are often sufficient for many people's needs.

TIP: *Often there is no need to change the file /etc/host.conf. Instructions on how to do so are included in case you have a need to change the default file.*

Do the following to accomplish this task:

1. Log in as **root**.
2. Edit the file /etc/host.conf.
3. Set the options that are appropriate for your network. The available options for host.conf are shown in Table 11.3.
4. Save and close the file.

TIP: *If edits are necessary, you must edit /etc/host.conf on each machine within the LAN, even if you do not intend to run a Domain Name Server locally. The exception to this statement is if the machine is entirely standalone.*

Table 11.3   Options for the file /etc/host.conf.

Option	Format of Setting	Purpose
alert	On or Off	Scan for attempts at IP address spoofing. Any such attempts, if the option is on, are listed in your system logs.
multi	On or Off	Determines whether hosts are allowed, for host query purposes, to have more than one IP address in /etc/hosts.
nospoof	On or Off	Prevent IP address spoofing by using reverse DNS resolution to match the connection's hostname to its IP address. The cost of using this option is increased load on your domain server.
order	hosts, bind, nis	Specify the order in which the various DNS resolution services are used. The *hosts* option tells the system to look in the /etc/host file. The *bind* option tells the system to consult a DNS server. *NIS* points to Network Information Service to try to resolve the hostname (see section "Determining If You Need NIS" for more details). You can use one, two, or all three of the settings. If you use more than one, separate them with a single space.
trim	domain name	Tell the system to remove the specific domain name and just look in /etc/hosts to resolve the IP address. This is useful for speeding up local resolution, especially if you are otherwise having DNS problems.

After you finish editing the /etc/host.conf file (if this was necessary), you need to configure the DNS itself. To accomplish this task, do the following:

1. Log in as **root**.

2. Edit the file /etc/resolv.conf.

3. Set the options that are appropriate for your DNS setup. The available options for resolv.conf are shown in Table 11.4.

4. Save and close the file.

Table 11.4   Options for the file resolv.conf.

Option	Format of Setting	Purpose
domain	domain name	Tell the DNS resolver what your LAN's domain name is.
nameserver	IP address(es) of nameserver	Tell your system where to look to resolve domains into IP addresses. You can list up to three nameserver IP addresses. If one fails, the resolver will try the next.
search	domain name(s)	Set default domains that people often use on the LAN. If a domain isn't included in a query, the resolver tries the domains listed with the search option. It is not necessary to place the LAN's domain name with the search variable.

Setting Up A LAN

Setting up a Local Area Network works best when a specific process is followed:

1. If the LAN is going to be connected to the Internet, register the domain name.

2. Choose and install the networking hardware.

3. Configure the Internet Protocol (IP) addresses for each machine, or node, on the network as discussed in "Setting The IP Address" and "Setting The IP Address In The GUI."

4. Use the "ping" command in the format "ping *address*" between various randomly-selected machines to ensure that the networking is set up correctly at this point.

5. Name the machines and the domain throughout the network.

6. Configure routing.

7. Configure DNS.

8. Use the "ping" command in the format "ping *name*" between randomly selected machines within the network to ensure that it's set up correctly.

9. Make security adjustments.

10. Connect LAN to the Internet if necessary.

11. If connected to the Internet, first test pings on IP addresses outside the domain, then test them on names.

Configuring Printing Services

WARNING!   *It is highly recommended that you use the GUI tools for configuring printing services. Additional steps are included in this section to try to help avoid any major problems.*

To configure your printing services at the command line level, do the following:

1. Log in as **root**.

2. Choose the name you will call the printer within your LAN, for example, laser1.

3. Create a spool directory for the printer in /var/spool/lpd, for example /var/spool/lpd/laser1.

4. Make sure all three of the directories have their permissions set to 775.

5. Make sure all three of the directories are owned by **root**, and are set to the group daemon.

6. Change to the printer's directory. For example,

```
cd /var/spool/lpd/laser1
```

7. Create the empty files .seq, errs, lock, and status. For example,

```
touch .seq errs lock status
```

8. Make sure all three files have their permissions set to 664.

9. Make sure all three files are owned by **root**, and are set to the group daemon.

10. Edit a new file called simple_filter.

TIP: *This is a very simple filter. You can create more complex ones if you need to do so. This file is a shell script. You can learn more about shell scripting in Chapter 18.*

---

11. Add the following line to simple_filter so a carriage return will be added before every newline code:

```
while(<STDIN>)(chop $_; print "$_\r\n";);
```

12. Save and exit the file.

13. Make sure the filter's permissions are **755**.

14. Make sure the filter is owned by **root** and assigned to group **daemon**.

15. Make a backup copy of the file /etc/printcap.

16. Note the original file's permissions and set the copy's permissions to the same.

17. Read the help information for printcap by typing "man printcap".

18. Edit the file /etc/printcap.

19. If this is the first printer you are adding, delete all other printer definitions. Otherwise, go to the end of the file.

20. Let's continue the example one line at a time. First, you define what the new print spool is called. To name the spool either l1 or laser1, add:

    ```
    l1|laser1:\
    ```

21. To set the spool directory to /var/spool/lpd/laser1, add:

    ```
    :sd=/var/spool/lpd/laser1:\
    ```

22. To tell the system there is no maximum size for print jobs, add:

    ```
    :mx#0:\
    ```

23. To tell the system which physical device your printer is, in this case /dev/lp1, add:

    ```
    :lp=/dev/lp1:\
    ```

24. To include the filter you created earlier, add the line:

    ```
    :if=/var/spool/lpd/laser1/simple_filter:\
    ```

25. To tell the system not to include a banner page with the name of the user and other information, include the line:

    ```
    :sh:
    ```

26. Exit and save the file.

11. Configuring A LAN

27. Make sure the permissions remain the same as in the original /etc/printcap.

28. Restart the print daemon by typing "/etc/rc.d/init.d lpd restart".

Adding A Printer Within A GUI

Both Red Hat and Caldera provide tools for working with printers from a dialog box while in their GUIs. Their tools are slightly different, and so are covered separately.

Adding A Printer In Red Hat

To configure your printing information within Gnome, do the following:

1. Log in as **root**.

2. Start Gnome if necessary.

3. Click the Footprint box to open the system menu.

4. Click System to open the System submenu.

5. Click Control Panel to open the system Control Panel.

6. Click the Printer Configuration button on the Control Panel, as shown in Figure 11.13.

   The RHS Linux Print System Manager window opens, as shown in Figure 11.14.

NOTE: *You may get some warnings about not having Samba or other networking applications installed. Read the dialog boxes and then click OK. If the warnings apply to you, follow the instructions. If not, ignore them and continue on.*

---

7. Click the Add button to open the Add a Printer Entry dialog box, shown in Figure 11.15.

8. Click the option appropriate for the printer you are adding.

9. Click the OK button. If you chose a local printer, the system tries to auto-detect it.

10. If any intermediate dialog boxes open, read them carefully and then click OK. The dialog box for editing the printer type you entered appears.

11. Fill in the dialog box. Where defaults are given, these are usually acceptable values.

Figure 11.13   The Gnome Control Panel Printer Configuration button.

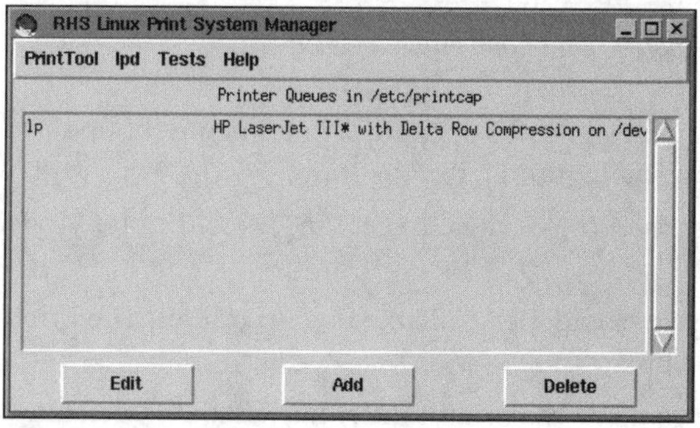

11. Configuring A LAN

RHS Linux Print System Manager

PrintTool   lpd   Tests   Help

Printer Queues in /etc/printcap

lp   HP LaserJet III* with Delta Row Compression on /dev

Edit   Add   Delete

Figure 11.14   The Gnome RHS Linux Print System Manager.

Add a Printer Entry

Printer type:

◆ Local Printer

◇ Remote Unix (lpd) Queue

◇ Lan Manager Printer (SMB)

◇ NetWare Printer (NCP)

OK   Cancel

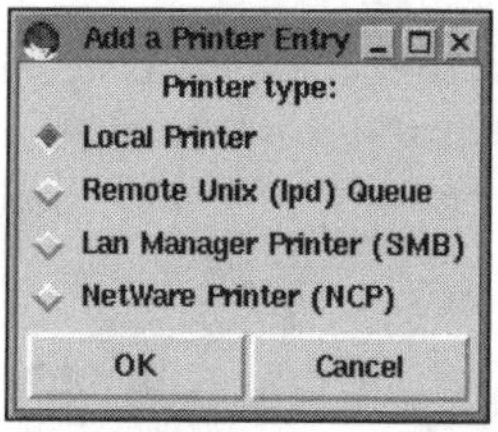

Figure 11.15   The Add a Printer Entry dialog box.

12. Click the OK button to save the changes.

13. If you have another printer to add, return to Step 7.

14. To close the window, click the PrintTool menu, then the Quit option.

Adding A Printer In Caldera

To configure print services within Caldera Linux, do the following:

1. Click the COAS icon (see Figure 11.7) to open the COAS menu.

2. Click the Peripherals menu option to open the COAS Peripherals menu.

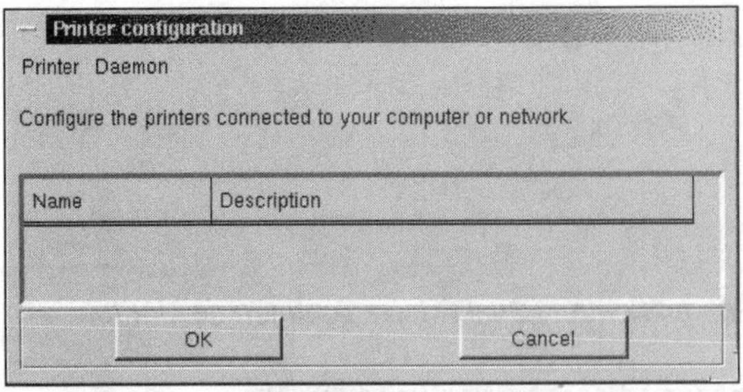

Figure 11.16   Caldera Printer Configuration dialog box.

3. Click the Printer option to open the Printer configuration dialog box, as shown in Figure 11.16.

4. Click Add in the Printer menu to get the "Select Printer Model" dialog box.

5. Choose the closest model available to your printer. The Printer name dialog box opens.

6. If you want to name the printer differently from the default, then change the name listed.

7. Click OK. The Printer attributes dialog box opens.

8. If the printer is connected to a machine other than the one you're configuring, enter its address under the Remote host text box.

9. Click OK to get the Save dialog box (shown in Figure 11.9).

10. Click Save to keep the information and get the Create printer queue dialog box.

11. It is recommended that you click OK in this dialog box so you don't have to create the queue by hand. After clicking OK, the program automatically stops and starts the print daemon, which needs to be done after making any print changes.

Editing A Printer Entry In The GUI

Both Red Hat and Caldera provide tools for working with printers from a dialog box while in their GUI. Their tools are slightly different, and so are covered separately.

Editing Print Entries In Linuxconf

To edit a printer entry within Gnome, do the following:

1. Log in as **root**.

2. Start Gnome if necessary.

3. Click the Footprint box to open the system menu.

4. Click System to open the System submenu.

5. Click Control Panel to open the system Control Panel.

6. Click the Printer Configuration button (see Figure 11.13) on the Control Panel.

   The RHS Linux Print System Manager window opens (see Figure 11.14).

7. Select the printing device whose entry you want to edit.

8. Click the Edit button. A dialog box opens with the current settings.

9. Change the setting as necessary.

10. Click OK to change the settings.

11. To close the window, click the PrintTool menu, then the Quit option.

Editing Print Entries In Caldera

To configure print entries within Caldera Linux, do the following:

1. Click the COAS icon (see Figure 11.7) to open the COAS menu.

2. Click the Peripherals menu option to open the COAS Peripherals menu.

3. Click the Printer option to open the Printer Configuration dialog box, (as shown in Figure 11.16).

4. Click the printer entry you want to edit.

5. Click Edit in the Printer menu to get the Printer attributes dialog box, as shown in Figure 11.17.

6. Edit the attributes of interest. There are many items available here that were not available when you created the printer entry.

7. When finished, click OK to get the Save dialog box, as shown in Figure 11.9.

8. Click Save to keep the changes.

9. Click OK to close the Printer Configuration dialog box.

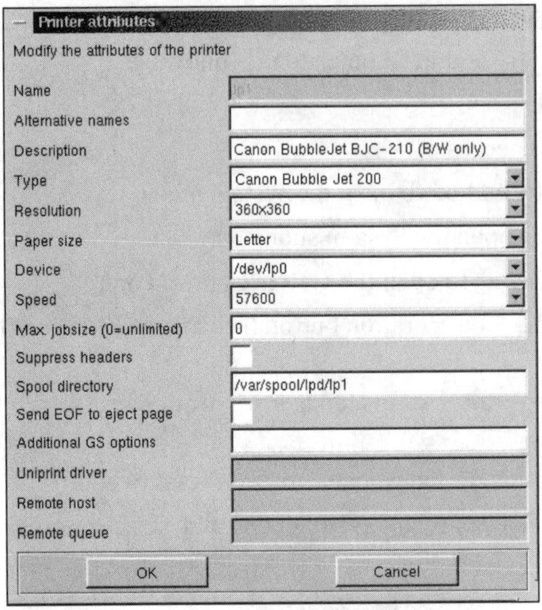

Printer attributes

Modify the attributes of the printer

Name	lp1
Alternative names	
Description	Canon BubbleJet BJC-210 (B/W only)
Type	Canon Bubble Jet 200
Resolution	360x360
Paper size	Letter
Device	/dev/lp0
Speed	57600
Max jobsize (0=unlimited)	0
Suppress headers	
Spool directory	/var/spool/lpd/lp1
Send EOF to eject page	
Additional GS options	
Uniprint driver	
Remote host	
Remote queue	

| OK | Cancel |

Figure 11.17   The Printer attributes dialog box.

Deleting A Printer Entry

To delete a printer entry by hand, do the following:

1. Log in as **root**.

2. Edit the file /etc/printcap.

3. Delete the printer's entry from the file.

4. Erase the printer's spool directory.

Deleting A Printer Entry In The GUI

Both Red Hat and Caldera provide tools for working with printers from a dialog box while in their GUIs. Their tools are slightly different, and so are covered separately.

Deleting Print Entries In Red Hat

To delete a printer entry in Linuxconf, do the following:

1. Log in as **root**.

2. Start Gnome if necessary.

3. Click the Footprint box to open the system menu.

4. Click System to open the System submenu.

5. Click Control Panel to open the system Control Panel.

6. Click the Printer Configuration button on the Control Panel, as shown in Figure 11.13.

   The RHS Linux Print System Manager window opens, as shown in Figure 11.14.

7. Select the printing device whose entry you want to delete. A dialog box opens asking if you really want to delete the entry.

8. If you want to delete, click Continue (if not, click Cancel). A dialog box opens, reminding you to delete the printer's spool file.

9. Click OK to close the dialog box.

10. To close the window, click the PrintTool menu, then the Quit option.

Deleting Print Entries In Caldera

To delete print entries within COAS do the following:

1. Click the COAS icon (see Figure 11.7) to open the COAS menu.

2. Click the Peripherals menu option to open the COAS Peripherals menu.

3. Click the Printer option to open the Printer Configuration dialog box as shown in Figure 11.16.

4. Click the Remove option in the Printer menu to open the Remove printer dialog box, as shown in Figure 11.18.

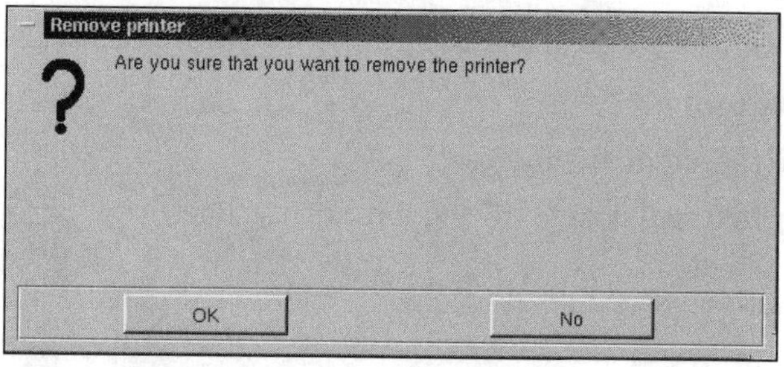

Remove printer

? Are you sure that you want to remove the printer?

OK   No

Figure 11.18   The Remove printer dialog box in COAS.

5. To remove the printer, click OK. The Remove printer queue dialog box appears, as shown in Figure 11.19.

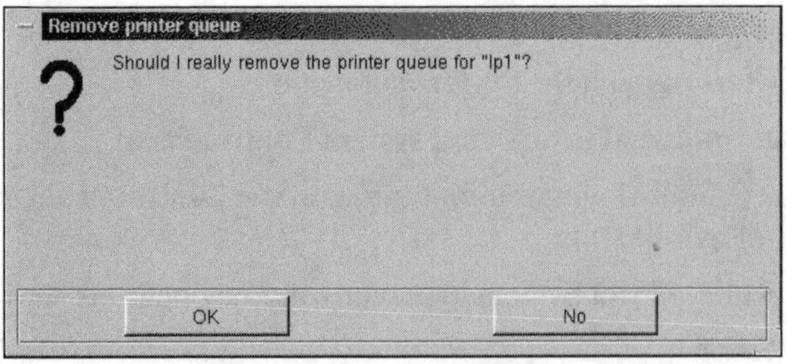

Figure 11.19   The Remove printer queue dialog box in COAS.

6. If you want to remove the queue associated with this printer, click OK. If not, click No, and the printer will be deleted but its queue will remain until you delete it by hand.

7. Click OK to close the Printer Configuration dialog box.

Configuring An NFS File Server

If your network contains a number of operating systems, then you might want to configure Network File System (NFS) file sharing. This essentially allows you to mount partitions across operating systems.

TIP: *If you choose to use NFS, you must use TCP/IP as your network protocol.*

To configure a Linux box as an NFS file server, do the following:

TIP: *Your NFS file server does not need to be a Linux machine.*

1. Log in as **root**.

2. Edit the file /etc/rc.d/init.d/inet.

3. Directly before the large "if" section, add the line:

```
/sbin/portmap
```

4. Save and quit the file. Now **portmap** will be run automatically at bootup.

5. Type "/sbin/portmap" to run **portmap** for the moment.

6. Edit the file /etc/exports.

TIP: You must edit the exports file on each machine where you want to make partitions available to mount.

7. Create an entry for each file system on the machine that you want available to outside systems. For example, if you want to make the directory /home and its contents available to be mounted with read access on blue.colors.org by any machine on colors.org, then you would add the following:

```
/home    *.colors.org(r)
```

The full listing of options available is shown in Table 11.5.

8. Save and exit the file.
9. Edit the new file /etc/exportfs.
10. Enter the following text:

```
#!/bin/sh
killall -HUP /usr/sbin/rpc.mountd
killall -HUP /usr/sbin/rpc.nfsd
```

11. Change the permissions of the file exportfs to 555.
12. Type "exportfs".

TIP: You need to run exportfs each time you change the exports file.

Table 11.5   NFS mounting options.

Option	Purpose
secure*d	Only accepts export requests from Internet ports below 1024. On by default.
insecure	Accept export requests from any Internet port.
ro	Do not allow NFS users to write to the exported volume.
rw	Allow NFS users to write to the exported volume. On by default. Be careful with this option, don't pair it with making the volume accessible to everyone.
noaccess	Prevents the NFS client from seeing or accessing directories below the current point.
link_relative	Change all symbolic links whose assignments start with a slash (/) into relative links by adding the appropriate number of leading slashes and dots to point to the proper directory (e.g. ../../../).
link_absolute	Leave symbolic links intact. On by defaullt.

13. Change to the directory /usr/sbin.

14. Run **mountd** by typing "rpc.mountd".

15. Run **nfsd** by typing "rpc.nfsd".

Configuring An NFS Client

To automount NFS partitions that are available to your machine, do the following:

1. Log in as **root**.

2. Edit /etc/fstab.

3. Add an entry for each partition you want to mount. Continuing with the example in the section Configure An NFS Server, say that you are configuring the machine yellow.colors.org to mount the /home partition on blue.colors.org. You would add the line:

```
blue:/home /mnt/blue nfs rsize=1024,wsize=1024,hard,intr 0 0
```

TIP: *To just mount the NFS file system temporarily, use the format "mount host:/directory /mountpoint". For example, to NFS mount the directory /home/bruce on the machine purple.colors.org to the mount point /mnt/bruce within the same domain, type "mount purple: /home/bruce /mnt/bruce".*

Determining If You Need NIS

NIS (Network Information Service) is used when you need to keep local host information in a central location. NIS is especially useful if:

1. You have a standalone LAN.

2. You have a large LAN and want to store all workstation addresses on a central machine to simplify administration.

3. You want to give all users the same login account and password for every machine on the LAN automatically.

Configuring NIS

To configure your LAN for NIS, you must configure a Master server and the clients. You also have the option of configuring Slave servers which contain copies of the NIS databases.

NOTE: *The portmap daemon must be running for the NIS software to run properly. Also, ensure that the time service is marked to run in /etc/inetd.conf. It's necessary for secure portmapping.*

Installing The Packages

The NIS package is available as an RPM on both the Red Hat and Caldera CD-ROMs. Install the packages just as you would install any other RPM. Their locations are:

- In Red Hat, you can find the code necessary to activate an NIS client in the authconfig package. The NIS server itself is in the package ypserv, and the client software is in yp-tools and yp-bind. All of these files are available in /RedHat/RPMS/.

- In Caldera, NIS is broken into two different packages. For a server, install the package nis-server. If you want to install a client, use nis-client. These packages are both available in /Packages/RPMS/.

NOTE: *During the Red Hat install process you were given the option of installing an NIS client in the Authentication Configuration dialog box.*

It is possible that these packages are already installed. RPM will tell you if this is the case.

NOTE: *Shadow passwords and NIS don't mix. If there are only certain people who need access to the NIS server then remove them from the shadow database and copy their passwords from /etc/shadow and back to /etc/passwd. Otherwise, you will need to remove shadow passwords from your system.*

Related solutions:	*Found on page:*
Installing The Shadow Password Package	159
Installing An RPM Package	295

Configuring The Master Server

The NIS server itself is the program "ypserv" in Red Hat, or "nis-server" in Caldera. To configure the machine that you intend to use as the NIS master server, do the following:

1. Log in as **root**.

2. Edit the file /var/yp/securenets.

3. Leave the line for the local host alone; you need that one in place so you can use a client to test NIS from the server machine.

4. Delete the line that leaves NIS open to all comers. Replace it with one of the following types of entries, or a combination of them:

   • To specify an entire network that uses one string of IP addresses, use the format "*netmask-openings IP-openings*". For example, if you have a class C network owning 192.168.15, then the entry would be "255.255.0.0 192.168.15.0". The zeros represent items that are available to be changed.

   • To specify a segment of a set of IP addresses, use the same format as above but adjust the netmask-openings term to allow movement within the IP addresses. For example, if you have a class C network spanning 192.168.15.0 through 192.168.17.255 that you want to allow access to the NIS server, add the entry "255.253.0.0 192.168.15.0". The 253 allows the second part of the IP address to grow by two from the starting point—the second entry—and the ending zeros allow the full range of changes in the addresses.

5. Save and close the file.

6. Edit the file /etc/ypserv.conf.

7. If you are using DNS instead of simply filling out the host files, then change the DNS entry to "yes".

8. Save and exit the file.

9. In Red Hat type "/etc/rc.d/init.d/ypserv start". In Caldera type "/etc/rc.d/init.d/nis-server start".

10. Generate the NIS database by typing "/usr/lib/yp/ypinit -m".

Configuring The Clients

The NIS client exists of the program ypbind, which must be running at all times. It's a good idea to do this on all of the machines, including the servers, since they will need clients as well. To set the NIS client up on a machine, do the following:

1. Log in as **root**.

2. Edit the file /etc/rc.d/rc.local.

3. Go to the end of the text in the file. If using vi, the command for this is "G".

4. Add a new line (if using vi, the command is "o") with the following:

```
/usr/sbin/ypbind
```

5. Save and exit the file. In vi, do this with ":wq". Now the client daemon will start whenever the computer boots.

6. To start the daemon by hand without rebooting at the moment, type "/usr/sbin/ypbind".

TIP: *On Red Hat Linux boxes you can run "authconfig" from the command line to enable NIS clients.*

Related solution:	*Found on page:*
Writing A Script	327

Configuring The Slave Servers

A slave NIS server is not necessary, but it is useful in large networks, or in networks where connections or machines are unreliable and access to the master NIS server cannot be guaranteed. To set up the slave server, do the following:

1. Log in as **root**.

2. Edit the file /etc/yp.conf. It should be initially empty.

3. Add a single line to point the NIS slave server to the NIS master server in the format "ypserver *ipaddress*". Using the IP instead of the name reduces access time, as it avoids the issue of name resolution.

4. Change to the /var directory.

5. Create the "yp" directory.

6. Edit the file /etc/rc.d/rc.local.

7. At the end of the file add the line:

```
/bin/domainname fictdomain
```

The fictdomain entry is a fictitious name used only for the purpose of NIS, not the one used in your LAN's DNS. For example, while you may be using the DNS domain colors.org, you could use anything for the NIS domain whether it was related or not. You could use purple.edu for fictdomain, or glass.org or anything else that feels appropriate. This tactic is multipurpose, but in general it is used either for internal networking reasons, or to gain the slight benefit in security because intruders listening on the network will not be able to easily find the NIS server to try to gain access to your password files.

8. Save and exit the file.

9. Restart the machine to activate and test the changes.

10. If the Master server has been set up on the LAN, and the NIS client has been set up on the slave machine, then type "/usr/lib/yp/ypinit -s masterhost" to activate the slave server.

Chapter 12

Integrating Into Windows Networks With Samba

In Brief

If your Linux box resides on a network where it must share drives and printers with Windows machines or other dissimilar operating systems, Samba (SMB, or the Session Message Block protocol) is a very useful tool. Samba is one implementation of Common Internet File System (CIFS), which is based on the file and printer access protocol Microsoft Windows uses internally. CIFS tools are also available for a number of other operating systems, making sharing across diverse networks easier.

TIP: *If there are a lot of people who will be accessing files over the service, and there is a high probability of people trying to access files at the same time, then use Samba instead of NFS. NFS does not do file locking, so multiple people can access a file at the same time and all try to change it at once, ending up with only one user's changes being stored. However, CIFS clients and servers track file access, "locking" a file while it is in use so others cannot open it until it is saved and exited.*

Also, and this is often the primary reason to choose Samba over NFS, MS Windows machines do not use NFS so you cannot use that service to access data across Linux/Windows networks.

Samba Components

Samba comes with two server components (daemons), two client components, and an administration tool. Each of these distinct parts has a specific function within the Samba suite.

Drive And Printer Sharing

The server component smbd enables drive and printer sharing. The client component for accessing the smbd server is smbclient.

NOTE: *If you installed Red Hat Linux with the Server installation class, smbd is already installed and should be currently running on your system. It is also already configured to run directly in the system startup scripts.*

Name Resolution And Browsing

The server component nmbd enables the management and distribution of NetBIOS information. It also provides a list of file and print services available for sharing across the network. This list is available for browsing by the other machines on the network. The client that accesses nmbd is nmblookup.

NOTE: *If you installed Red Hat Linux with the Server installation class, nmbd is already installed and should be currently running on your system. It is also already configured to run directly in the system startup scripts.*

Samba Configuration Procedure

This section provides a general breakdown of the procedure for configuring Samba. Once you have it installed, you must:

1. Determine how you want to run the Samba daemons. There are several ways to actually run the daemons. You can choose to:

   • Start the daemons by hand when necessary.

   • Configure your system's startup scripts to start them at boot time.

   • Configure inetd to start the Samba daemons for you.

TIP: *If you intend your Samba server to run continuously, it is best to configure the daemons to run from within inetd. This ensures that they will run each time the computer is booted, and they will be restarted if they fail or crash for some reason.*

2. Set the Samba daemons to run via the method you chose (see the appropriate daemon configuration section).

3. Configure Samba to share drives across the network:

   • Share Linux drives with Windows machines (see the section "Configuring Drive Sharing, Linux to Windows").

   • Share Windows drives with Linux machines (see the section "Configuring Drive Sharing, Windows to Linux").

4. Test drive sharing (see the appropriate drive testing section).

5. Configure Samba to share printers across the network:

   • Share a Linux printer with Windows machines (see the section "Configure Print Sharing, Linux to Windows").

   • Share a Windows printer with Linux machines (see the section "Configure Print Sharing, Windows to Linux").

6. Test printing (see the section "Test Print Sharing").

Immediate Solutions

Finding The Latest Version Of Samba

While both Red Hat and Caldera ship with SMB, you can download the latest version of the source from **www.samba.org**.

Checking To See If Samba Is Installed

You may have installed Samba when you installed the Red Hat or Caldera distributions. If so, type "rpm -q samba" to determine if the package is already on the hard drive.

Related solution:	Found on page:
Listing What RPMs You Have Installed	295

Installing The Samba Package From The Red Hat CD-ROMs

Samba is provided as an RPM (Red Hat Package Manager format, discussed in more detail in Chapter 15) on the Red Hat CD-ROM. You can either install the RPM by hand, or via the Control Panel's Package Manager. To install by hand, do the following:

1. Mount the Red Hat CD-ROM onto the filesystem.

2. Change to the directory RedHat/RPMS/ on the CD-ROM (for example, /mnt/cdrom/RedHat/RPMS).

3. Install the package by typing "rpm -ivh samba*" since there is only one Samba package among the RPMs.

Related solutions:	Found on page:
Installing An RPM Package	295
Mounting Onto The File System	168

Installing The Samba Package From The Caldera CD-ROMs

Samba is provided as an RPM on the Caldera CD-ROM. You can either install the RPM by hand or via the kpackage utility. To install by hand, do the following:

1. Mount the Caldera CD-ROM onto the filesystem.

2. Change to the directory Packages/RPMS on the CD-ROM (for example, /mnt/cdrom/Packages/RPMS.

3. Install both the samba package and the samba documentation package by typing "rpm -ivh samba*".

Related solutions:	Found on page:
Installing An RPM Package	295
Mounting Onto The File System	168

Installing The Samba Package From The Source

If you want or need to use the latest source instead of the packages provided on the CD-ROMs, follow this procedure:

1. Download the source from **www.samba.org/**.

2. Unpack the source into the directory of your choosing.

3. Read the README file for up-to-date information on install procedures and additional options.

4. Compile the source as instructed in the README.

5. Follow any additional instructions regarding permissions or file moving in the README.

6. Configure Samba as detailed in this chapter unless the README instructs otherwise.

NOTE: *When new versions of programs become available, both Red Hat and Caldera make RPMs and post them on their sites.*

Related solutions:	Found on page:
UnGZipping A File	300
Untarring A File	298
Installing An RPM Package	295

Determining If The Samba Daemons Are Running

To determine if the two daemons Samba needs are running, log in as root and type the command combination "ps -aux | grep *bd". If you see smbd and nmbd in the process list, both of the daemons are properly running.

Configuring The Samba Daemons To Run From Inetd

To configure the daemons smbd and nmbd to run from within inetd, do the following:

1. Log in as **root**.

2. Make a backup copy of inetd.conf.

3. Edit the file /etc/inetd.conf.

4. Move to where you want to place the code in the file; at the end is fine.

5. Build the smbd statement. The ordering for what appears in the inetd.conf code is:

```
[Service] [Socket] [Protocol] [Flags] [User] [Server Path]
    [Arguments]
```

To build the statement for smbd:

• The service smbd provides is netbios-ssn.

• The type of socket used by smbd is stream.

• The protocol used by smbd is tcp.

• The flag you need for this service is **nowait**.

- The user running smbd is **root**.
- The location of the daemon is /usr/sbin/smbd.
- The argument to run the program is smbd.

The resulting statement is:

```
netbios-ssn stream tcp nowait root /usr/sbin/smbd smbd
```

6. Build the nmbd statement. Following the same process as with smbd, the resulting statement is:

```
netbios-ns dgram udp wait root /usr/sbin/nmbd nmbd
```

7. Save and exit the file.
8. Restart inetd by typing "kill -HUP 1".

Configuring The Samba Daemons To Run From System Startup Scripts

If you installed Samba from an RPM then all of the proper links are in place. However, if you installed from source and just want to make sure, then do the following:

1. Log in as **root**.
2. See if you already have the necessary smb script in place by changing to the directory /etc/rc.d/init.d/ and seeing if the file smb is there.
3. See if you need to set up symbolic links by first typing "ls -la smb".
4. Look in the listing at the number directly after the permissions. This number represents the number of links to the file. If the number is one then you may need to create the three links.
5. Type "ls -l /etc/rc.d/rc1.d *samba". If there is a Samba listing there then proceed to the next step. If not, create the first link by typing "ln -s /etc/rc.d/init.d/smb /etc/rc.d/rc1.d/K33smb". This link sets the Samba process to be killed when entering runlevel 1, or single user mode.
6. Type "ls -l /etc/rc.d/rc3.d *samba". If there is a Samba listing there then proceed to the next step. If not, create the second link by typing "ln -s /etc/rc.d/init.d/smb /etc/rc.d/rc3.d/S91smb".

This link sets the Samba process to be started when entering runlevel 3, or command line mode.

7. Type "ls -l /etc/rc.d/rc6.d *samba". If there is a Samba listing there then you are done. If not, create the third link by typing "ln -s /etc/rc.d/init.d/smb /etc/rc.d/rc6.d/K33smb". This link sets the Samba process to be killed when entering runlevel 6, or reboot mode.

If no links are required, then your system is already configured to run the daemons from the startup scripts.

Related solution:	Found on page:
Creating Links	88

Stopping The Samba Daemons From Running From The Startup Scripts

If you want smbd and nmbd to run from within inetd, and your system is running them by default from the startup scripts, you will first need to set the daemons so that they will not run from the system startup scripts. To accomplish this, do the following:

1. Log in as **root**.

2. Type "ls -l /etc/rc.d/rc1.d *samba". If there is a link there, delete it with "rm /etc/rc.d/rc1.d *filename*".

3. Type "ls -l /etc/rc.d/rc3.d *samba". If there is a link there, delete it with "rm /etc/rc.d/rc3.d *filename*".

4. Type "ls -l /etc/rc.d/rc6.d *samba". If there is a link there, delete it with "rm /etc/rc.d/rc6.d *filename*".

Starting The Samba Daemons By Hand

To start smbd and nmbd by hand, log in as root and then type one of the following:

- If using Red Hat Linux, type "/etc/rc.d/init.d/smb start".

- If using Caldera OpenLinux, type "/etc/rc.d/init.d/samba start".

Defining Hosts For SMB Access

One important feature of Samba is the ability to define specific host access, so it is necessary to understand the process involved in doing so. To create a host access definition, do the following:

1. Determine whether you want to explicitly allow or deny access to the host in question. Then you can begin writing the statement as "hosts allow" or "hosts deny".

NOTE: *You can add host definitions to local or global segments of the Samba configuration file. Global always overrides local in this context.*

---

2. While you can use domain names or IP addresses, it is often best to use IPs to avoid name resolution slowdown or outage problems. Determine which IP address or string of addresses you want to allow or deny.

3. Fill out the host entry with the form of the IP address that properly defines the string of hosts desired:

   • To allow an entire class IP address, simply don't fill in the last entry. For example, allowing an entire class A might be "hosts allow 10.152.62.". This example can go as far as "10.152." or "10." as well.

   • Disallow one specific untrusted host with the EXCEPT clause, such as "hosts allow 10.152.62. EXCEPT 10.152.62.13".

   • Allow machines in a particular IP class range which also have a specific hostmask by using a slash (/) such as "hosts allow 10.152.62.0/255.0.0.0".

   • Include multiple entries with a comma surrounded by spaces, such as "hosts allow localhost, 10.152.162.".

   • Disallow specific host names to connect to the Samba share in the format "hosts deny purple, red".

4. Add additional host entries if necessary.

NOTE: *More about formatting host entries is available in "man smb.conf" and "man 5 hosts_access".*

Building A Samba Configuration File

There are a number of subtleties when it comes to building a share statement. One process to follow is:

1. Log in as **root**.

2. Edit the file /etc/smb.conf.

3. Begin a statement that defines the server defaults with the code:

   ```
   [global]
   ```

4. There are a large number of parameters available for use globally. A full listing is available by typing "man smb.conf". Table 12.1 lists a selection of the more interesting ones. A number of the Samba parameters have nuances depending on how they are combined. The man page outlines them well.

5. Fill out the global section with the items you need to assign. For example,

   ```
   add user script = /home/samba/bin/createsmbuser %u
   hosts allow = localhost
   ```

Table 12.1   Global parameters for the file /etc/smb.conf.

Parameter	Purpose	Argument	Dependencies
add user script	If a lot of users from Windows NT will be accessing the file system and do not have accounts on the Linux box, this parameter will create the necessary Linux accounts on the fly. You have to write a script that creates a Linux user given the argument %u, which is the user name.	Full path to the script. Thoroughly test this script because it is going to run as root.	The security option must be set to "server" or "domain", the password server parameter must be defined, and if you want the user to be deleted in the end then set the parameter delete user script.
encrypt passwords	If using Windows NT 4. OSP3 or above this option is necessary to allow clients to negotiate encrypted passwords with the Samba server.	Create a local smbpasswd file or set security to "server" or "domain".	None.

(continued)

Table 12.1   Global parameters for the file /etc/smb.conf (continued).

Parameter	Purpose	Argument	Dependencies
hosts	Set specific hosts which are allowed or denied access to shares. Global host settings override local ones.	The options are "allow" or "deny", along with the host definition. See the section "Defining Hosts For SMB Access".	None.
password server	The NetBIOS name of the LM1.2X002 or LM NT 0.12 protocol password server Samba should look to. Be very sure that this password server can be trusted, and do not point this option back to the Samba server itself.	Name of the password server.	The security option must be set to "server" or "domain".
security	Outlines how the Samba server handles user authentication requests. There are many nuances to this command; be sure to read the man pages and test it thoroughly before trusting it does what you think.	The options are "user" (the default), "share", "server", or "domain".	Can include "NetBIOS aliases", "include", "guest only", "guest account", "username map", "encrypted passwords", "map to guest", and/or "password server" depending on what you are trying to accomplish.

6. To begin the statement, give it a share name and then define the path to that share location. The code might look like:

```
[userhomes]
    path = /home
```

TIP: *In fact, there is a special feature in Samba that will create shares for user home directories on the fly. Naming a definition section [homes] activates this feature.*

---

7. Fill out the rest of the share definition. To give people accessing the share write access but prevent them from being able to see

12. Integrating Into Windows Networks With Samba

what is in the subdirectories /bin and /priv, use the following combination of code:

```
writeable = yes
dont descend = /bin,/priv
```

Table 12.2 lists some of the local parameters defined in the man page for smb.conf.

8. Fill out the rest of the share definitions.

9. Save and exit the file.

10. Restart the samba daemon by typing "/etc/rc.d/init.d/smb stop" then "/etc/rc.d/init.d/smb start" in Red Hat, or use "samba" instead of "smb" in Caldera.

Related solution:	Found on page:
Writing A Script	327

Table 12.2   Global parameters for the file /etc/smb.conf.

Parameter	Purpose	Argument
dont descend	Tell the Samba server to always show certain directories as empty to someone accessing the specific Samba share.	Comma-separated path list, no spaces.
follow symlinks	Prevent the Samba server from letting people accessing the particular Samba share from following the symlinks within that portion of the filesystem.	The options are "Yes" (default) and "No".
hide dot files	Show Linux files starting with a period (.) as Windows "hidden" files.	The options are "Yes" and "No" (default).
read only	People accessing the Samba share cannot write to it.	The options are "Yes" (default) and "No".
writeable	People accessing the Samba share can write to it.	The options are "Yes" and "No" (default).

Configuring Drive Sharing, Linux To Windows

To configure which Linux drives are available to MS Windows machines, do the following:

1. Log in as **root** on the Linux box that will serve as the Linux side Samba server.

2. Edit the file /etc/smb.conf.

3. Put the text "[global]" in the beginning.

4. On the next line begin setting the global options according to the section "Building A Samba Configuration File".

5. Create the individual shares in their own sections. See the section "Building A Samba Configuration File" for the details on how to create a share statement. Create a statement for each drive you want to share. For a more detailed example than in the statement-building section, you might want to offer a share to the general public named "public". You need to assign it a space in your file system. It's often recommended that public areas are given their own partition to tighten the security a bit, so a partition named "/public" is added to the drive. Perhaps you don't want the general public to have write access, but you do want them to be able to read the files there.

```
[public]
    comment = Items available to the general public.
    path = /public
    public = yes
    readable = yes
    writeable = no
```

6. Save and exit the file.

7. Restart the samba daemon by typing "/etc/rc.d/init.d/smb stop" then "/etc/rc.d/init.d/smb start" in Red Hat, or use "samba" instead of "smb" in Caldera.

TIP: *A tool that tests whether smb.conf is assembled properly or not comes with the Samba suite. To run this tool, type the command "testparm".*

Configuring Drive Sharing, Windows To Linux

To make sure that Samba on the Linux machines can see drives from Windows machines, do the following:

1. Open the Windows Control Panel.

2. Double-click the Network control panel.

3. Click the Configuration tab.

4. Click the File and Print Sharing button to open the File and Print Sharing dialog box.

5. Make sure the "I want to be able to give others access to my files" option is selected. This item is usually selected by default.

6. Click OK to close the File and Print Sharing dialog box.

7. Click TCP/IP in the network components list box.

8. Click the Properties button to display the TCP/IP Properties dialog box.

9. Click the WINS Configuration tab.

10. Select the Enable WINS Resolution radio button to select it.

11. Enter the IP address of the machine your Linux Samba server is on.

12. Click the Add button to add this IP address to the WINS list.

13. Click the OK button to close the TCP/IP Properties dialog box.

14. Click "File and printer sharing for Microsoft networks" in the network components list box.

15. Click Properties to open the File and printer sharing for Microsoft Networks Properties dialog box.

16. Click Browse Master in the Property list box.

17. Select Disabled in the Value drop-down list box.

18. Click the Access Control tab.

19. Make sure the Share-level access control radio button is selected. This item is usually selected by default.

20. Click OK to close the Network control panel. Wait while Windows builds its new drivers.

21. Configure any drives or folders you want to have accessible to the Samba clients in Linux as sharable, using Windows Explorer or your preferred Windows file manipulation tool.

Testing Drive Share Setup From A Windows Box

To test whether a Windows machine is seeing shared Linux drives properly, do the following:

1. Log into the Windows machine you want to test.

2. Double-click the Network Neighborhood icon on your desktop (or it might have the specific name for your LAN). The Linux drives and directories configured as accessible on the Samba server are displayed as clickable icons.

Testing Drive Share Setup From A Linux Box

1. Log into the Linux box you want to test as the user you want to test from.

2. Type "rpm -q samba" to see if you have the client installed. If not, mount the distribution CD-ROMs, go to the RPMS directory—"/mnt/cdrom/RedHat/RPMS" in Red Hat or "/mnt/cdrom/Packages/RPMS" in Caldera—and type "rpm -ivh samba*" to install.

3. Type "smbclient –L" to see what shares are available to the account you logged into. Compare the list you see with what you know you configured on the Windows side of the network.

4. Enter one of the shared directories following the instructions in the section "Accessing A Windows Drive".

Related solutions:	Found on page:
Mounting Onto The File System	168
Listing What RPMs You Have Installed	295
Installing An RPM Package	295

Configuring Print Sharing, Linux To Windows

To configure a Linux printer for use by a Windows machine via Samba, do the following:

1. Ensure that the printer works properly under Linux.

2. Log in as **root** on the machine hooked up to the printer.

3. Edit the file /etc/smb.conf.

4. Go to the end of the file.

5. If you want to allow users to connect to any printer already configured on the Linux network, create a section called "[printers]" and fill in its values. In general, the section would look like:

```
[printers]
    path = /usr/spool/public
    writeable = no
    guest ok = yes
    printable = yes
```

6. If you would rather do it by hand so as not to include all of the printers, create a printer statement for each Linux printer you want available to the Windows machines. Begin this statement with a name for the printer such as the text "[laser1]".

7. Fill out the statement with the options you want to apply to the printer definition. Table 12.3 outlines the statements that specifically apply to Samba print shares.

8. Save and exit /etc/smb.conf.

9. Restart the samba daemon by typing "/etc/rc.d/init.d/smb stop" then "/etc/rc.d/init.d/smb start" in Red Hat, or use "samba" instead of "smb" in Caldera.

Table 12.3   Printer parameters for the file /etc/smb.conf.

Parameter	Purpose	Argument	Dependencies
load printers	Whether or not to load all printers from /etc/printcap.	The options are "yes" or "no".	None.
lprm command	The program or script used to delete print jobs from the queue.	Path to program or script, plus the arguments. Useful arguments are %p for the name of the printer, and %j for the print job number.	None.

(continued)

Table 12.3   Printer parameters for the file /etc/smb.conf (continued).

Parameter	Purpose	Argument	Dependencies
print command	Print a spooled file.	Path to program or script. Useful arguments are %p for printer name, %f for the print spool name without its associated path, and %s for print spool name including the path.	At least one instance of %s or %f must be used.
Printable	Share clients can use the printer.	The options are "yes" or "no".	None.
printer name	Assign the specific printer a descriptive name.	Name for the printer.	None.

Configuring Print Sharing, Windows To Linux

To configure a printer attached to a Windows machine to be accessible from a Linux box via Samba, do the following:

1. Log into each Linux box as **root**.

2. Add an entry for each Windows printer to the /etc/printcap file on each Linux box. You can generate these entries using the printing tools in Red Hat or Caldera's GUIs, or create one by hand. A simple /etc/printcap file might contain:

```
#Name of printer
laser1:\
#Print spool directory
:sd=/var/spool/lpd/laser1:\
#Suppress the extra header page if you want with the
#next one.
:sh:\
#Print files up to 10MB in size.
:mx#10:\
#Use the log file /var/log/laser1.
:lf=/var/log/laser1:\
```

3. Determine if you want to convert your ASCII files into Post-script. If so, log in as **root** and type "find / -name "nenscript" to see if the Postscript converter is somewhere on your Linux system (it is likely to be in /usr/bin if it is already installed).

   If this script is found, make a note of its location. If it is not, you need to install a copy of this script, which is included among the RPM packages on your CD-ROM (the "enscript" RPM on both the Red Hat and Caldera CD-ROMs).

NOTE: *The latest versions of these scripts (nenscript and smbprint) can also be found at www.samba.org.*

---

4. If you installed the samba package from the Caldera or Red Hat CD-ROM then the smbprint script is already on your hard drive in /usr/sbin. You will need it to process the print jobs coming in from the Windows machines. This script is quite well docu-mented with internal comments. To use it, include a line in the /etc/printcap file adding an input filter to the printer you want to use it for:

```
:if=/usr/bin/smbprint:\
```

TIP: *If you're only pointing the Windows machine to one Linux printer, make a special print entry in your printcap that's for Samba.*

Related solutions:	Found on page:
Mounting Onto The File System	168
Listing What RPMs You Have Installed	295
Installing An RPM Package	295

Testing Print Sharing

Try printing a file from a machine on the Linux side if you are printing to Windows, or the Windows side if you are printing to Linux.

Accessing A Windows Drive

To access an MS Windows drive from within Linux, you use smbclient in the following manner:

1. Log into the user account you want to access the drive from.

2. Determine the name of the service you want to access. (Hint: Type "smbclient –L" to see a list of available drives.)

3. Mount the Windows drive onto your Linux filesystem with the following command:

```
/usr/sbin/smbmount //machinename/path mount_point
```

4. Access the files as desired.

5. When finished, detach the mounted drive with the following command:

```
umount mount_point
```

12. Integrating Into
Windows Networks With
Samba

Connecting To The Internet

In Brief

One of the first things many people want to do after they get their Linux box set up is to connect it to the Internet. Machines that are not hooked up to a LAN that is already net-connected generally have to be configured to use a modem to make their connections. They might even be serving as the connection between the LAN itself and the Internet. This chapter covers making this connection to the Internet, as well as how to use some of the Linux Internet clients.

See the section "Connecting To Your ISP" for the basic steps on how to proceed.

The PPP Dialers

Connecting to the Internet with a modem generally involves configuring a PPP connection. Fortunately, both distributions provide you with tools to help with this process:

- The Caldera distribution comes with the GUI tool **kppp**. See the section "Setting Up A PPP Connection With **kppp**" for more information.

- The Red Hat distribution's **Linuxconf** GUI tool can set up your PPP connection as well. See the section "Setting Up A PPP Connection with **Linuxconf**" for more information.

- The tool **pppsetup** is also available at the command-line level for both distributions.

The Internet Clients

Each operating system has its own selection of Internet clients; Linux is no exception. In general, two different types of tools are available: graphical tools and command-line tools. Which type you use is entirely up to you and your needs. As usual, command-line tools are sometimes cryptic, and GUI tools take up more RAM—and therefore might slow down your system.

TIP: *The command-line tools can also be used in a terminal window in the GUI.*

The Command-Line Tools

The command-line Internet tools supplied with the Red Hat and Caldera distributions are listed in Table 13.1.

The GUI Tools

The GUI-based Internet tools supplied with the Red Hat and Caldera distributions are listed in Table 13.2.

Table 13.1   Linux command-line Internet tools.

Tool	Service
ftp	FTP
irc	IRC
lynx	WWW browsing
pine	Email
tin	Usenet news
trn	Usenet news

Table 13.2   Linux GUI-based Internet tools.

Tool	Service	Distribution
gftp	FTP	Red Hat
kmail	Email	Caldera
krn	Usenet news	Caldera
ksirc	IRC	Caldera
Netscape	Email	Caldera and Red Hat
Netscape	Usenet news	Caldera and Red Hat
Netscape	WWW browsing	Caldera and Red Hat
xchat	IRC	Red Hat

Immediate Solutions

Connecting To Your ISP

The process involved in connecting your machine to your ISP is:

1. Get the following information from the ISP:

   - User ID

   - Password

   - DNS Server address

   - Authentication type (PAP, CHAP—Challenge-Handshake Authentication Protocol—or script)

2. Utilize the **minicom** program to walk through the login process once by hand, making note of the exact prompts you encounter and what you answer to each. See the section "Preparing To Write A Login Script" for instructions.

3. Configure your machine with the information it needs to complete the connection, using:

   - In Caldera and KDE, **kppp** (see the section "Setting Up A PPP Connection With **kppp**").

   - In Red Hat and Gnome, **Linuxconf** (see the section "Setting Up A PPP Connection With **Linuxconf**").

   - At the command line for either distribution, **pppsetup** (see the section "Setting Up For PPP Dial-Up With **pppsetup**").

Setting Up A PPP Connection With **kppp**

KDE comes with a handy dialer called **kppp**. **kppp** is easy to configure and can manage multiple dial-up numbers and accounts. To configure this dialer, do the following:

1. Log in as **root** into Caldera's GUI.

2. Click the large K button to bring up KDE's menu.

3. Choose the Internet menu item.

4. Choose **kppp** on the Internet submenu to bring up the **kppp** program, shown in Figure 13.1.

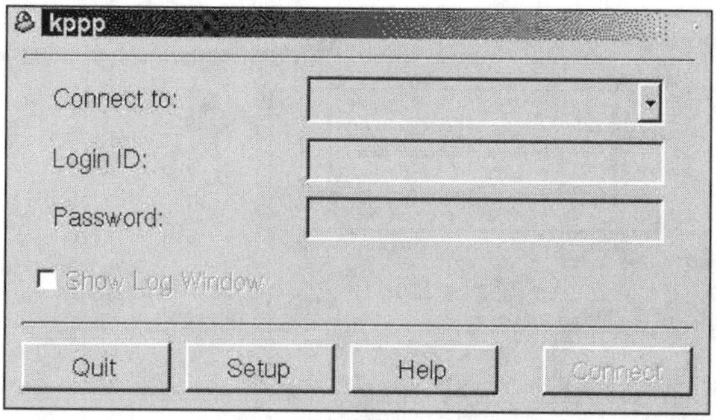

*Figure 13.1   The **kppp** PPP dialer program for Caldera's KDE GUI.*

5. Click on the Setup button to get the **kppp** Configuration dialog box, shown in Figure 13.2.

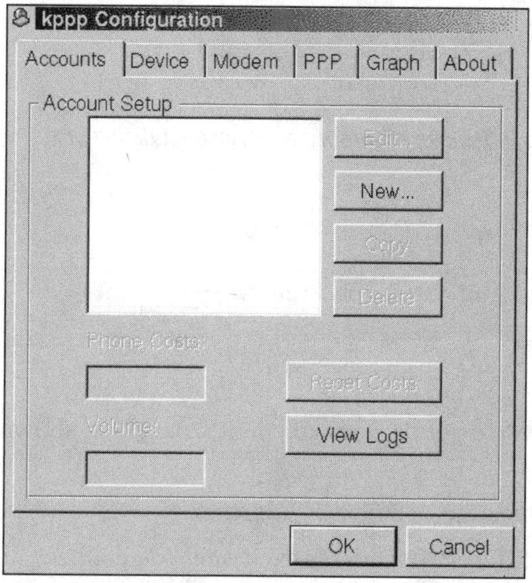

*Figure 13.2   The **kppp** PPP dialer program's Configuration dialog box, Accounts tab.*

6. Click the New button under the Accounts tab to get the New Account dialog box, shown in Figure 13.3.

7. Fill in the Connection Name and Authentication text boxes.

8. Choose the authentication protocol from the Authentication drop-down list. You will need to get this information from your ISP, either from Technical Support or their Web site. The choices are:

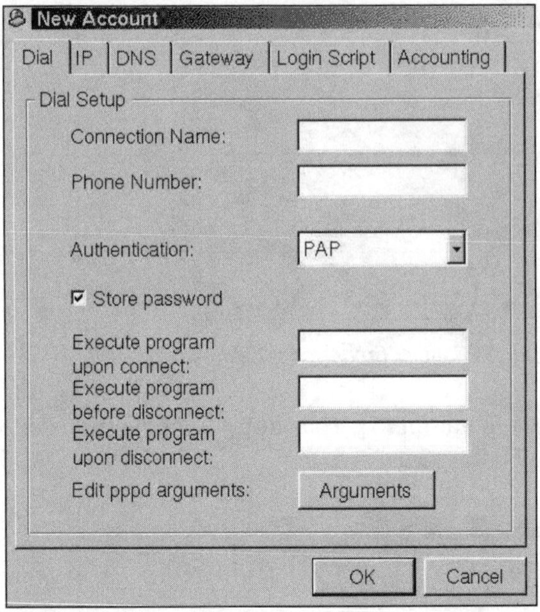

*Figure 13.3 The **kppp** PPP dialer program's New Account dialog box, Dial tab.*

- Script-based
- PAP (Password Authentication Protocol)
- Terminal-based
- CHAP

9. Click on the IP tab to get the New Account dialog box, shown in Figure 13.4.

10. Choose either Dynamic or Static IP Addressing:
    - If you have a different IP address each time you connect, choose Dynamic.
    - If you have a permanently assigned IP address that you get every time you connect, choose Static and fill in the IP Address and Subnet Mask text boxes.

11. Click on the DNS tab to get the dialog box shown in Figure 13.5.

12. Fill in the Domain Name your ISP gave you.

13. Enter the DNS IP Address your ISP gave you.

14. Click the Add button to add the Domain Name Server to your list of servers. If you have more to add, return to Step 13.

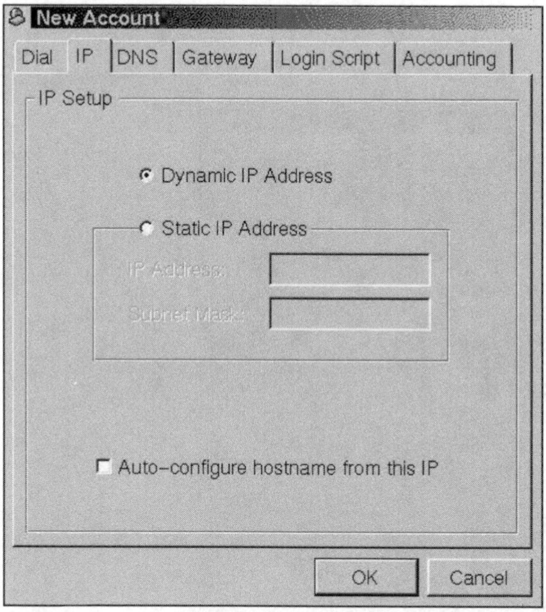

*Figure 13.4   The **kppp** PPP dialer program's New Account dialog box, IP tab.*

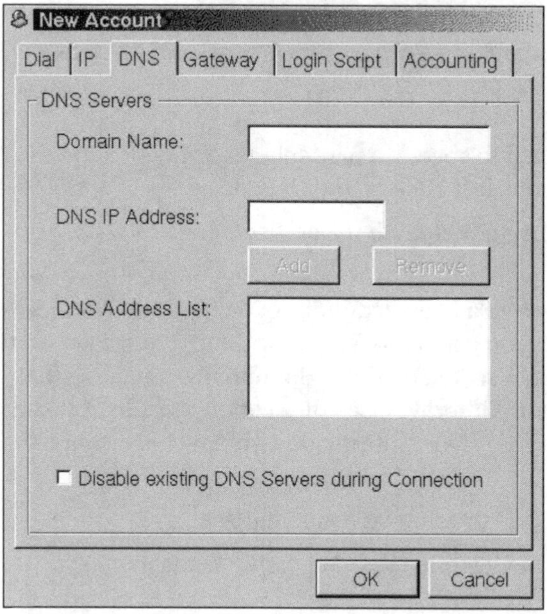

*Figure 13.5   The **kppp** PPP dialer program's New Account dialog box, DNS tab.*

15. Click on the Gateway tab to get the dialog box shown in Figure 13.6.

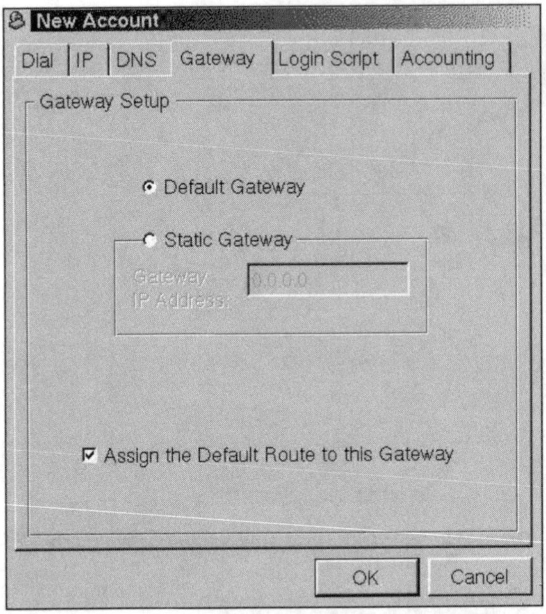

*Figure 13.6   The **kppp** PPP dialer program's New Account dialog box, Gateway tab.*

16. Unless you need to specify a particular gateway IP address assigned by your ISP, click on the Default Gateway option.

17. Click on the Login Script tab to get the dialog box shown in Figure 13.7.

18. Whether you need a login script or not depends on your ISP's login process. You can try logging in without it; if it fails, do the script. You can also just do the script initially, assuming that you will need it. Either way, see the section "Writing A Login Script In **kppp**" for more information on how to accomplish this task.

19. Click OK to close the New Account dialog box.

20. Click on the Device tab to get the dialog box shown in Figure 13.8.

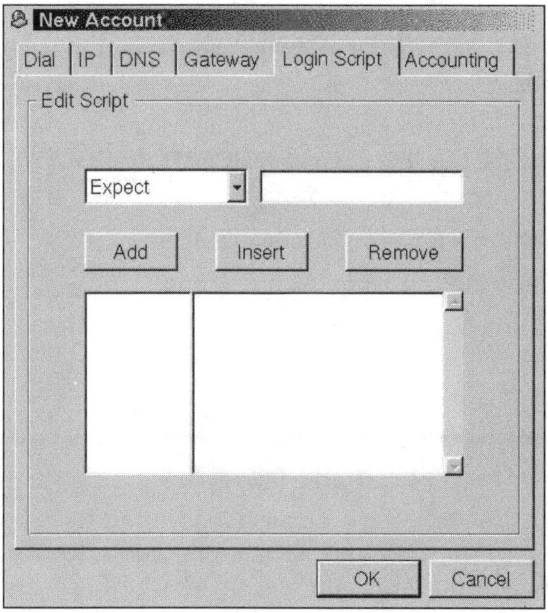

*Figure 13.7   The **kppp** PPP dialer program's New Account dialog box,
                Login Script tab.*

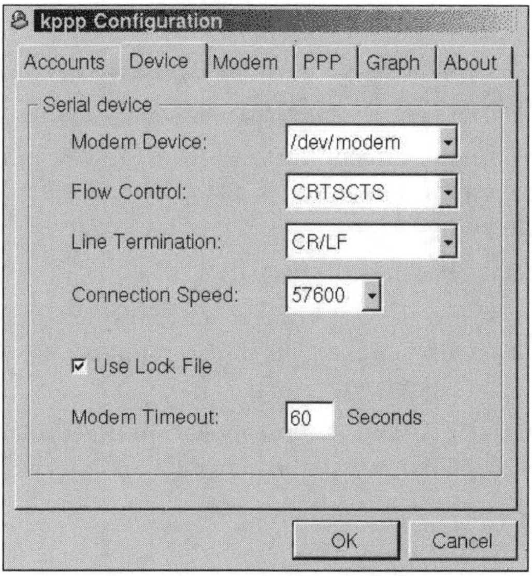

*Figure 13.8   The **kppp** PPP dialer program's Configuration dialog box,
                Device tab.*

13. Connecting To The
Internet

21. Click on the Modem Device drop-down box and choose one of the devices listed. A breakdown of what these cryptic device types refer to is:

    - The ttyS# or cua# devices are the same as Windows COM devices, but offset by one number. So, COM1 is /dev/ttyS0, and COM2 is /dev/cua1.

    - The ttyI# devices refer to ISDN modems.

22. Click OK to close the Configuration dialog box.

23. Click Quit to close **kppp** for now.

Preparing To Write A Login Script

Regardless of which tool you use to connect to your ISP, there is the possibility that you will need to write a login script for it. To prepare to write this script, you need to know exactly what text appears on the screen to prompt you at each step of the login process. You can get this information from the ISP, or you can dial into the account from a machine that is already configured and watch the steps.

Writing A Login Script In **kppp**

Writing a login script is not a difficult process. To write your script while in the **kppp** program's New Account dialog box, at the Login Script tab, do the following:

1. Make sure Expect is chosen in the drop-down list box.

2. Type part of the first prompt that **kppp** needs to respond to in the box to the list's right. For example, if the prompt says "Enter User ID:", you would type "ID:".

3. Click the Add button. The Expect term appears in the text box on the bottom of the dialog box to the left, and the ID: term appears to its right.

4. Choose Send in the drop-down list box.

5. Enter the text that **kppp** needs to send in response to the prompt. In this case it is the User ID or login name. For example, if the ID is "author" then you would type "author\r" in the text box. The \r tells **kppp** to press Enter afterwards.

6. Click the Add button. The Send term appears on the left, and author\r appears on the right below the previous entry.

7. Continue this process, choosing Expect each time **kppp** needs to look for a prompt and choosing Send author each time it needs to answer a prompt.

8. When you're finished writing the script, proceed with the rest of the **kppp** configuration process.

Setting Up A PPP Connection With **Linuxconf**

Red Hat's Gnome comes with the **Linuxconf** tool, which has sections to use to configure your PPP dial-ups. To use this tool, do the following:

1. Log in as **root** to Red Hat's GUI.

2. Click on the Gnome menu foot icon.

3. Choose the System submenu.

4. Choose **Linuxconf** from the System submenu to get the **Linuxconf** tool, shown in Figure 13.9.

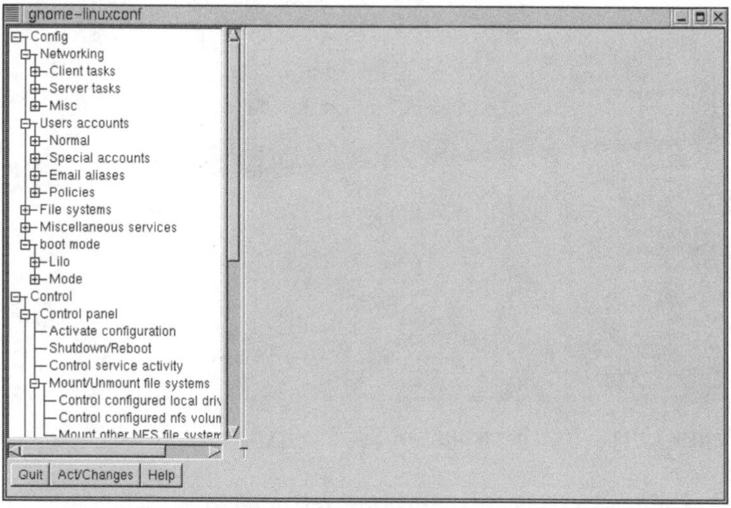

Figure 13.9   The **Linuxconf** *tool in Red Hat Linux.*

5. Under the Config, Networking hierarchy, click the PPP/SLIP/ PLIP option to get the PPP/Slip/Plip configurations tab, shown in Figure 13.10.

6. Click the Add button to continue to the interface selection tab, shown in Figure 13.11.

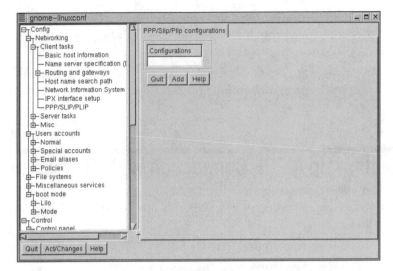

*Figure 13.10   The **Linuxconf** PPP/Slip/Plip configurations tab.*

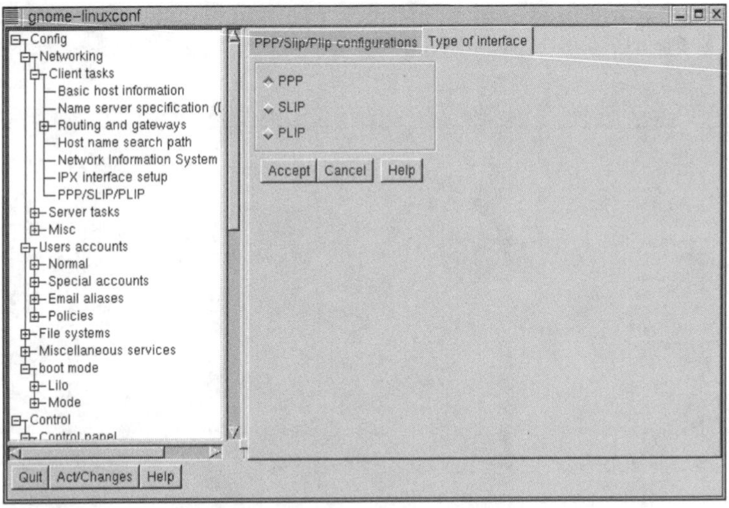

*Figure 13.11   The **Linuxconf** PPP/Slip/Plip Type of interface tab.*

7. Choose the type of connection you need to make according to your ISP's offerings.

8. Click the Accept button to continue. From here you will be taken to the appropriate configuration tab. Because most dial-up configurations these days involve PPP, Figure 13.12 displays the PPP interface ppp0 tab.

9. Fill in the Phone Number, Login Name, and Password text boxes.

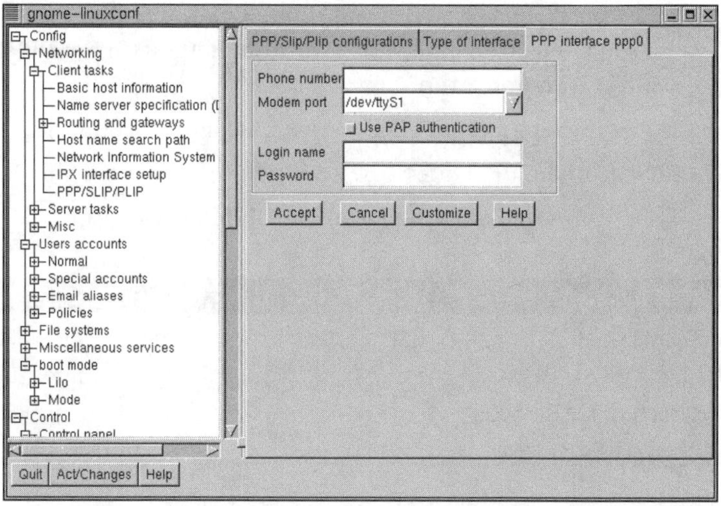

*Figure 13.12   The **Linuxconf** PPP/Slip/Plip PPP interface ppp0 tab.*

10. Select or enter the device that points to your modem. If it is a standard modem, then to refer to it in terms of COM ports, a modem on COM 1 is /dev/ttys0, one on COM 2 is /dev/ttys1, and so on. An ISDN modem is /dev/ttyI# instead.

11. If your ISP says it uses Password Authentication Protocol (PAP) for login authentication, check the Use PAP authentication option. This option is unchecked by default.

12. Click Accept and you are returned to the Configurations dialog box.

Getting And Installing **pppsetup**

A good command-line tool for setting up a PPP dial-in connection is **pppsetup**. To get this package, do the following:

1. FTP to **sunsite.unc.edu** and look in the directory /pub/Linux/ system/network/serial/ppp.

2. Download the **pppsetup** package.

3. Place the package in your temporary directory, or someplace like /usr/src.

4. Use the **gunzip** and **tar** programs to uncompress and unpack the package. It automatically creates its own subdirectory within the hierarchy where you unpack the package.

5. Type "rpm -q dialog" to determine if the **dialog** package is installed. If it is, continue to the section "Setting Up For PPP Dial-Up With **pppsetup**".

6. Mount the distribution CD-ROM with the **mount** command.

7. Change to the RPM directory.

8. Type "rpm -ivh dialog*" to install the **dialog** package.

Related solutions:	Found on page:
UnGZipping A File	300
Untarring A File	298
Mounting Onto The File System	168
Installing An RPM Package	295

Setting Up For PPP Dial-Up With **pppsetup**

To use the **pppsetup** program to set up your system for dialing in via PPP, do the following:

1. Change to the **pppsetup**-*version* directory with the **cd** command.

2. Two different README files are included with the documentation. Be sure to read both of them in case the instructions on using this package have been updated.

3. Type "./pppsetup" to run the script and get the opening screen, displayed in Figure 13.13.

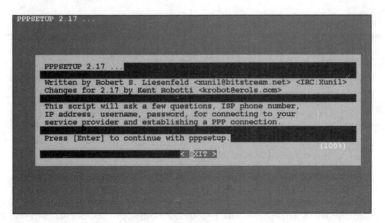

*Figure 13.13   The **pppsetup** opening screen.*

4. Press the Enter key to continue to get the Phone Number screen shown in Figure 13.14.

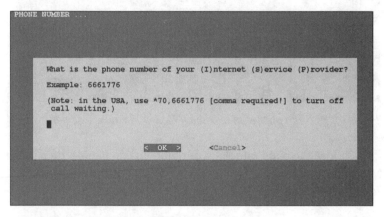

```
PHONE NUMBER ...




      What is the phone number of your (I)nternet (S)ervice (P)rovider?

      Example: 6661776

      (Note: in the USA, use *70,6661776 [comma required!] to turn off
       call waiting.)

      ▮


                        <  OK  >       <Cancel>
```

Figure 13.14   The pppsetup Phone Number entry screen.

5. Enter the phone number for the ISP, then press Enter to go to the Modem Device entry screen shown in Figure 13.15.

```
MODEM DEVICE ...




             Where is your modem /dev/ttys?

             ttyS0  =  (COM1:  under  DOS)
             ttyS1  =  (COM2:  under  DOS)
             ttyS2  =  (COM3:  under  DOS)
             ttyS3  =  (COM4:  under  DOS)


             <  OK  >       <Cancel>
```

Figure 13.15   The pppsetup Modem Device entry screen.

6. Choose the device that corresponds to your modem and then press Enter to go to the Maximum Modem Baud Rate screen shown in Figure 13.16.

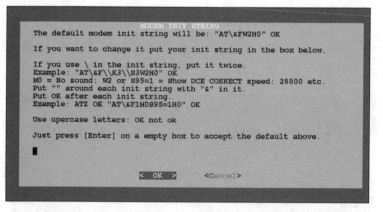

*Figure 13.16   The **pppsetup** Maximum Modem Baud Rate screen.*

7. Choose the baud rate that your modem can handle, then press Enter to go to the Modem Init String dialog box shown in Figure 13.17.

*Figure 13.17   The **pppsetup** Modem Init String dialog box.*

TIP: *There is a modem init string database at **www.in.net/info/modems/search.html**.*

---

8. Type in the init string for your modem or just press Enter to accept the defaults and then go to the DNS IP Address screen shown in Figure 13.18.

9. Type in the IP address for the DNS server your ISP told you to use, then press Enter to go to the PAP/CHAP or Script screen shown in Figure 13.19.

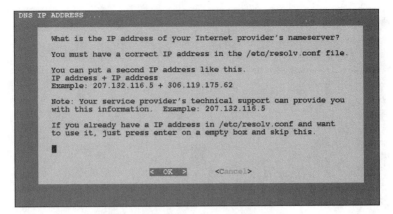

*Figure 13.18   The **pppsetup** DNS IP Address screen.*

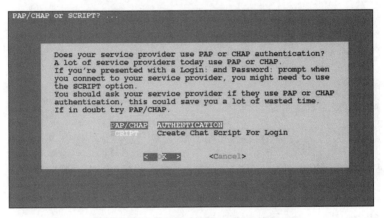

*Figure 13.19   The **pppsetup** PAP/CHAP or Script screen.*

10. If your ISP uses PAP or CHAP authentication, choose the PAP/CHAP option and fill in the login name and password when prompted, and you are done. Otherwise, choose the Script option and press Enter.

11. Read the explanation of what **pppsetup** wants you to do, and then press Enter once again to go to the Expect screen shown in Figure 13.20.

12. Enter the text that **pppsetup** needs to respond to. For example, if the prompt says Enter User ID: then you might type "ID:" in the text box. Press Enter when you have the text how you want it to go to the Send screen, as shown in Figure 13.21.

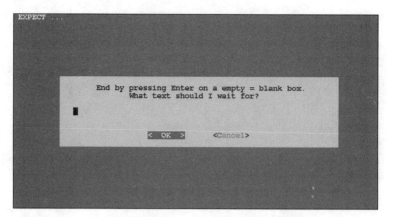

Figure 13.20   The **pppsetup** Expect script creation screen.

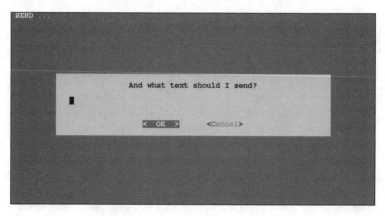

Figure 13.21   The **pppsetup** Send script creation screen.

13. Enter the response that **pppsetup** needs to send for the prompt. For example, in response to the Enter User ID: prompt you might need to send the login name *author*. However, you also need to have an Enter key pressed at the end of the term so the ISP knows you gave it an answer, so you add the text "\r" at the end, making it *author\r*. Press Enter when you have the text how you want it, which returns you to the Expect dialog box.

14. Continue entering each step of the login process until you have all of the prompts answered, and then press Enter in the Expect box without adding any text to continue.

15. Read the instructions given to you on how to correct any of these values at a later date.

16. Copy the **ppp-off** command from the **pppsetup** directory into /usr/sbin with the **cp** command.

13. Connecting To The Internet

Dialing In From The Command Line

To dial in from the command line, do the following:

1. Log in as **root**.

2. Type "ppp-go -c" to connect to the Internet.

3. Type "ifconfig" and see if a *ppp0* section is included. If so, you're up and running. If not, then you may need to work on the modem init string or connect script.

4. To hang up, type "ppp-off".

Dialing In From The Caldera GUI

To dial in from Caldera's **kppp** tool, do the following:

1. Log in as **root** in the GUI.

2. Open the **kppp** tool.

3. Choose the connection you want to use from the Connect To drop-down box.

4. Fill in the login ID and password if necessary.

5. Click the Connect button.

Dialing In From The Red Hat GUI

To dial in from Red Hat's **Linuxconf** tool, do the following:

1. Log in as **root** to the Red Hat GUI.

2. Click on the PPP/SLIP/PLIP option under Config, Networking.

3. Click on the entry in the configuration listings you want to use to dial. The PPP interface ppp0 dialog box comes up.

4. Click the Connect button to connect to the Internet.

5. When finished, click the Disconnect button.

Setting Up Internet Services

In Brief

Each Internet service now must be configured to your specifications. Some of them are automatically installed by the Red Hat and Caldera installers, which saves you some work on the installation front.

NOTE: *Although this chapter's title refers to Internet services, these same items may be necessary for your isolated LAN or your intranet, even without a permanent or dial-up Network connection.*

Connectivity

Connectivity issues come into play when you set up many Internet services. Each of these issues builds upon the other. These issues are:

- How many users are on the machine? Just one or multiple?
- Is the machine networked to other machines on a LAN?
- Does the machine or LAN connect to the Internet?
- Is the Internet connection permanent?
- If the connection is not permanent, how often is the machine or LAN connected? During specific hours? Only when Internet transactions must occur?
- If the Internet connection is permanent, are people going to be accessing your services from the Internet?

After you answer these questions, you have the information you need to choose how to set up each service.

Email Considerations

There is more than one type of email server available, and you may find that you need not one but both to handle what needs to be done. The two servers of interest are installed by default, which makes your job much easier. These two servers are Post Office Protocol (POP) and sendmail.

The POP server listens for connections from email clients. When a client connects, the POP server authenticates them and then allows them to download the mail they have waiting. This process prevents mail bouncing whenever a user is not immediately available to receive it.

POP is not meant as an outgoing mail server, although some versions do handle this task.

TIP: *If you want to assign users accounts that are for mail only, you can do so easily with the user management tools. The key issue is that a mail-only account has a login shell of /bin/false. This prevents any abuse of the account because users (or people who crack their passwords) cannot log in to an actual shell. In Red Hat's Linuxconf X interface there is an option that automatically creates specialized accounts for you, with POP-only being one of them.*

Outgoing mail (and incoming mail for people who are continuously connected) is the domain of sendmail. While sendmail is notoriously difficult to configure, current versions are installed with a default configuration file that you can alter to suit your own needs. Even better, a set of macros is available to help you set up a custom configuration file without needing to edit the main file. The things you likely want to change or add are:

- Create email address aliases (see the section "Configuring Sendmail Aliases").

- Set up your central mail server (see the section "Configuring Email On Your LAN").

- Set up machines on your LAN to forward to the central mail server (see section "Configuring Email On Your LAN").

- Set up mail delivery for virtual hosts (see section "Configuring Email For Virtual Hosts").

14. Setting Up Internet Services

TIP: *Email aliases allow your various administrators not to have to check multiple email accounts, which greatly decreases annoyance on their part and improves their response time. Aliases also help by eliminating the problem of mistyped email addresses, simplifying long and complex addresses, and creating simple mailing lists that have only a few members by assigning multiple people to one alias.*

Making Changes Cleanly

One thing to keep in mind when configuring your various network services is that when you change a configuration file, the changes will not take effect until you stop and start the service. Often these services can be found in the directory /etc/rc.d/init.d/. For example, to stop and restart inetd, you would first type "/etc/rc.d/init.d/inetd stop" to stop the service. If it stops cleanly, then start it again with:

```
/etc/rc.d/init.d/inetd start
```

If it doesn't stop and start cleanly, try stopping and starting it a few times more until it does.

Virtual Hosting

It is common today to have one machine providing services for more than one named domain. This process is called "virtual hosting". Whether you want to host two or two hundred different domains on the same machine or LAN, the process for setting them up is the same. See the section "Setting Up Virtual Hosting" to begin the general setup.

Immediate Solutions

Setting Up Virtual Hosting

In order to have a machine host services for more than one domain name, you need to configure it properly. To set up virtual hosting, do the following:

1. Log in as **root**.

2. Your kernel must be configured to support IP aliasing. Most 2.2.x kernels are already set up to do so. If it turns out yours is not, then see Chapter 10 for instructions on how to compile a new kernel with this option activated.

TIP: *In the xconfig tool, IP aliasing is toward the bottom of the Networking options dialog box.*

---

3. Get the MAC (Media Access Control) address for the Ethernet card in the machine by typing "ifconfig" and look for the line containing the term "HWaddr". The MAC address is a six part group of two units each, which looks something like "00-06-97-7F-33-46". Every Ethernet card has a unique MAC address.

4. Make a backup copy of the file you are about to edit, using the **cp** command such as "cp /etc/rc.d/rc.sysinit /etc/rc.d/rc.sysinit-original".

5. Use the **vi** command to open the file by typing "vi /etc/rc.d/rc.sysinit".

6. Go to the end of the file by typing "G".

7. Type "O" to start a new line after the cursor position and enter Insert mode.

8. For each virtual host you want to add, add a line in the format "arp -s *virtualhost MAC*"—where:

   - The *virtualhost* entry is either the full domain name plus machine name, or an IP address. Using an IP address is cleaner, because if you change IP and domain assignments later you will not have to come back and change them here as well.

   - The MAC address is separated with colons (:) and not dashes (-).

   For example, "arp -s 192.168.60.9 00:06:97:7F:33:46".

9. Save the file and exit by typing ":wq".

10. See Chapter 11, "Configuring Name Resolution For The Machine" for how to map the IP address to the virtual domain's name.

Related solutions:	See page:
Places To Look For Kernel Source	180
Installing A Kernel	188
Testing A Kernel Install	181

Configuring Email

Configuring your central email server is a vital step, whether you have networked machines or a standalone. There are a number of steps involved in this process. Which steps you choose to follow depends on what you want to do with your setup.

Configuring Email On Your LAN

To configure your LAN so it has a primary mail server that the others look to for delivery:

1. Log in as **root** on the machine that will serve as your LAN's primary mail server.

2. Edit the file /etc/sendmail.cw.

3. Add a listing for each machine on your network which will have its mail served by this server. This listing is simply the full name of your machine. For example, if the machine "red" is serving mail to the machine "purple" at colors.org you would add:

```
purple.colors.org
```

4. Log into each machine that will receive mail from the primary mail server in turn. For the sake of this example, the machine is purple.

5. Edit the file /etc/sendmail.cf on each machine in turn.

6. Locate the line that begins with "DR".

7. Add the name of the mailserver. For example,

```
DRred.colors.org
```

8. Locate the line that begins with "DM".

9. Add the domain name for the machine to masquerade as. For example,

```
DMcolors.org
```

Configuring Sendmail Aliases

To create email aliases within sendmail:

1. Log in as **root** on the computer you're using as your mail server.

2. Edit the file /etc/aliases.

3. Examine the aliases already there. For example, the person who should get root's mail. Change those that need customization to the user name of the person the alias should point to.

4. Add any new aliases you want. The location in the aliases file is not important, although it is useful to group them in a way you can easily find things later. The format should be:

```
currentusername: addressitshouldpointto
```

NOTE: *Try to avoid logging in as root as much as possible. This means that you don't want to send a lot of mail to the root account, including postmaster mail.*

For example, if you want to point all email sent to the postmaster address to a mail administrator with the address "mailboss," then you would add the line:

```
postmaster: mailboss
```

TIP: *You can have an alias point to more than one address. Separate the addresses with a comma and a space. For example, if you wanted to create a small mailing list for all of your system administrators, you could add a line such as:*

```
admins: root, alan, cindy, broom
```

14. Setting Up Internet Services

5. Save and exit the file.

6. Type "newaliases" to have the system load the new aliases file.

Configuring Email For Virtual Hosts

To set up email sending and delivery for a virtual host, do the following:

1. Log in as **root**.

2. Create the directory */virtualdomain* with the **mkdir** command.

3. Type "cp /etc/sendmail.cf */virtualdomain*/etc" to use the base sendmail.cf file you have already created.

4. Open the file with **vi** by typing "vi */virtualdomain*/etc/ sendmail.cf".

5. Search for the text "#Dj" by typing "/#Dj".

6. Use the arrow keys to move the cursor down to the line stating "#Dj$w.Foo.COM".

7. Press "i" to go into Insert mode.

8. Uncomment the line by removing the hash mark (#).

9. Change the line to list the virtual host's domain name instead. For example, "Djfruit.org".

10. Save and exit the file by typing ":wq" and pressing Enter.

Testing Email

Depending on your setup, you need to send email along the following lines to test whether it works or not:

- Send mail locally within a machine from one user to another from within your favorite mail client. You do this by specifying the specific user on the specific machine. For example, if you were on the machine "peach," you would send the test mail to **paul@peach.fruit.org**. (This example does not apply if the machine is not connected to any others. In that case you can test this feature by sending mail just to the user account—e.g. paul.) Or, you could send the mail to **paul@localhost**, since "localhost" is an alias for the specific machine you are on.

- Send mail locally within your LAN, from one machine to another. If you configured sendmail to forward all mail to the central server, then this should be possible by sending to a user without using a domain name (such as just "paul")—otherwise the mail is only sent within the particular machine and not along the LAN. To test whether this is working properly or not, send email to just the username, go to another machine, check mail for the same username on that machine, and see if the test mail arrived.

NOTE: *Sendmail is often configured by default to send mail every 15 minutes. So the test mail may not arrive immediately even if the configuration worked properly.*

- Send mail to another account of yours on the Internet, or to a friend's account where you know the person can respond quickly. Another trick is to send to an account that you know is running some kind of auto-response email system.

If one or more of these items fails, then it is time to go back through the following configuration issues:

- Is sendmail configured properly?
- Is the LAN configured properly?
- Is the DNS configured properly?
- Is the routing configured properly?

Tests such as pings, and using other services from the machine that is not working and other machines—FTP, Web, and more—should help you narrow things down.

Running POP Email

POP email is often part of the default installation. A quick way of determining whether you already have it or not is to do the following:

1. Log in as **root** on the machine you're using as your mail server.
2. View the contents of the file /etc/inetd.conf.
3. There is a section dedicated to POP packages. If the listings don't have a comment marker (#) in front, then you don't need to change anything. If there are comment markers, remove them and then restart inetd.

Configuring The Apache WWW Service

Apache is already installed for you. What you need to do now is configure your primary Web server, and any other machines where you want to run secondary or tertiary servers.

NOTE: *After making changes in any of the configuration files for Apache, be sure to restart the http daemon by typing "/etc/rc.d/init.d/httpd restart". Otherwise, the changes will not go into effect.*

Setting Your Web Site's Document Locations

To customize where the Web server looks to find Web pages to display, do the following:

1. Log in as **root**.

2. Edit the file /etc/httpd/conf/srm.conf.

3. Change the path on the line that begins with DocumentRoot. The default is /home/httpd/html. This means that whenever someone accesses the Web server from outside, the server looks in the directory /home/httpd/html for either index.html, or the specific file the user requested. Any subdirectories created for the Web site are created inside this directory. A user accessing **www.fruit.org/citrus/** tells the Web server to look in /home/httpd/html/citrus.

   So, the new directory must be the place where you want to store any Web files. Perhaps you created a partition to hold Web documents which is mounted as /Web, and have created subdirectories there for the various people who have Web sites on your system. You could change the DocumentRoot line to "DocumentRoot /Web".

Changing The Port Your Web Server Watches On

To change which port your Web server uses do the following:

1. Log in as **root**.

2. Edit the file /etc/httpd/conf/httpd.conf.

3. Locate the line that begins with Port and change the value after it.

NOTE: *If you use a nonstandard port (80 in the case of httpd) for Web service, then people accessing your site must include the port number in the URL. For example, to access the main server at colors.org, which you've placed on port 150, they would type "www.colors.org:150."*

Setting The Web Administrator's Email Address

To set the email address displayed for Web server administrator contact information, do the following:

1. Log in as **root**.
2. Edit the file /etc/httpd/conf/httpd.conf.
3. Locate the line that begins with ServerAdmin and change the email address after it.

Configuring Web Server Error Logging

You have the option of customizing your Web server's logs:

1. Log in as **root**.
2. Edit the file /etc/httpd/conf/httpd.conf.
3. If you want to change where the Web server's error log is stored, then locate the line that begins with ErrorLog and change the path listed.

NOTE: *If there is no leading / then a start location of the server root directory is assumed—so the default log location is /home/http/logs/error_log.*

---

4. If you want to change the number of messages stored in the Web server's error log, locate the line that begins with LogLevel. The various levels available and their functions are shown in Table 14.1. Each level displays its own messages, plus the messages of the level above it. For example, using the lowest level of debug means that every level available will be recorded

Table 14.1   What type of data each log level specifies to write to the log file.

Level	Data Written To Log
emerg	The system has encountered an emergency and can no longer run. This could be a Linux issue, such as permissions, that has nothing to do with the Web server.
alert	The system can continue to function, but will not be able to function properly. Unpredictable behavior may result.
crit	The system can continue to function correctly, but this functionality will degrade over time.
error	There is an error (potentially just a typo) in your system configuration.
warn	There are no obviously significant errors, but warnings generated could possibly be a symptom of something more critical.
notice	Significant day-to-day operations.
info	Informational messages regarding normal operation of your Web server.
debug	Messages useful when debugging problems. Includes minor issues such as the opening and closing of files.

in your log files. Using the highest level of emerg only logs messages that explain why the Web server has crashed.

TIP: *Be careful about logging too much information. The more information logged, the bigger the log files are going to get, and they can eventually overrun their allotted disk space. If they are not on their own partition they can overrun the whole file system.*

---

5. If you want to change where the Web server's Web access log is stored, then locate the line that begins with CustomLog and change the path listed.

6. If you want the agent log (which browser the person accessing the page is using) and the referrer log (which URL the user came from within your own site to get to the current page) to be separate from the access log, you can uncomment the referrer and agent log CustomLog entries. If you want agent, referrer, and access logs all together in one file, then uncomment the CustomLog line with the combined tag at the end.

Setting Up Virtual Web Sites

To configure Apache to be able to serve Web documents for each of your virtual Web sites, do the following:

1. Log in as **root**.

2. Edit the file /etc/httpd/conf/httpd.conf.

3. Go to the end of the file.

4. At the end of the VirtualHost section, add an entry for the host(s) you want to include Web service for.

NOTE: *You may find that Web service for your main site no longer works properly after you configure virtual hosts. Add an entry for your main site in the VirtualHost section if this problem occurs.*

Fine-Tuning Your Server

There are some things you can change in order to fine-tune and customize your server's performance:

1. You can tell Apache not only to log the IP addresses of the servers that access your site, but to resolve the domain name as well. Doing this slows down access time slightly as the server resolves the domain, but it can be useful if you want access to this data. To accomplish this, edit the file /etc/httpd/conf/

httpd.conf and change the HostnameLookups value to be "on" instead of "off."

2. If your Web server is meant for large-scale service—around 1,000 hits per day or more—examine the default values in httpd.conf for MinSpareServers, MaxSpareServers, StartServers, and MaxClients, and determine whether you want to adjust these or not. Considerations to keep in mind include:

- The speed of the Web server's CPU.

- The amount of RAM in the Web server.

- How many other services the machine also hosts.

- The projected number of Web pages and sites hosted.

- The projected number of people accessing the pages.

TIP: *The Squid caching server is of valuable use when you are operating a large scale installation. This server stores the results of DNS resolutions so that DNS lookups do not need to be repeated.*

Testing Web Services

To ensure that your Web server is running properly, do the following:

1. Log in as **root**.

2. Create a dummy index.html in your document root directory.

3. As any user, use a Web browser to access your domain. For example, if you created a new page on **www.colors.org** and added this page to /home/httpd/html, then you should be able to access it with a Web browser by typing "www.colors.org/".

4. If you created any virtual sites, be sure to check each one individually with the same method, creating an index.html in each virtual site's root directory.

Configuring An FTP Server

You may have chosen to include FTP during the initial install process, or you may need to install the appropriate services.

Installing Anonymous FTP

Anonymous FTP is not usually included in the initial install process. If you want to run an anonymous FTP server, you need to install both the wu-ftp and anonftp Red Hat Package Manager packages (RPMs) from the Red Hat CD-ROM.

NOTE: *Don't install anonymous FTP unless you have a particular reason to use it. Otherwise, you open yourself to potential security holes or abuse of your system.*

Related solution:	Found on page:
Installing An RPM Package	295

Configuring FTP Access

To configure who can log in to your FTP server, do the following:

1. Determine whom you want to allow into your FTP server.

2. Log in as **root**.

3. Edit the file /etc/ftphosts.

4. Create allow statements for the hosts you want to specifically allow access to. For example, if you wanted to allow all users from your own site, colors.org, then you would use the line:

```
allow     *        *.colors.org
```

5. Create deny access for the hosts you specifically do not want to allow in. For example, if you have had a problem in the past with the user alice from the site machine1.test.com, then you would use the following to prevent her from entering in via FTP:

```
deny      alice    machine1.test.com
```

Configuring FTP Welcome Messages

To change the messages users see when they FTP into your server, do the following:

1. Log in as **root**.

2. Change to the directory /home/ftp, or whichever subdirectory you want to add a welcome message to.

3. Create the file ".message" and enter the text you want displayed when the user FTPs into the directory.

4. Save and exit the file.

Testing FTP Setup

To test your FTP setup, do the following:

1. Log in as any user.

2. FTP to the machine you configured as an FTP server. For example, if you installed anonymous FTP software on the machine "yellow" on colors.org, then you would type "ftp yellow.colors.org".

3. Try uploading files.

4. Try downloading files.

5. Try entering directories.

Configuring NFS

NFS is installed by default. What is necessary is to spend a few moments setting up user access for security.

Defining NFS Exports

To define the volumes available for exporting under NFS, do the following:

1. Log in as **root** on the machine you want to export volumes from.

2. Edit the file /etc/exports.

3. Build a statement for each file system you want to export. Each statement consists of two parts: the path being mounted, and the rules for mounting. For the sake of an example, say that you want to export the entire root directory (/) on the machine red.colors.org with full access to only the machine green.colors.org. And you also want to export as read only the directory /workfiles to any machine on colors.org. The two lines you might build would look like the following:

```
/        green
/workfiles    *.colors.org(ro)
```

Chapter 15

Package Management

In Brief

As you look for new files and programs to download, and prepare to send files or programs to other people, package management becomes a serious issue. Understanding the ins and outs of package and file formats can help reduce your own frustration and confusion, because you can much more easily determine the fastest route to accomplishing things.

This chapter covers the various types of packaging you will encounter in your explorations and how to choose among them.

Choosing Package Formats To Download

Often you have the opportunity to download a package in more than one format. The common choices you are given when downloading Linux software are:

- Source
- Binaries
- RPMs

Which one you choose depends on your level of expertise with programming, how standard your setup is, and whether you want to customize things highly or try them as they come by default.

Downloading Source

Choosing to download the source code for a package is in many ways the most complex solution available. It is complex because if you download the source, you must then compile it before you can install it. Reasons to go this route are:

- You are familiar with programming and know ahead of time that you want to make some adjustments to the source before compiling it.
- You have tried the other options available and for various reasons they did not work properly.
- Source is the only format through which the program is available.

Once you have the source you will need to compile it. This topic is covered in more detail in Chapter 16.

Downloading Binaries

Choosing to download a binary is often a simple procedure. This is because the binary is the already compiled version of the program, saving you the potential headaches of trying to compile it yourself. The issues you have to deal with when installing a binary are:

- The binary may not be fully compatible with your particular Linux setup.

- You cannot alter the binary itself.

- How quickly you get the binary properly installed depends on the quality of the README file that comes with it.

NOTE: *If the product is Open Source, then the source code is available to you if the binary is not compatible with your system, although it might be in an alternate download area.*

Downloading RPMS

The current format of choice for downloading for both Caldera and Red Hat is the Red Hat Package Manager (RPM) file. However, don't always trust that because it's an RPM means it is safe. The most trustworthy sources for RPMs include, but are not exclusive to:

- Red Hat's Web and FTP sites.
- Caldera's Web and FTP sites.
- The company or group who created the software's Web and FTP sites.
- Well-known and trusted Linux software download sites.
- RPMs that are PGP (Pretty Good Privacy, an encryption program) -signed by trusted sources.
- RPMs you make yourself.

TIP: *A trustworthy site is one that takes care to ensure that the downloads it offers are what they claim to be. This is especially a concern when the general public is allowed to upload packages. Each package must be tested for its validity and safety. Even so, it is wise to check each package yourself as much as you can, rather than blindly trust what you get.*

These principles apply to any downloads, not just RPMs.

Related solution:	See page:
An Example: Installing PGP	306

Packaging Schemes

When you download files or prepare to send files to other people, you encounter a number of cryptic file extensions.

NOTE: *In general, when downloading these packages you will want to put them all in a standard place. Some people like to use the /tmp directory. Others create a /download directory somewhere in their filesystem.*

Tar Archive

Tar is used to bundle files together while maintaining their directory structure. This archiving program does not do any file compression—unless called with the -z flag, in which case it utilizes the GZip program to compress the archive when it is finished. Its function is to bundle the files or directories specified with their associations and locations intact. Therefore, tar is often used in conjunction with a compression program or the compression flag to reduce the amount of space the archive uses.

NOTE: *Using tar with gzip as described above is only a GNU tar feature, not a standard tar feature. It will not work under Unix systems that use the standard tar.*

You can recognize a tar file by the .tar extension.

TIP: *A common practice is to create a "tarball," which has either a .tgz extension or .tar.gz. To open a tarball, follow the instructions for unzipping a file, then untarring it.*

GZip Compression

A popular form of file compression among Linux users is the program GZip, which is GNU's compression program. You can recognize a file compressed with GZip by the .gz extension. Sometimes, although rarely, a .z (note the lower case) extension is used instead.

Z Compression

Another form of file compression (available across Unix platforms) is done with the program compress. You can recognize a file compressed with the compress program by the .Z extension.

Zip Compression

Useful for creating or opening a pkzip-compatible compressed file. You can recognize a file compressed with the zip program by the .zip extension.

Red Hat Package Manager

Another method of transmitting programs or groups of programs to install is via the Red Hat Package Managers, which are discussed earlier in this chapter. You can recognize an RPM by the .rpm extension.

XWindow RPM Tools

If you find having to memorize all of the appropriate switches to manage your RPM packages frustrating, or if you simply prefer to work with more graphical interfaces, don't despair. RPM tools that cover the most commonly used tasks do exist.

Red Hat X RPM Manager

Red Hat provides an X tool for its default Gnome window manager called *GnoRPM* to make managing your RPMs easier, as shown in Figure 15.1.

Caldera X RPM Manager

Caldera provides an X tool for its default KDE window manager called *KPackage* to assist in managing your RPMs, as shown in Figure 15.2.

Figure 15.1   GnoRPM, the Gnome RPM graphical manager.

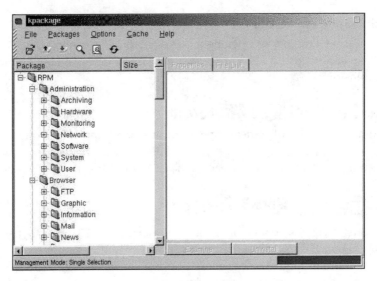

Figure 15.2   KPackage, the KDE RPM graphical manager.

Immediate Solutions

Managing RPMs

You can manage your RPMs either by hand on the command line or via Red Hat and Caldera's X tools. This section refers to the command line unless explicitly stated otherwise.

NOTE: *While the basics of RPMs are covered here, more aspects are included in Chapter 16.*

Installing An RPM Package

There are three primary flags for installing an RPM package:

- **rpm -i** is used to install a new package.
- **rpm -U** is used to upgrade a package or to install it if it is not already installed.
- **rpm -F** is used to upgrade a package, but not install it if it is not already installed.

Supplemental flags commonly used with the primaries are:

- **-v** is used to see verbose messages.
- **-h** is used to see hash marks (#) as progress markers during the install.

A common combination to use is:

```
rpm -Uvh package-name.rpm
```

This command upgrades or installs new packages, using verbose messages and hash marks for progress. You can replace the **i** or **F** with the **U**.

Removing An RPM Package

To uninstall an RPM, use the **-e** flag. For example,

```
rpm -e package-name
```

Listing What RPMs You Have Installed

To get information on what RPMs you have installed, you use the query flag (**-q**). To see all RPMs you've installed, type "rpm -qa".

If you want to know if a particular package is already installed, type "rpm -q package-name".

Determining What Files Are In An RPM Package

To get a listing of the files within a package, you have the following options:

- If you have not installed the package, then the command is

```
rpm -qlp package-name.rpm
```

- If you have installed the package, then the command is

```
rpm -ql package-name
```

Determining What RPM Package A File Is In

If there is a particular file on your system and you want to know what package it is in, perhaps so you can upgrade that package to upgrade the file, first find that file with its full path. Then, type "rpm -qf file-with-full-path".

For example, if you wanted to find the daemon httpd, which lives in /etc/rc.d/init.d/, you would type "rpm -qf /etc/rc.d/init.d/httpd".

Determining What An RPM Package Is For

You can query a package before installing it to find out what it is, who built it, and other such pertinent information. To accomplish this, type "rpm -qip package-name.rpm".

Verifying A PGP Signed RPM

If you downloaded an RPM that is PGP signed, you need to verify it before you continue. To verify this package, do the following:

1. Download and install the PGP package, as shown in Chapter 16.

2. Add PGP to your path, as shown in Chapter 16.

3. Locate the directory containing your public keyring.

4. Create an environment variable named PGPPATH, which is equal to the directory name determined in Step 3. How this task is accomplished depends on the shell you are using. If you are using the default (**bash**) shell, then you do this by typing "PGPPATH=path_from_3".

For example, if in step 3 you found the keyring in /etc/pgp/rings then you would type "PGPPATH=/etc/pgp/rings".

NOTE: *To test and make sure the path was set properly, type "echo $PGPPATH".*

---

5. Verify the package by typing "rpm -K —checksig *package*.rpm".

Verifying That An Installed RPM Package Has Not Been Changed

You can verify that a package is not missing files or changed without your knowledge by checking it against the original RPM used to install it. To do so for a single package, type "rpm -V package-name".

If there is nothing wrong, then no data will be given. If some form of change is detected, then it is given in the form of:

```
SM5DLUGT c file
```

What each of these stands for is shown in Table 15.1.

Look for the following in the results:

- If a necessary file is missing, the complete path for that file is shown.

- If a dependency is missing, the necessary package name is given.

- Any SM5DLUGT listings. Some of these could have been changed simply along the lines of normal system maintenance and are fine. However, changes also could be the symptom of a problem.

Table 15.1   The meaning behind rpm -V output.

Code	Meaning
S	File size.
M	File mode.
5	MD5 checksum value.
D	Major and minor file numbers.
L	Symbolic links.
U	File owner.
G	File group.
T	File modification time.
c	Displayed if the file is a configuration file.
file	The complete path to the file that failed verification.

15. Package Management

Other useful variants are:

- **rpm -Va** is used to verify all installed RPM packages.

- **rpm -Vf** *path-to-program* is used to verify the package that a particular malfunctioning program belongs to. For example, if you are having difficulties with the **korn** shell, which is installed to /bin/ksh, then you might type "rpm -Vf /bin/ksh".

- **rpm -Vp** checks installed packages against packages on your CD-ROM or other media. It is used if you want to verify your RPM database, but have lost it.

TIP: *Running rpm -Vp regularly—perhaps in a cron job—is a good way of making sure no one has changed the packages you installed. This action requires that the CD-ROM be in the machine when the cron job will run.*

Related solution:	See page:
Setting Backups To Run At Specific Times	368

Working With Tar Archives

The tar archiving program has many useful features. It is worthwhile to look through the tar man pages if you find yourself heavily using this program.

Listing The Contents Of A Tar Archive

If you want to see what is in a tar archive before you take it apart, use the command

```
tar -tf filename.tar
```

to see just a listing of the file names, or

```
tar -tvf filename.tar
```

to see a listing of the contents as in the same format ls -l uses.

Untarring A File

To **untar** a file, the basic flag is the letter **x** (extract). A common combination of flags used in file extraction is **xvf**, for example:

```
tar -xvf filename.tar
```

The **v** flag is for verbose, and the **f** flag tells **tar** you are going to give it a file's name.

TIP: *Where you open a tar archive depends on how it was initially created. Looking at the contents (see the second option in the section "Listing The Contents Of A Tar Archive") helps to determine how this was done. This action will allow you to see the directory structure stored within the tar archive so you can choose accordingly where to put the file.*

If you are still unsure, untar it in a temporary area and see what kind of structure it opens with. You can then untar it again in the appropriate location.

Extracting Only The README File From The Tar Archive

Often it is useful to extract only the README file from a tar archive, so you can see where the instructions tell you to unpack the archive without needing to do it twice. To accomplish this task:

1. Enter the directory the tar file is stored in.
2. Type the second option listed in the section "Listing The Contents Of A Tar Archive."
3. Note the format and location of the README file within the archive.
4. Use the following command in full, substituting the appropriate file names where necessary:

```
tar xf archive.tar dir/README > README
```

For example, if you had the archive file program.tar and within its directory structure you saw listed home/bruce/Read.me, then you would type something to the effect of "tar xf program.tar home/bruce/Read.me > README".

NOTE: *You can do this without the redirection, but if so then the file will be created with the archived directory structure intact. So if you followed the example without the redirection at the end, the file Read.me would be extracted into the directory home/bruce, which would be created for that purpose.*

---

5. Read the file README and learn where you are instructed to open the tar archive.

Creating A Tar Archive

To create a tar archive, do the following:

1. Locate the directories or files you want to archive.

2. Determine whether you want the archive to be restored to a relative or absolute path.

NOTE: *If you intend to share archives with others, it is not recommended that you create archives that will extract to an absolute path. However, if the archives are exclusively for your own backup use, then you may find it beneficial to use absolutes.*

---

3. Change to the parent directory that contains the files or directories you want to archive. For example, if you want to archive the directory /var/spool/mail, change to the directory /var/spool.

4. Create the archive by typing "tar cvf archive.tar directory", where *archive.tar* is the name of the new archive file, and *directory* is the name of the file or directory you want to archive. Continuing the example, to archive /var/spool/mail to the file mail-archive.tar, you would type, from within /var/spool, "tar cvf mail-archive.tar mail".

Appending Files To An Existing Tar Archive

To append files or directories to an existing tar archive, follow the instructions for creating a new tar file, but use the flags **rf** instead of **cvf**, such as

```
tar rf mail-archive.tar mail-to-add
```

Working With GZip Compression

Data compression is a wondrous thing when it comes time to put files on a disk where they would not otherwise fit. GZip is one of the most popular forms of compression in the Linux community.

GZipping A File

To GZip a file, type "gzip *file*".

For example, if you wanted to GZip file1, you would type "gzip file1"and the file file1.gz would be created.

NOTE: *If you want to Zip multiple files together, see the section "Creating A Tarball."*

UnGZipping A File

To unzip a GZipped file, type "gunzip file".

Creating A Tarball

To create a tarball, do the following:

1. Follow the steps in the section "Creating A Tar Archive" to create the .tar file.

2. Follow the steps in the section "Gzipping A File" to compress the tar archive. Be sure to give the target a .tar.gz extension.

3. If you prefer, rename the file so instead of having a .tar.gz extension, it has a .tgz extension.

15. Package Management

Chapter 16

Installing New Software

In Brief

As you become more comfortable with your system, you will find more uses for it. Perhaps you will simply want to see what other software is out there. You will quickly find that adding Linux software is not always as straightforward to the novice as in other operating systems. If what you download is an RPM, you are in luck; the installation work is done for you by the package manager. If not, you have more work ahead of you.

Fortunately, the task of installing binaries and source becomes easier the more you deal with the issue.

Choosing Where To Install Software

If you are the only person using your Linux box, then where you install software is not as large an issue as in multiuser boxes or on a LAN. But some of these principles still apply, because software must be installed in a place that allows it to be used as necessary. Haphazard and inconsistent file system policies can eventually cause problems.

Within The Linux File System Standard

The Linux file system standard (FSSTND) lays out the structure of the Linux directory tree. It is not necessary for you to follow this standard, but there are some compelling reasons to do so:

- If you stay within the standard, all of your packages remain together whether you place them by hand or with a package manager, such as RPM.

- Staying within the standard allows you to become familiar with the layout of other Unix file systems that also follow the standard, which is most of them. This makes your system administration skills portable, and it also makes it easier if you have to have someone look after your system when you are unavailable.

- Using the standard when you place files manually makes it easier for programs to find other programs. Otherwise, you need to modify configuration files or source code to tell new programs where to look.

A brief look at the Linux file system standard is shown in Table 16.1.

Table 16.1   The Linux FSSTND layout.

Directory	Use
/	The root directory of your file system.
/bin	Binaries necessary for proper command function.
/boot	Files needed by your boot loader (LILO).
/dev	Device files used to tell Linux how to access the different aspects of your hardware.
/etc	Configuration files that apply only to the specific machine.
/home	Home directories for your users.
/lib	Shared libraries needed by programs within the root file system.
/mnt	Location to mount temporary file systems, usually each with its own identifying subdirectory.
/opt	Used by some to house add-on binaries.
/root	Home directory for the root user.
/sbin	Binaries necessary for proper system function.
/tmp	Temporary files for both users and programs.
/usr	Public applications for use by most or all users. This portion of the file system is sometimes kept centrally on a specific server and then mounted by all machines in the LAN, to allow one central /usr management point.
/var	Variable data such as program logs.

NOTE: *To see the complete FSSTND, go to **www.pathname.com** or do a Web search on the acronym and you will get a number of detailed and general breakdowns.*

Permission Issues

One important item to consider when installing software is what permissions are necessary. The issues involved in these considerations are:

- Is the program meant to only be run by root? Or by a specific user or group? Or by all users?

- What is the program trying to do? Does it need to run as a specific user or group?

- What file or directory resources does this program need to access during operation?

- Do you want the program to be within your default path? The average user's default path?

An Example: Installing PGP

To demonstrate the full process of finding and installing software, we will run through an example of installing the encryption package called Pretty Good Privacy (PGP). Using this package can increase your security, especially in conjunction with other programs—such as RPM's ability to verify the validity of packages with a PGP signature (see Chapter 15 for more information).

In order to make this a worthwhile example, we include some twists and turns to show how to recover from otherwise confusing problems.

Follow these steps to add PGP to your system and then use it:

1. Locate and download a reliable version of the package. This step is often best accomplished by going to the Web site maintained by the package's creators or to one of the trusted Linux download sites. Otherwise, you risk fetching an altered version of the package, which could damage your system.

2. Install the package. Sometimes this means properly placing a binary or using RPM. Or you might need to compile the source, and use **make install** at the end of the process to put the compiled binaries in place.

3. Locate and read the documentation for the package.

Finding And Downloading PGP

Locating software packages can be a simple or complex process. The actual location of this package is in Step 4. This example serves to detail what steps you might go through to find and download PGP. The process might be the following:

1. PGP is not included among the initial RPMs that came with your Red Hat or Caldera CD-ROM because of encryption export reasons, so you will not find it there.

2. PGP is not on Red Hat or Caldera's Web sites for the same export reasons.

3. Normally you would next locate the primary PGP Web site. This task can sometimes take some Web searching, though sometimes it is simple. In the case of PGP it is **www.pgp.com**. However, this site mentions nothing about the Linux version of PGP.

4. Going to Red Hat's Web site at **www.redhat.com** and searching on the terms "PGP and download" leads to a statement that PGP

is considered a "munition" and therefore cannot be offered by Red Hat. The FTP site **ftp.replay.com** offers PGP instead.

5. Finally, an RPM of the PGP package is available under the Unix section at the replay FTP site. Download that package to a temporary directory.

Installing The PGP RPM

Now that you've downloaded the PGP RPM, you can install it by typing "rpm -ivh pgp*", unless you have more than one item in the directory that starts with "pgp". A line of hash marks later, and the PGP package is properly installed on your machine. This process may seem anticlimactic if you are used to compiling source or installing binaries.

What Now?

To learn more about the package and how to use it, you now have access to:

• Man pages for the package. In this case, type "man pgp".

• Additional text files that are installed along with PGP. To locate them, type "rpm -ql pgp".

   If there is a file in any form that resembles *"Read me first"* (maybe *readme.1st*), accept the advice and read that file first. It will have the most up-to-date information. Some of the other files may be one or two versions behind that of the program you just downloaded and installed.

• Use what you've learned to put the program into action. Sometimes the best way to learn a program is to fool around with it. Just be careful and don't run programs capable of large-scale damage as the root user.

In the case of PGP, although it can be used as a standalone program, its primary uses are integrated with other packages. The first step many take after installing PGP is to create their private and public keys, and collect keys from those they wish to exchange encoded information with. PGP is also used to verify PGP-signed RPM packages, which is why PGP was chosen as an example.

16. Installing New Software

Immediate Solutions

Locating A Software Package

Here are some useful strategies for locating Linux software packages:

- If you are on the hunt for new software but don't have anything specific in mind, start surfing the Web. You can spend hours, even days, following the links within these sites.

- If you are looking for software that accomplishes a specific task, first try your favorite Linux software repositories. If you can't find what you're looking for there, try a well-worded Web search. Include the word "Linux" plus other keywords that apply to the type of software you want to find. Sometimes it's necessary to keep trying different keywords until you get the results you're looking for, or to filter out certain keywords that are muddying your search efforts.

- If you know the package you want, it is often best to start at the creator's Web site, whether it is an individual hobbyist or a company. This site will have the latest version available and, although nothing is one hundred percent reliable, it is likely to have a secure version of the software.

TIP: *There is much discussion in Chapters 15 and 16 of being sure that packages are secure. It is important to remember that, although some of the reasons many people move to this operating system include the cooperation within the Linux community and the small number of viruses aimed at Linux, it is still only as secure as you make it.*

Linux security issues are discussed in more detail in Chapter 21.

Determining If Source Will Compile On Your Machine

If you choose to download the source for a particular package, (or if you have no other choice), you need to take a look and make sure it will compile on your machine without needing changes. Look first in the documentation, then in the makefile, to see if there is a Linux target available. If not, do the following:

NOTE: *Well-constructed makefiles are full of helpful instructions, letting you know when to comment out or uncomment code for specific setups.*

- If available, choose a BSD compile option. This choice will usually give you the least items to change within the makefile.

- If there is no BSD option, or if the BSD option will not compile, try the SysV (System V) compile target.

- There may not be a named operating system target at all in the makefile—meaning that there may not be a series of segments that allow you to choose which operating system to compile the code for (for example, Linux, BSD, or Sys V). In that case, just try the compile, see what happens, and then edit from there.

TIP: *Source code gets easier to work with through practice. If you are uncomfortable with the process of preparing and compiling source, it is advisable to download source that is not mission-critical, practice checking to see if it has compile options for your machine, and then compile it. Using this method takes some of the pressure off and allows you to give up if you get stuck, coming back later after you have learned more from playing with source for other packages.*

Waiting to deal with source for the first time when you are in a rush and really need to get a package installed and working is a recipe for frustration.

Altering A Makefile

Altering a makefile, if you are not familiar with programming, can be a confusing and nontrivial procedure. There are some particular issues to keep in mind when fussing with makefiles:

- There are often comments scattered throughout a makefile to explain what segments you may and may not want to change.

- It is a good idea to make a backup of the original makefile, especially if you are unused to programming.

- The more C programming you know and understand, the more makefiles make sense.

Compiling Source Code

Although it is not possible to give a generic set of step by step instructions for compiling all source code, it is possible to give a series of guidelines for how to go about it. These guidelines are:

- It is a standard with GNU software to include an INSTALL file with the source for a program. Read this file carefully if it is there. If the instructions are step by step or very useful, leave them open in a virtual terminal while you work in another.

- If there is no INSTALL file, read the README file that comes with the source, along with any other text documents sent along with it. If the instructions are step by step or very useful, keep them open in a virtual terminal to follow while you work. Even if there is an INSTALL file, it is good to look at any README files as well.

- Carefully pay attention to versions of libraries and other programs that may be required for the software you're compiling. You may be fortunate and find that what you need to satisfy dependencies is available as an RPM you already have on CD-ROM.

- Although it is not necessary to watch the screen during every moment of a software compile, it can definitely help you to spot errors if you are having difficulties getting source to compile properly. If there is too much information and you cannot scroll back far enough, append the following to the end of the make statement:

```
> output
```

This addition places all of the output from the make process into the file named output, so you can go through it at your leisure when attempting to debug the compile.

The commands you might use while compiling source are listed here, in the order you would likely use them:

NOTE: *If the README or INSTALL file does not mention the list of make targets available, look through the makefile. They will all be in there. It is possible that there will be an "all" option within the makefile that automates the entire process if it runs properly.*

---

1. **make config**—Examines your system setup and builds the specific configuration file necessary to build the program for your installation.

2. **make clean**—Removes any files left over from previous failed attempts to compile the program.

3. **make**—Uses the default target, which usually actually compiles the program.

4. **make install**—Places all of the program's components into place, giving them the proper ownerships and permissions.

Installing A Binary

Do the following to install a binary package:

1. Uncompress it into a temporary directory, if it is compressed and/or archived.

2. Read any README or INSTALL documentation that comes with the package. It does not hurt to look in the makefile as well. Here is where you can do things like edit the default paths for the installation if you so choose.

3. Type "make install".

Adding A Package To Your Path Statement

If you are using the **bash** or **korn** shell, you add a new directory to your path statement by doing the following:

1. Log into the account whose path you want to change.

NOTE: If you want to alter the path for all users at once, edit the file /etc/profile as **root**.

---

2. Type "PATH=$PATH:additional_path" to append a path to the account's current path statement. For example, if you wanted to append the path /usr/local/bin to your path statement, you would type "PATH=$PATH:/usr/local/bin".

NOTE: To see your full path statement, type "echo $PATH".

---

16. Installing New
Software

Recognizing A Runnable Program

There are a few ways you can recognize a runnable program:

- One of the fastest ways to recognize a runnable program is to look at its permissions. If the executable (x) bit is set, then it is a runnable program. However, if the permissions are improperly set for some reason, this method will not suffice.

- If you think a program might be an executable, try looking at its man page by typing "man program".

- One way to test whether something is runnable or not is simply to try to run it. This can be a bit risky in some ways, depending on what the software or script does.

Chapter 17

C Programming Tools

In Brief

Many Linux users either choose the operating system because they enjoy programming, or find that they become at least rudimentary programmers over time as they learn more about how to work with their systems and compile the source code they download for their system. The more you get into programming, the more important it is to know the tools at your disposal and how to upgrade them, because the day eventually comes when source you downloaded requires you to use them.

C Programming Tools

A programming language such as C is compiled, not interpreted. This means that it requires a compiler at the very least in order for you to be able to utilize the language. On top of this, one of the great advantages of the C language is its ability to use shared libraries. These libraries contain chunks of code that keep programmers from having to reinvent the wheel in order to accomplish basic tasks. There are also specialized libraries available for industry-specific programming, such as computer telephony libraries. Some specialized libraries come on the distribution CD-ROMs; others are available on the Internet, either for download or for sale.

NOTE: *The C programming language is a complex instrument. This chapter in no way claims to teach you how to use it. The focus here is to show you what tools are available and how to find and install them.*

C Programming In Linux

If you come from an MS Windows programming environment where you are used to using project files, then programming in C in Linux is going to take some getting used to. You will now need to learn how to build a *Makefile* by hand. See the section "Building A Simple Makefile" for a starter example.

Immediate Solutions

Installing The C Compiler

To install the GNU C compiler, do the following:

1. Log in as **root**.
2. Place the distribution CD-ROM in the CD-ROM drive.
3. Mount the distribution CD-ROM with the **mount** command.
4. Change to the package directory with the **cd** command. You'll find this directory in:
   - /mnt/cdrom/RedHat/RPMS on the Red Hat CD-ROM
   - /mnt/cdrom/Packages/RPMS on the Caldera CD-ROM
5. Type "ls egcs*" to see which package is the base *egcs* package. This base package has nothing else attached to it and will look something like *egcs-1.1.2-12.i386.rpm*.
6. Install the package by typing something similar to "rpm -ivh egcs-1.1.2-12.i386.rpm", using the specific text for the package you are using instead of the version listed here, if different.

Related solutions:	Found on page:
Mounting Onto The File System	168
Unmounting Off The File System	170
Installing An RPM Package	295

Installing The Initial C Libraries

To install the base libraries used by the C compiler, do the following:

1. Log in as **root**.
2. Place the distribution CD-ROM in the CD-ROM drive.
3. Mount the distribution CD-ROM with the **mount** command.
4. Change to the package directory with the **cd** command. You'll find this directory in:
   - /mnt/cdrom/RedHat/RPMS on the Red Hat CD-ROM
   - /mnt/cdrom/Packages/RPMS on the Caldera CD-ROM

17. C Programming Tools

5. Type "rpm -ivh glibc-devel*" to install the standard C libraries.

Related solutions:	Found on page:
Mounting A File System	XX
Unmounting A File System	XX
Installing An RPM Package	XX

Installing The Kernel Libraries

To install the kernel source code, which is necessary to compile many C programs aside from the kernel itself, do the following:

1. Log in as **root**.

2. Place the distribution CD-ROM in the CD-ROM drive.

3. Mount the distribution CD-ROM with the **mount** command.

4. Change to the package directory with the **cd** command. You'll find this directory in:

   • /mnt/cdrom/RedHat/RPMS on the Red Hat CD-ROM

   • /mnt/cdrom/Packages/RPMS on the Caldera CD-ROM

5. Type "rpm -ivh kernel-head* kernel-source*" to install the packages containing both the kernel's C header files and its source code.

Related solutions:	Found on page:
Mounting Onto The File System	168
Unmounting Off The File System	170
Installing An RPM Package	295

Installing The Build Manager

To install the **make** program, which acts as a type of manager for the compilation of many of the programs you will download as source, do the following:

1. Log in as **root**.

2. Place the distribution CD-ROM in the CD-ROM drive.

3. Mount the distribution CD-ROM with the **mount** command.

4. Change to the package directory with the **cd** command. You'll find this directory in:
   - /mnt/cdrom/RedHat/RPMS on the Red Hat CD-ROM
   - /mnt/cdrom/Packages/RPMS on the Caldera CD-ROM

5. Type "rpm -ivh make*" to install the **make** package.

Related solutions:	Found on page:
Mounting Onto The File System	168
Unmounting Off The File System	170
Installing An RPM Package	295

Installing The C Preprocessor

To install the C preprocessor (cpp) package, which provides tools that allow the creation of macros for small pieces of C code, conditional compiler options, and the includes of items like header files, do the following:

1. Log in as **root**.

2. Place the distribution CD-ROM in the CD-ROM drive.

3. Mount the distribution CD-ROM with the **mount** command.

4. Change to the package directory with the **cd** command. You'll find this directory in:
   - /mnt/cdrom/RedHat/RPMS on the Red Hat CD-ROM
   - /mnt/cdrom/Packages/RPMS on the Caldera CD-ROM

5. Type "rpm -ivh cpp*" to install the package.

Related solutions:	Found on page:
Mounting Onto The File System	168
Unmounting Off The File System	170
Installing An RPM Package	295

17. C Programming Tools

Installing The File Comparison Tools

To install the diffutils package, which includes applications like the
diff program—which you can use to create source code patches—do
the following:

1. Log in as **root**.

2. Place the distribution CD-ROM in the CD-ROM drive.

3. Mount the distribution CD-ROM with the **mount** command.

4. Change to the package directory with the **cd** command. You'll
   find this directory in:

   • /mnt/cdrom/RedHat/RPMS on the Red Hat CD-ROM

   • /mnt/cdrom/Packages/RPMS on the Caldera CD-ROM

5. Type "rpm -ivh diffutils*" to install the package.

Related solutions:	*Found on page:*
Mounting Onto The File System	168
Unmounting Off The File System	170
Installing An RPM Package	295

Installing The Patch Applicator

To install the **patch** program, which applies patches to source code
in order to update it, do the following:

1. Log in as **root**.

2. Place the distribution CD-ROM in the CD-ROM drive.

3. Mount the distribution CD-ROM with the **mount** command.

4. Change to the package directory with the **cd** command. You'll
   find this directory in:

   • /mnt/cdrom/RedHat/RPMS on the Red Hat CD-ROM

   • /mnt/cdrom/Packages/RPMS on the Caldera CD-ROM

5. Type "rpm -ivh patch*" to install the package.

17. C Programming Tools

Related solutions:	*Found on page:*
Mounting Onto The File System	168
Unmounting Off The File System	170
Installing An RPM Package	295

Finding Specialized Libraries

If you get more into programming and are interested in finding more specialized libraries, try the following methods:

* Look in the RPM packages that came with the distribution for the libraries contained there. Typing "ls *lib*" is a quick way to take a look at which libraries exist. Then typing "rpm -qip *packagename*" gives you the information on the package itself.

* View the libraries listed at **www.linuxprogramming.com**.

* Check out the Linux Commercial HOW-TO at **metalab.unc.edu/ LDP/HOWTO/Commercial-HOWTO.html** for a listing of commercially available libraries for a variety of tasks.

Related solutions:	*Found on page:*
Mounting Onto The File System	168
Unmounting Off The File System	170
Installing An RPM Package	295

Building A Simple Makefile

This section assumes that you know how to build the necessary header (.h) and C code (.c) files and are now ready to attempt your first build in Linux. Because builds tend to have to be done more than once during the debugging process, it is more efficient to write a Makefile now than to follow through the entire build process by hand every time. To create a simple Makefile, do the following:

1. Change to the directory where the source files you want to compile are.

2. Type "vi Makefile" to create the Makefile with the **vi** editor.

3. Press *i* to enter **vi**'s Insert mode.

4. Each entry in a Makefile is in the following format:

```
target : prerequsite (s)
    command
```

A Makefile essentially breaks down into a string of these statements. The order in which they are entered into the Makefile is not important, but for ease of use many people enter them from the most complex to the least complex. The first target to build is often the *all* target, which is unusual because it does not contain any commands and looks like this:

```
all : main_target
```

The main_target item is generally the name of the binary you want to produce.

5. From here you create the main_target statement, which would look something like:

```
main_target : target1.o target2.o target3.o
    cc -o main_target target1.o target2.o target3.o
```

6. Now, build statements for each of the smaller targets. These statements might be:

```
target1.o : target1.c
    cc -c target1.c

target2.o : target2.c
    cc -c target2.c

target3.o : target3.c
    cc -c target3.c
```

Keep in mind that the command does not have to be a C compiler command. It can be anything that needs to be run at that stage in the **make** process.

7. Save and exit the file by typing ":wq".

8. Type "rpm -q make" to see if the **make** package is installed. If it is not, see the section "Installing The Build Manager."

9. Type "make all" or "make *main_target*" to build the file.

Chapter 18

Writing Shell Scripts

In Brief

The Shell script is an immensely useful administrative tool. It can be used to automate repetitive or complex tasks usually done at the command line. Scripts can also be used to automate basic tasks for users who do not have much knowledge of Linux, or more complex user tasks that only those who have a solid grounding in Linux could otherwise accomplish.

The Shells

A shell is an interface between you and the Linux kernel itself. It is your working environment, and you can choose which shell you prefer to work with. Each shell has its own specialized features that make it interesting and useful to people according to their personal needs. Each shell also has its own syntax for dealing with commands, environment variables, and more:

- The bash shell is the default in Linux, as well as the shell most often used for the root account.

- The C shell is so named because its syntax is much like the C programming language; it is popular among C programmers for this reason.

- The Korn shell used in Linux is not actually the standard Korn shell, but a public domain version called *pdksh (Public Domain Korn Shell)*. It shares some features with the C shell and also has a number of new features that make it a favorite of many people who write a lot of shell scripts. It is available on the Red Hat and Caldera CD-ROMs in its own package.

Related solutions:	Found on page:
Mounting Onto The File System	168
Installing An RPM Package	295

Good Scripting Habits

Although there is no universal set of instructions for writing shell scripts, here are some good habits to follow along the way:

- It is often wise to put all of your shell scripts together in one place, for both file and path management purposes. This fact is true regardless of what account you write them for, superuser or normal user. Many people create a subdirectory in their home directory called bin (~/bin).

- A caveat to the above is that if you write scripts as a system administrator for use by a number of people or by all users, you need to determine where the script needs to live according to the same principles you would use to choose a location for a program.

- Don't trust that you will have a perfect memory for what each section of your script does and how. It is wise to comment your work as best you can to avoid confusion if you need to update the script months or years later.

- Indent conditional statements so that you can easily see what commands belong to which clauses. An example of this formatting is in the section "Writing Conditional If Statements."

An Example

Let's build a short example script to walk through the process. Included in these steps are the behind-the-scenes considerations you must make as you plan and write shell scripts. Don't worry, this process gets easier with practice.

Script Purpose

This basic script automates the task of making bulk, identical changes to a Web file on one of your Web hosts. Because the example administrator does not have time to build a complex script, this example is written to handle only the initial change that needs to be made. The script could then be built upon over time to handle larger and more complex tasks, such as changing the contents of every Web file in a grouping of selected directories.

Plan The Script

It might seem most efficient to start building the script right away. However, the process of building is much easier once some planning has gone into it. Otherwise, you could find yourself going back to make repeated changes as you realize some other aspect needs to be dealt with. The steps involved for this script are as follows:

1. First, you need to decide which shell the script interpreter will run under. Because this is an administrative script and the default shell is bash, this example sticks with the bash shell.

2. Before you build the script, you should determine the set of commands you would normally use to accomplish the task at

the prompt. In this case, the point is to search and replace a URL within a Web page as a springboard toward eventually making a more complex package. To accomplish this search-and-replace, you use the **sed** command.

3. Read the man page and other available resources for **sed**. It is possible to accomplish your task by using **sed** without a script around it, but creating a script will make it easier for you to do the same or a similar task again without having to relearn how to use the complexities of the **sed** editor.

4. The first thing you may notice is that to separate the components of the search-and-replace terms requires a delimiter character. The default delimiter is the front slash (/). However, because the search-and-replace terms are URLs, there will be slashes within these terms. This issue leaves two choices:

- *To escape the front slash with the escape character, the back slash (\\).* Escaping a character lets the interpreter know that the character typed is meant just as it is, and not as a special character (like a delimiter). For example, to search for the URL **www.green.org/lime**, you would type the search term:

```
www.green.org\/lime\/
```

In the example this option is chosen because it is the standard format used for programs that accept regular expressions.

- *To use an entirely different delimiter.* You are not required to always use the front slash. For example, because there is no need to use the **http://** part of the URL in the search-and-replace term, a colon (:) could be used as a delimiter.

TIP: *A meta-character is a character that gives information about other characters. It is a "special character"; rather than just being the character it is, it has a special purpose. For example, the front slash (/) is often a meta-character when used to build **sed** commands because it is used to break the command into its components.*

---

5. Now, to build the **sed** statement. The specific thing you want to search for and replace is the URL **www.peach.org**, changing it to **http://watermelon.com/pink**. Because the first part, http://, does not need to be changed, the statement looks like this:

```
s/www\.peach\.org\//watermelon\.com\/pink\//
```

To break this statement down:

- s/ tells **sed** that this command is for a substitution.

- www\.peach\.org\// is the text we want to find. There are so many escape characters (\) because the periods (.) and the final slash for the URL (/) must be escaped. Note that there is still one last slash to mark that the search part of the command is finished.

- watermelon\.com\/pink\/ is the text we want to put in place of the original.

- The final slash signifies the end of the **sed** statement.

Create The Script File

To build this script we first must open and edit a text file:

1. Create a bin subdirectory in your home directory by typing "mkdir ~/bin".

2. Change to the bin directory by typing "cd ~/bin".

3. Add this bin directory to your path by typing "PATH=$PATH:~/bin".

4. Open the file in your favorite editor. If the editor is **vi**, then you might type "vi webchange".

Write The Script

Now that the commands and syntax are determined, it is time to write the script:

1. The first line in every shell script is the interpreter declaration. For this script the interpreter will be the bash shell. So the first line in the Web change script is:

```
#!/bin/bash
```

From this point on, everything you add to the script must be specific to the bash shell's interpreter.

2. Because this script is originally built to do one task, but the intention is to expand its use in a more generic sense, it is important not to forget the lessons learned while researching the complexities of **sed**. You add comments to a script by starting the line with a hash mark (#).

18. Writing Shell Scripts

NOTE: When you start a line in a shell script with the characters #!, the shell knows that you are about to declare the program used to run the script.

An example comment for this script is:

```
# Sed statement built to search for the first URL and
# replace it with the
# second. Notice the escape
  # characters ensuring that the periods and front
# slashes are seen as actual characters and not meta-
  characters.
```

3. Now for the **sed** statement itself:

```
sed s/www\.peach\.org\//watermelon\.com\/pink\// test.html
```

Rather than risking one of the production Web files, copy one to a test file (in this example called test.html) so you can ensure the script causes no unforeseen problems before applying it to important data.

4. Save and exit the file.

5. Change the permissions so the file is an executable with, for example, "chmod +x webchange".

Test The Script

Now to test the script to ensure it runs properly. If you:

• Added the script's directory to your path statement

• Copied or created a test file in your ~/bin directory

• Made the script file executable with, for example, "chmod +x webchange"

then you can test the script by typing its file name, "webchange".

Immediate Solutions

Writing A Script

There are a number of basic steps for writing a shell script:

1. Begin by editing the text file that will contain your script.

2. Add the shell identifier line so Linux knows which shell language you are using.

3. Build your shell script.

4. Save and exit the script file.

5. Change the permissions and ownerships of the script so it is executable by the right user accounts with, for example, "chmod +x webchange".

6. Run the script to test it.

7. Take steps to debug if necessary, then return to Step 6.

8. Move the completed script to its new home if necessary.

9. Add to your path statement if necessary.

Assigning Value To A Variable

You can either assign values directly to a variable, or assign the variable to be the output of a command. Whether you do one or the other is mostly dependent on where the value you want to assign is coming from.

Assigning Value Directly

To assign a value to a variable directly, use the format:

```
variable=value
```

Remember that if you want to use meta-characters within the value you need to cancel or ignore them (see the section "Ignoring Meta-Characters"). Also, if you want to use a string of characters that involves spaces you need to put them in double quotes (" "), for example,

```
name1=" Smith, Adam"
```

Assigning Value Through Command

To assign the value of a variable to be the result of a command, put that command in back quotes (") using the format:

```
variable='command'
```

For example, using

```
now='date'
```

sets the value of the variable "now" to the output of the date command, which is the current day, date, and time.

Using The Value Of A Variable

To utilize the value of a variable, type the variable in the format:

```
$variable
```

Prompting And Receiving Input

You can also prompt the user within the script itself to enter necessary information. To do so, first prompt using the **echo** command (see Echo under "Debugging A Script"). Then utilize the **read** command in the format:

```
read variable_name
```

The **read** command tells the script to pause and wait for user input, then continue along with the script after Enter is pressed.

Ignoring Meta-Characters

The following is a list of meta-characters that must be cancelled by a backslash if you wish to use them as normal characters, perhaps in an echo statement:

```
/ . > * ? $
```

Other methods of normalizing meta-characters are:

- Surround the character or the string associated with it in single quotes (' '). For example,

```
echo '--> Cut Here and send $8 With Application <--'
```

- Surround the character or string in double quotes (" "). However, this tactic will not normalize the dollar sign ($) or back quote ('). To get the same result as the example above with double quotes, you must type this instead:

```
echo "--> Cut Here and send \$8 With Application <--"
```

Writing Conditional If Statements

When you add an if statement to a script, it can have the components shown in Table 18.1.

As long as you follow the appropriate statement closure rules (discussed below), you can nest these commands as much as necessary to accomplish your goals.

NOTE: *Nesting statements means using statements within statements.*

If-Then

These components are assembled in a number of combinations that follow certain patterns. The most basic involves simply the conditions and the result:

```
if conditions
   then result
fi
```

NOTE: *An if statement must always be closed with fi.*

Table 18.1   Components of an if statement.

Component	Purpose	Required?
if	Beginning of statement.	Yes
fi	End of statement.	Yes
then	Task to complete if the if statement is true.	Yes
else	Task to complete if the if statement is false.	No
elif	"Else if." If the initial if statement is false, begin this next if statement.	No

If-Then-Else

Often, it is good to include some form of result that occurs when the conditions are not met. The format for that kind of statement, which adds the else clause, is:

```
if conditions
    then result
    else alternate_result
fi
```

If-Then-Else-Elif

Sometimes the conditions are too complex for a straightforward if-then-else structure. Perhaps you need to use multiple ifs within the same statement. In this case you add an elif (else if) clause, such as:

```
if conditions
    then result
    else alternate_result
    elif secondary_conditions
        then secondary_result
    fi
fi
```

NOTE: An elif statement must be closed with fi just like an if statement.

Accepting Command Line Input

If you want to accept arguments for a script, you pass them as you invoke the script at the command line. These arguments are assigned a value from $1 to $9 in most shell scripting languages, with the script name itself being $0. A space between the arguments signifies that you're moving to the next one, unless you use double quotes (" ") to mark it off. Here are two examples to clarify the point:

- The first example is:

```
myscript a b cdef g
```

In this example, the script name and the value of $0 is myscript. The value of $1 is a, $2 is b, $3 is cdef, and $4 is g.

- The second example is:

```
myscript "a b" cdef g
```

In this example, the script name and value of $0 is still myscript. The value of $1 is a b. The value of $2 is cdef, and $3 is g.

Adding Comments

A comment is signified in a shell script by the hash mark (#). The comment begins directly after this symbol and ends at the end of the line when you press Enter. See the two examples below for an idea of what options you have:

1. A comment can begin at the beginning of a line and span several lines.

```
# Comments are very useful in scripts, since you might learn
# a lot while writing them but forget it by the next time
# you look at the code.
```

2. A comment can exist only at the end of the line, after existing code.

```
echo "Hello world." # Prints Hello world.
```

Adding A Help Component

It is often useful to add a help component to a script that has complex data to be included on the command line. You should do this whenever the script has anything to it that you think you might forget before you run it.

To add a help component, do the following:

1. Choose the one or more ways you would like the help component to be accessed. Some of the more common ones are:

   • Typing nothing except the name of the script.

   • Typing the name of the script and then the word "help".

   • Typing the name of the script and then the term "--help".

   In the example, the first option is used because it is a common option among the shell scripts and programs in Linux.

2. Determine the text for your help statement.

3. Create a conditional if loop in the beginning of the script. The test condition looks for an empty $1 (for more on $1, see the section "Accepting Command Line Input"). A simple version of this loop could look like:

```
if $1 = ""
    then echo "Here is how to use this script."
    exit
fi
```

4. You can either make the rest of the script an else statement within the if clause but before the exit statement, or place it after the fi.

Adding A For Loop

If a loop needs to execute a certain number of times (say, for each argument on the command line, each file in a directory, or each day of the week) a good option is a for loop. The basic structure of a for loop is:

```
for item_to_count do
    Commands to execute within loop
done
```

NOTE: *You can have other loops or conditionals within a for loop.*

Adding A While Loop

If you want to run a loop until it reaches a particular condition, use a while loop. The basic structure of a while loop is:

```
while item_to_watch do
     Commands to execute within loop
done
```

Adding A Menu

If you want to add a menu where the user can select a single option, use the **case** command. The general structure used with and surrounding **case** is:

```
echo "Choose one of the following options:"
echo series of options
...
read variable
case $variable in
     potential_value) Action;;
     ...
esac
```

For example, perhaps you have a number of users who are not familiar with using Linux. You might write them a script that contains the following:

```
echo "Choose one of the following options to work with files:"
echo "[E]dit or create a file"
echo "[D]elete a file"
echo "[M]ove a file"
echo "[R]ename a file"
read action
case $action in
     E|e) echo "Name of file to edit? Please provide full path."
          read filename
          pico $filename;;
```

```
        D|d) echo "Name of file to delete? Please provide full path."
             read filename
             rm $filename;;
        M|m) echo "Name of file to move? Please provide full path."
             read filename
             echo "Where do you want to move the file to?"
             read moveto
             mv $filename $moveto;;
        R|r) echo "Name of file to rename? Please provide full path."
             read filename
             echo "What do you want to rename the file to?"
             read newname
             mv $filename $newname;;
    esac
```

NOTE: *Keep in mind that this script does nothing to make sure that the user entered a valid menu entry.*

Double-Checking User Entries

While you cannot completely proof a script against problems, you can attempt to anticipate where they might crop up and have methods in place to deal with them. One of the tools provided in many shells is the **test** command. It is also useful in conjunction with conditional statements.

The most basic form of this command (which tests for True) is:

```
test option_flag item_to_test
```

If the test succeeds, the value returned is 0 (True). A failure yields a 1 (False). You can test for either value. If you want to test for False instead, use the format:

```
test ! option_flag item_to_test
```

Testing Files

One of the most useful tests to help avoid errors is the ability to test files the user chooses to ensure that the script can manipulate them. The file-testing flags available are shown in Table 18.2.

Table 18.2 The *test* Command File Testing Tags.

Tag	Is the file ...?	0	1
-a	Does the file exist?	Yes	No
-b	Is it a block device file?	Yes	No
-c	Is it a character device file?	Yes	No
-d	Is it a directory?	Yes	No
-f	Is it a regular file?	Yes	No
-g	Is the setgid bit set?	Yes	No
-k	Is the sticky bit set?	Yes	No
-p	Is it a pipe or FIFO file?	Yes	No
-r	Is it readable?	Yes	No
-s	Does it have any content?	Yes	No
-u	Is the setuid bit set?	Yes	No
-w	Is the file writeable?	Yes	No
-x	Is it executable, or is it a directory that can be searched?	Yes	No
-G	Does it share the shell owner's group ID?	Yes	No
-L	Is it a symbolic link?	Yes	No
-O	Is it owned by the shell's user ID?	Yes	No
-S	Is it a socket?	Yes	No

For example, if you wanted to have the user input a file name, but then check to see if the file

- Exists
- Belongs to the user
- Is not a directory

then you might write:

```
echo "Enter the name (with full path) of the file you wish to
delete:"
read filename
# Does the item exist?
if test -a $filename
    then
    # The item exists. Does it belong to the user?
    if test -O $filename
        then
        # The item exists. Is it a directory? If it is, the test
gives False.
        if test ! -d $filename
            then
            # All tests passed. Delete the file.
            rm $filename
```

```
                   else
                   echo "The item is a directory, not a file."
                   exit 1
               fi
           else
           echo "The item is not yours to delete."
           exit 1
       fi
       else
       echo "The item does not exist."
       exit 1
   fi
```

Testing Strings

You can also test strings of text to ensure that the user entered data when asked. The flags available for string tests are shown in Table 18.3.

For example, you might use it for something like the following:

```
echo "Enter last name:"
read last
# If user entered no data, go into a loop that keeps requesting
# data until the user types something before they press Enter.
while test -z $last do
        echo "Enter last name:"
        read last
done
```

*Table 18.3   The **test** Command String Testing Tags.*

Tag	Is the string …?	0	1
-n	Anything but empty?	Yes	No
-z	Empty?	Yes	No

Comparing Files, Strings, Or Regular Expressions

Sometimes, for sorting or other purposes, it is useful to be able to compare items to one another. This issue brings us back to the **test** command (see "Double-Checking User Entries" for more information). This command has a comparison feature as well as a one-item testing feature.

The basic format for a comparison with **test** is:

```
test item1 option_flag item2
```

Comparing Files

While **test** does not handle comparisons of actual file contents, it is useful for making some basic checks of files against one another. See Table 18.4 for a specific list of the options available.

An example of **test** using one of these comparisons is:

```
test workdata -nt work_data
```

Comparing Strings

You can use **test** to compare strings of characters to one another. See Table 18.5 for a specific list of options available.

For example, the following is True, or 0:

```
test cart = ca?t
```

TIP: *A pattern is a set of characters where you include wildcards. A wildcard allows you to put unknown quantities within the characters. The wildcards available in a pattern are:*

- *An asterisk (*), which means one or more unknown characters. The pattern c*t would work for cat, cart, court, and more.*

- *A question mark (?), which stands for one unknown character. The pattern c?t would work for cat. The pattern c??t would work for cart.*

- *Brackets ([ ]), which contain a range of characters. The pattern c[a-c]t would work for cat, but not cart or cot.*

Comparing Mathematical Expressions

You can use **test** to compare equations and numbers. See Table 18.6 for a specific list of the options available:

For example, the following is False, or 1:

```
test 1+4 -eq 5-2
```

Table 18.4 The test Command File Comparison Tags.

Tag	Compares	0	1
-nt	Which file is newer.	File 1 is newer.	File 2 is newer.
-ot	Which file is older.	File 1 is older.	File 2 is older.
-ef	Are they the same file?	Yes, they are the same.	No, they are not.

Table 18.5 The test Command String Comparison Tags.

Tag	Compares	0	1
=	Does the string match the pattern?	Yes	No
!=	Are the string and the pattern different?	Yes	No
<	Does the first string come before the second in alphabetical order?	Yes	No
>	Does the second string come before the first in alphabetical order?	Yes	No

Table 18.6 The test Command Mathematical Comparison Tags.

Tag	Compares	0	1
-eq	Are the expressions equal?	Yes	No
-ne	Are the expressions equal?	No	Yes
-lt	Which term is smaller?	Term 1	Term 2
-gt	Which term is greater?	Term 1	Term 2
-le	Is the first term less than or equal to the second?	Yes	No
-ge	Is the first term greater than or equal to the second?	Yes	No

Ending A Script

There is no specific signal or code that you must use at the end of a script file. When the shell reaches the end of the script or an error, it quits automatically, using the results of the last command it ran for the exit status. For more on the basics of the exit status, see the section "Debugging A Script."

An example:

```
if test $value9 -eq 0
    then
        exit 1                   # Division by 0 error would result.
    else
        value16='expr $value5 / $value9'
        echo "$value5 divided by $value9 equals $value16."
        exit
fi
```

In this example, the *then* part of the statement has an explicit exit value assigned, but the *else* value does not. However, its exit value is 0 because there are no errors within it.

Testing A Script

When testing a script, keep the following practices in mind:

- Don't make and save changes to production files (meaning files that are important and in use on the system) unless the script is fully tested. Save changes to an intermediate file or run the script on a test file instead.

- It is wise to test scripts incrementally. Add one new piece of functionality, then test the script. Add another, then test again. This method makes it far easier to narrow down problems than writing a long script all at once and testing it for the first time as one large unit.

Debugging A Script

This section outlines a number of useful practices to follow when debugging a script. These practices can help turn what could be a maddening procedure into a calm search that narrows down the possibilities that could cause the problem.

In the bash shell, a handy command-line tool is "set -o xtrace" or "set -x". If you type this before testing shell scripts, the shell outputs all commands and arguments to the screen as the script executes. To then shut this feature off, use either "set +o xtrace" or "set +x".

Echoing, Or Printing Text To The Screen

You can trace what is happening to the variables in your script by adding statements to display pertinent information as the script runs by using the **echo** command. For example, if you suspect there is a problem with the handling of the variable count, you could add the statement

```
echo "The value of the variable count after step one is $count."
```

after the first step of your script. The script interpreter properly sees $count as referring to the value of the variable because of the dollar sign ($). If the value of count were 14, the script would display

```
The value of the variable count after step one is 14.
```

when it reaches the echo statement.

Unexpected EOF

When you try to run a script and see Unexpected End Of File (EOF), you likely did not properly close all of your if and elif statements.

Giving Exit Status

The shell notices whether a script exits successfully or not, meaning that it finishes with no errors, hidden or obvious. To have a script print the exit status as it finishes, add the statement:

```
echo $?
```

A more useful variant if a script has a lot of output is:

```
echo "The exit status is $?"
```

If the status is 0, the script finished properly. If it is a 1, there was an error.

Commenting Out

If you cannot seem to locate the bug in your script, it can be useful to start commenting out sections of code so they will not run. Then you can see whether the error persists without those sections.

The one problem with this method is that the code may break in a new way when you comment out segments. Be sure to look and see if something done in the section you want to ignore is vital to another part of the script.

Chapter 19

Perl

In Brief

There are times when shell scripts (covered in Chapter 18) easily suffice for the task you need to accomplish. At other times, however, you might need something more powerful. One step up from writing shell scripts is Perl, the Practical Extraction and Report Language. It is a mix of shell scripting languages and C programming, taking advantage of the strengths of both. Perl is especially popular among Linux system administrators for writing applications to run on the Web.

Why Use Perl?

There are a number of reasons to use Perl, or not to use it, depending on how the items on the list appeal to you:

- The Perl structure is similar to the C programming language, not a completely new construct.

- The rules are fairly loose (or nonexistent) regarding such things as line length, variable name length, and how far nested subroutines can be.

- The Perl interpreter detects insecure data sources, important assistance for any system administrator.

- If you find yourself using a lot of pipes in a shell script to move between countless programs and back again, Perl would be a cleaner option.

Perl Programming Example

Let's write an example program to demonstrate both the Perl programming process and how the language works. Many of the considerations and good practices are the same or similar to writing shell scripts.

Program Purpose

The purpose of this Perl program is to input the data necessary to create a small phone book, and store that data in a file that can be appended later by using this same application.

Plan The Program

Before you write the program, it's important to consider how you want to put it together. Doing this can save you time rewriting large segments when you realize they cannot handle the functionality the application needs. Some of the planning issues considered for this program are:

1. What data does the program need to accept? At the very least, this is a name and phone number.

2. What format should the name be in? For the sake of future flexibility, break it into first and last.

3. What format should the phone number be in? Include area code plus seven digits. Display a sample format so the user knows how to type it in.

4. How will the program know when to stop asking for more data? The user will not likely know ahead of time how many entries he or she wants to include. Include an iterative loop that stops when the assigned exit condition is reached.

5. What kind of exit condition should be used? Rather than forcing the user to remember a specific word to type in at the end, include a question that says to enter *y* if they want to add another entry, or *n* if not.

6. Include error checking to ensure that the query is answered.

7. When doing the file handling, because this program is meant to build a database of records, you will likely want to allow people to keep growing this database over time. Therefore, opening the file for write access will be done in the format of "Create it if it does not exist, or append it if it does."

Create The Program File

To build the program, you must first open and edit a text file, just as with a shell script:

1. Choose where you want to store and work on your programs. The same directory used for working on shell scripts, ~/bin, is a good place to store Perl programs as well. If you like to keep everything segregated, then consider creating ~/bin/shell and ~/bin/perl. For this example, we'll store the file in ~/bin.

2. Change to the ~/bin directory.

3. Edit the file with your favorite text editor—for example, *vi phonebook*.

Related solution:	Found on page:
Writing A Script	327

Write The Program File

Now to write the program itself:

1. The first line in every Perl program, because it is a text file, is a declaration telling the shell that the file contains Perl code by pointing to the Perl interpreter:

```
#!/usr/bin/perl
```

2. Before beginning the main loop, print the instructions for the user:

```
print "For each person whose phone number you want to
   store,\n";
print "you will be prompted for the following information:\n";
print "First Name, Last Name, and Phone Number.\n";
print "\n";
```

3. Initialize the query and counter variables so the loop does not exit before running:

```
$continue = "y";
```

4. Open the file:

```
open (FILE, ">>phonebook.dat") ||
    die "Can't open phonebook.dat.\n";
```

5. Because the loop needs to continue until the user enters an *n* at the query prompt, let's use a while statement to contain it. This statement might be:

```
while ($continue eq "y") {
   #Entering data.
   print "Enter first name: ";
   $first = <STDIN>;
   print "Enter last name: ";
        $last = <STDIN>;
   print "Enter phone number in the format 2135551234: ";
   $phone = <STDIN>;
   #Finished entering. Printing data to file.
        print FILE "$first";
```

```
print FILE "$last";
print FILE "$phone";
#Determine if user wants to add more data.
print "Do you want to add another entry (y/n)? ";
$continue = <STDIN>;
#Perl trick to make sure we're only using the first
#letter from the input, ignoring newlines and carriage
   returns.
$continue = substr($continue, 0, 1);
#Test to see if user wants to add more data. Returns
   "False"
#for any value that is not "y".
while ($continue eq "") {
    print "\nDo you want to add another entry (y/n)? ";
}
}
```

6. Close the file:

```
close (FILE);
```

7. Save and close the Perl program.
8. Make the Perl program an executable by typing "chmod +x *filename*".

NOTE: There is an alarming lack of error checking in this program. If this were meant for actual production use, it would need to verify that there was data in each item entered, and that the data was of the proper type.

Related solutions:	Found on page:
Understanding File And Directory Listings	86
Changing File And Directory Permissions	86

Test The Program

To test this program, run it by typing its name. In this case, just type "phonebook" at the prompt, or "./phonebook" if it's not located in a directory that's in your $PATH.

Related solution:	Found on page:
Adding To Your Path Statement	99

19. Perl

Immediate Solutions

Creating A Perl Program

There are a number of basic steps for writing a Perl program:

1. Create the text file that will contain the program.

2. Add the interpreter identifier line so Linux knows what program to use to run your code.

3. Build your Perl program.

4. Save and exit the file.

5. Change the permissions and ownerships of the program so it is executable by the right user accounts with the command "chmod +x *filename*".

6. Test the program.

7. Take steps to debug if necessary, then return to Step 6.

Related solutions:	Found on page:
Understanding File And Directory Listings	86
Changing File And Directory Permissions	86

Running A Perl Program

There are two different ways to run a Perl program:

- Make the text file that contains the program an executable by typing "chmod +x *filename*". Type the name of the file at the command line to run the program.

- Leave the text file as a nonexecutable. Type it as an argument for Perl, such as "perl *filename*".

Related solutions:	Found on page:
Understanding File And Directory Listings	86
Changing File And Directory Permissions	86

Advancing The Output Display To The Next Line

To advance the items your Perl program prints out down to the next line, add the control character \n. For example, consider the following code:

```
print "Enter your favorite color:\n";
$color=<STDIN>;
print "\n";
```

The output might look something like:

```
>Enter your favorite color:
>Red
>
```

NOTE: *If you try this by putting the string in single quotes, the newline control code (\n) will be printed literally instead of seen as a code.*

Accepting Command Line Input

To accept command line input with Perl, assign the value of the variable that contains the input to be equal to the Standard Input (keyboard) as follows:

```
$variable=<STDIN>
```

Assigning Value To A Variable

To assign a value to a variable in Perl, use the following format:

```
$variable=value;
```

When assigning strings of characters as the value, be sure to put them in quotes. For example,

```
$name="Janet Smith";
```

Using The Value Of A Variable

To utilize the value of a variable, type the variable in the format "$variable".

Testing For True Or False

Just as with shell scripts, testing for true using operators yields a value of zero or one. However, the zero in the case of Perl is false, and one is true.

NOTE: *In fact, any nonzero integer is true.*

Testing Files

Perl offers a number of flags that allow you to test file (and sometimes directory) conditions, as shown in Table 19.1.

The format of a file testing statement is:

```
-flag "full path to file"
```

For example, to determine if the file ~/data exists, you would use:

```
-e "~/data"
```

Table 19.1   File test flags used in Perl.

Flag	Tests	1	0
-B	Is the file binary?	Yes	No
-d	Is it a directory?	Yes	No
-e	Does the file exist?	Yes	No
-f	Is this a regular file?	Yes	No
-r	Is the file readable?	Yes	No
-s	Does the file have contents?	Yes	No
-T	Is it a text file?	Yes	No
-w	Is the file writeable?	Yes	No
-x	Is the file executable?	Yes	No
-z	Is the file empty?	Yes	No

Using Mathematics

Each computer language has its own specific ways of handling mathematical calculations, and Perl is no exception.

Mathematical Operators

Perl understands a wide selection of numeric operators, as shown in Table 19.2.

For example, consider the following:

```
$value=9;
$power=4;
$valuetopower=$value ** $power;
```

Mathematics With Variables

When including variables in the mathematical mix, be sure they are not variables that contain alphabetical characters (letters). These letters will be converted into zeros for the sake of calculation.

Table 19.2   Mathematical operators used in Perl.

Operator	Result
+	Adds the values.
-	Subtracts the preceding value from the following one.
*	Multiplies the values.
/	Divides the preceding value from the following one.
**	Calculates the value of the preceding to the power of the following.
%	Determines the modulus, or division remainder, of dividing the preceding by the following.

Comparing Values

Each computer language has its own twists and turns for comparing values. Be careful not to confuse those Perl uses with scripting or commands with their own specific phrasings.

Comparing Numbers

Perl offers a number of operators to use for mathematical comparisons, as shown in Table 19.3.

An example statement might look like this:

```
if ($value1==$value2) {
    print "The values are equal";
}
```

Comparing Strings

Perl can compare strings of characters as well as numbers. It converts strings to the ASCII code of each character and then compares the ASCII numerically. Perl uses the operators shown in Table 19.4 for string comparison.

An example statement might look like this:

```
if ($string1 ne $string2) {
    print "The strings are identical";
}
```

Table 19.3   Mathematical comparison operators used in Perl.

Operator	Tests	1	0
==	Are the values equal?	Yes	No
!=	Are the values equal?	No	Yes
<	Is the first value less than the second?	Yes	No
<=	Is the first value less than or equal to the second?	Yes	No
>	Is the first value greater than the second?	Yes	No
>=	Is the first value greater than or equal to the second?	Yes	No

Table 19.4   String comparison operators used in Perl.

Operator	Tests	1	0
eq	Are the strings identical?	Yes	No
ge	Is the first string greater than or equal to the second?	Yes	No
gt	Is the first string greater than the second?	Yes	No
le	Is the first string less than or equal to the second?	Yes	No
lt	Is the first string less than the second?	Yes	No
ne	Are the strings identical?	No	Yes

Manipulating Strings

Perl provides operators to do two types of string manipulation: repetition and concatenation.

Repeating A String

To repeat a string, use the format:

```
$string x number_of_repetitions
```

For example, perhaps you want to make a divider for the output of a program. If the width of the output is 72 characters, you could use the following segment of code to print out the divider:

```
$break="-";
print $break x 72;
```

This saves the onerous task of having to type the print statement with exactly 72 dashes.

Concatenating Strings

To concatenate strings, or join them together, use the format:

```
$string1 . $string2
```

For example, perhaps you inputted the value of $first and $last names and want to store the entire name as a unit, in the format "last, first".

To create this new variable, use the line:

```
$whole= $last . ", " . $first
```

Using Arrays

Since Perl is a full-blown programming language, it offers the ability to use data arrays. These arrays allow you to store indexed lists for easy retrieval. For example, if you have a list of 100 items and several aspects of each item on the list (perhaps name, price, and description), an array is a perfect storage tool.

Normal Arrays

A normal array is a limitless (limited by the amount of RAM in the system, not by Perl) storage facility for a stack of related data. You define a normal array by beginning it with an at (@) symbol. The format looks like:

```
@array = (item1, item2, item3, item4, ...);
```

Then, to call data from the normal array, you refer to the position of the data piece you want. These positions are numbered from zero up, the first position being 0, the second 1, and so forth. The format to call data from the normal array is:

```
$array[position]
```

The following code sample illustrates how such an array might be used in a meeting tracking program:

```
@months = ("January", "February", "March", "April", "May");
@week = ("Monday", "Tuesday", "Wednesday", "Thursday", "Friday");
@days = (1, 2, 3, 4, 5, 6, 7, 8, 9, 10, 11, 12, 13, 14, 15, 16,
17, 18, 19, 20, 21);
print "The first meeting is on $week[0] $months[3] $days[8].";
```

The output of this code piece would be:

```
The first meeting is on Monday April 7.
```

Adding Values To Normal Arrays

There are two quick ways to add values to a normal array. One method involves explicitly stating what slot to put the value into in the format:

```
$array[new_slot] = new_value;
```

For example,

```
@array = (1, 2, 3, 4, 5);
$array[5] = 6;
```

The other quick way is to use the function called *push*. The format to use push is:

```
push(@array, new_value);
```

To continue this example:

```
push(@array, 7);
```

Using For Statements

One form of iterative statement available is the for loop. This statement continues cycling through until a set condition is reached. The format used in a for statement is:

```
for (set start value; set conditions; set iteration steps) {
    actions...;
}
```

The following snippet of code shows an example of using a for statement:

```
print "How many entries are there?\n";
$number = <STDIN>;
for ($i = 1; $i < $number; $i = $i + 1) {
    print "Enter item $i: ";
    $item{$I} = <STDIN>;
    print "\n";
}
```

Using Foreach Statements

Another iterative statement available to the Perl programmer is foreach. A foreach statement is given an array or list of items, and the statement executes for each item it contains. The format of a foreach statement is:

```
foreach $variable (@array) {
    actions...;
}
```

In this case, the variable contains the contents of the array for the current iterative sweep through the statement.

For example, consider the following section of code:

```
@prices = (1, 2, 3, 4, 5);
foreach $total (@prices) {
    print "The price of \$$total with tax is ";
    $total = $total * .07 + $total;
    print "\$$total.\n";
}
```

Using If Statements

An if statement is one type of conditional available in Perl. The format of a general if statement is:

```
if (conditions) {
    actions...;
}
```

You can use a number of clauses with an if statement.

NOTE: *Notice that the "then" in Perl is implied instead of explicitly stated.*

For example, you might use it to run a routine that checks to see if an item has sales tax applied to it. You could store the item data in a normal array with the following structure:

```
@item = (Item Type, Item Code, Price, Taxable?)
```

An example of item contents is:

```
@item = ("Book", 15301, 14.30, 1)
```

The statement that checks for and applies tax would be as follows:

```
if ($item[3]) {
    $price = $item[2] * .06 + $item[2];
}
```

If-Else Statements

One form of an if statement includes the else clause. The format used with this clause is as follows:

```
if (conditions) {
    actions...;
```

```
}
else {
    actions...;
}
```

To expand upon the previous code example, you could add as an error statement:

```
if (-e file) {
    rm -f file;
}
else {
    print "File not found\n";
}
```

If-Else-Elsif Statements

You can add another level of testing complexity by using the if-else-elsif combination. The format for these combined clauses is:

```
if (conditions) {
    actions...;
}
elsif (other conditions) {
    actions...;
}
else {
    actions...;
}
```

For example, perhaps you want to allow the option of either creating or deleting a file:

```
print "Press D to delete the file, or R to rename the file\n";
$input=<STDIN>;
if ($input = "D") {
    rm -f $file;
}
elsif ($input = "R") {
    print "Enter new file name\n";
    $newname = <STDIN>;
    mv $file $newname;
}
else {
    print "Incorrect input\n";
}
```

Using Unless Statements

Another type of conditional available in Perl is unless. With unless, the statement is executed if the condition is false (0).

The format of an unless statement is as follows:

```
unless (conditions) {
    actions...;
}
```

For example, perhaps you don't want to allow people to delete particular files. One item you might include could be:

```
unless ($file = "~/.profile") {
    print ".profile is necessary for logging in.\n";
    print "Choose another file to delete.\n";
    $file=<STDIN>;
}
```

Using Until Statements

An until statement is another iterative clause offered in Perl. The statement continues to execute until the conditions become true (1). The format for an until statement is:

```
until (conditions) {
    actions...;
}
```

For example, consider the following code:

```
$count = 0;
print "Enter no more than 10 items.\n";
until ($count = 10) {
    $data{$count} = <STDIN>;
    $count = $count + 1;
}
```

Using While Statements

Also available among Perl's iterative statements is while. This loop continues while the conditions listed are true (1). The format for a while statement is:

```
while (conditions) {
    actions...;
}
```

For example, perhaps you want to have the user input a list of data without needing to ask how many items there will be:

```
print "Enter data now. If this is the final item, use the word
END.\n";
$input = " ";
while ($input ne "END") {
    print "Enter term: ";
    $input = <STDIN>;
    print "\n";
}
```

Writing Data To A File

In order to write data to a file, you must deal with some additional issues. The file has to be opened before writing, then closed when you are finished. While writing the data, you use the same command you would use to write to the screen, except this time you add a file handle to it.

NOTE: *There are many complex factors and lots of nuances to writing data to files with Perl. The very basics are touched on here in order to allow you to get a running start.*

The format used to open, write to, then close a file in this method is:

```
open (FILE, ">>file.dat") ||
    die "Can't open file.dat.\n";
print FILE "$value\n";
close (FILE);
```

You may find it useful to specially indent everything between the open and close statement in order to be sure you've remembered both aspects of dealing with the file.

19. Perl

Reading Data From A File

When reading data from a file, you must use the same sequence as you would when writing to one. Open the file, read from the file, then close it. To read data one line at a time from a file, you use the format:

```
$value = <FILE>;
```

So, the format for the whole statement might be:

```
open (FILE, "file.dat") ||
    die "Can't open file.dat.\n";
$value = <FILE>;
close (FILE);
```

Chapter 20

Configuring System Backups

In Brief

Having recent system backups makes the greatest difference between a traumatic system crash and a minor annoyance. You can use a number of backup hardware, software, and timing options, depending on the importance of the machine and each segment of its file system.

Backup Hardware

A variety of hardware is available for creating system backups. Each type has its strengths and drawbacks when it comes to issues like price, storage space, and ease of use. Be sure before obtaining any new hardware for backups that you check the Hardware Compatibility List for your distribution and ensure that there are drivers available.

When choosing what medium to use for backups, keep in mind not only the price of the drive, but the price of the storage components (tapes, disks, and so forth) as well.

Floppy Disks

One medium most computer users have access to is the floppy disk. Although it is not convenient for backing up large volumes of data, the floppy disk is useful for smaller backups, even those that span multiple disks.

Advantages of using floppy disks for backing up are:

- They are inexpensive.
- They can be used in almost all machines that have floppy drives and recognize the formatting used.
- They are reusable.
- They can be stored separately in a safe or other secured location.

Disadvantages of using floppies are:

- The disks hold a small volume of data.
- The contents of floppy disks can degrade over time.

Tape Drives

A wide range of tape drives is available on the market. These drives come in many prices, access speeds, and storage sizes. The higher end tape drives can store a number of individual tapes and auto-load them when necessary.

NOTE: *To use a tape drive you must install the ftape driver.*

Advantages of using tapes are:

- There is no mistaking backup tapes for available media and accidentally overwriting them.
- They are reusable.
- Tapes can be stored separately in a safe or other secured location.
- With autoloader tape drives, backups can be automated and run unattended.

Disadvantages of using tapes are:

- If for some reason the tape drive does not see the End Of Tape (EOT) properly, the tape can actually be disconnected from the spool as it continues to turn. However, instructions are often available in the manual that comes with the drive for fixing this problem if it occurs.
- Tapes can stretch over time. It is important to remember to re-tension them before first using them, and before backups. This process needs to be done on a regular basis, even if it is not done every time the tape is used. Otherwise the stretching can distort the data on the tapes and make it difficult to retrieve.
- Only the most expensive tape drives operate quickly.

Hard Drives

Spare hard drives also can moonlight as system backup devices. If you have nothing else at hand and don't want to use floppies, consider putting an old smaller hard drive to work storing important data.

Advantages of using hard drives for backing up are:

- If a partition fails and there is an exact duplicate of it as of a certain backup time, you can mount the backed-up version directly to take the place of the damaged one.
- They are reusable as a backup device.
- They can be used as part of the file system if there is need to replace it with a different backup device.
- If you use removable-rack hard drives, they are changeable.

- If you use removable racks, you can move the drives from one machine to any other one that has the proper bays.

NOTE: *However, moving any drive complete with an operating system on it from one machine to another brings up configuration issues for specific hardware components.*

- If you use removable racks, the media can be stored separately in a safe or other secured location.
- They are the fastest of all available backup options.

Disadvantages of using hard drives for backing up are:

- Hard drives are good backup tools for certain situations, but not necessarily for heavy use.
- If the backup is required because of serious damage to the machine that contains both hard drives, the backup drive could be damaged as well. However, it is also possible to back up to a hard drive in another machine.
- If you do not use removable racks, the media are not changeable.
- If the backup drive uses the last potential hard drive connector position, then it usurps space that could be used by adding a second drive for the file system.
- If you don't use removable racks, the media cannot be stored separately in a safe or other secured location.

Zip Drives

Zip drives can use both regular floppies and Zip disks, which hold 100 or 250MB. People often already have them installed on their machines. So when it comes time to make backups, the Zip drive is an option to explore if you already have one.

Advantages of using Zip drives for backups are:

- The Zip disks are reusable.
- They can be stored separately in a safe or other secured location.
- Zip drives work fairly quickly.
- Using a Zip drive is no more difficult than using a floppy.

Disadvantages of using Zip drives for backups are:

- A Zip disk may not hold enough for some large-scale backups.
- Zip disks are considerably more expensive than tapes or floppies on a per-byte basis.

CD-ROM Writers

CD-ROM drives that are able to write to CD-ROMs have gone from high-tech wonders to affordable alternatives to normal nonwriteable CD-ROM drives. As such, they are a potential backup device for those who already have one and don't want to run out and buy specialized hardware for that purpose.

Advantages of using CD-ROM writers are:

- They are excellent for data you want to store for long periods of time, because they are not prone to degrading.

- It is easy to store large volumes of CD-ROMs in a small amount of space.

- Data stored to CD-ROM can be easily shared on other machines as long as they have CD-ROM drives.

- The CD-ROM and writer can be used for other purposes if they are replaced with a new backup medium.

- They can be stored separately in a safe or other secured location.

- Writeable CD-ROMs are almost as inexpensive as floppy disks, although rewriteable CD-ROMs cost more.

Disadvantages of using CD-ROM writers are:

- If the drive is not a re-writer, a CD-ROM can only be used once. This is not a good choice if system backups are frequent.

- Writing to CD-ROMs is a slow process and requires precise timing. If your computer is busy running other CPU-intensive tasks, this timing can be thrown off, and the entire CD-ROM is ruined.

- Compared with tapes, the storage capacity of a single CD-ROM is small (about 680Mb).

Immediate Solutions

Getting The Ftape Driver

Download the most up-to-date version of the ftape driver from the ftape home page at **www.math1.rwth-aachen.de/~heine/ftape/ftape.html**.

Installing The Ftape Driver

It is not necessary to install ftape if you are using kernel version 2.2 or later. To determine the kernel version you have installed, type "uname -r".

If you are using an earlier version of the kernel and want to use ftape without upgrading, then you need to compile ftape into the kernel source, then compile the kernel. The general steps to install ftape are:

1. Download the latest ftape driver (see "Getting the Ftape Driver"), keeping any warnings about hardware or software issues on the page under consideration.

2. Read the documentation that comes with ftape.

3. If you are using a kernel before version 2.0, follow the instructions for patching the kernel to work with ftape.

4. Set any environment variables you are instructed to define.

5. Ensure that the source code for the kernel you are using is installed to /usr/src/linux.

6. Follow the instructions for making (compiling) the ftape driver.

7. Follow the instructions for installing the ftape driver.

8. Follow the instructions for inserting ftape into the kernel.

Choosing A Backup Scheme

There are various theories regarding how to do backups most efficiently. Which scheme is best for your system depends on your needs and how heavily the system is used. Here are some methods that highlight some of the ways of handling system backups.

Full Regular Backups

The Grandfather-Father-Son (GFS) backup scheme requires eleven media for the first month, then an additional one for each subsequent month. Say that you have backups scheduled to run at 3 A.M. each day. You might handle the GFS scheme as follows:

1. Monday through Sunday before 3 A.M. you insert backup media, labeling each one with its appropriate day.

2. When you remove the Sunday media, you label it "Sunday Week 1" and put it aside.

3. On Monday through Saturday you re-use the exact same media as you did the previous week.

4. On Sunday you use a new media.

5. When you remove the Sunday media, you label it "Sunday Week 2" and put it aside.

6. On Monday through Saturday you re-use the same media as you did the previous weeks.

7. On Sunday you use a new media.

8. When you remove the Sunday media, label it "Sunday Week 3" and put it aside.

9. Continue with the cycle.

10. When you remove the fourth Sunday media, label it "Month, Year" and put it aside for permanent or at least long-term storage.

11. Repeat the process, always using the same media for Monday through Saturday—until wear and tear makes it time to replace them—then the same media for the first three Sundays, then saving the last Sunday media for long-term storage.

In the GFS backup scheme, the "son" is the daily, the "father" is the Sunday weekly, and the "grandfather" is the monthly.

Incremental Backups

On many systems, especially those that are not often changed at a basic level, frequent backups are mostly necessary for particular parts of the file system. In this case, you might choose to do incremental backups. This process requires five media for the first month, then one additional media each month. An incremental backup might work like the following:

1. Determine which parts of the file system change frequently and which remain the same within most months. For example, the /home part of the file system usually changes on a regular basis, as well as the logs stored under /var.

2. Once per week, back up the parts of the file system that change often.

3. Once per month, back up the entire file system.

4. When a new month begins, re-use the weekly tapes.

Mixing Schemes

Which backup scheme is right for your system depends entirely on your needs and how the system is used. Often a mix of schemes is useful—for example, doing an incremental backup, except backing up partly every day and then fully each week.

Creating A Manual Backup: General

To create a manual backup, do the following:

1. Choose what segments of the file system you want to back up.

2. Determine when these segments will be most idle so files will not be in use during backup.

3. Mount the backup media into the file system.

4. Use the tar package to bundle related files.

5. If space is an issue, **gzip** the tar package.

TIP: Be sure the bundled archive has a meaningful name, including whatever information helps you know it at a glance: version number, program name, any key terms that might serve as a reminder.

6. Place the bundle on the backup media if you didn't archive it directly there.

The sidebar reads: **20. Configuring System Backups**

7. Label the media with information, such as the date of the archive and what is on it.

8. Store the media in a safe, easily located place.

Related solutions:	Found on page:
Creating A Tar Archive	299
GZipping A File	300

Doing A Full Backup To Floppy Disks Or A Tape Drive

When backing up to floppy disks, often the tar program is used to create the backup files. Part of the reason for this is that tar can spread the file across multiple disks. To create a backup to floppy disk, do the following:

1. Determine which device driver your floppy is attached to. The example that follows assumes /dev/fd0. If you have a tape drive instead, use the driver for the tape system.

2. Make a file system (format) the number of floppy disks or tapes you project that you will need. To format each disk, type "mke2fs /dev/*driver*". For example, "mke2fs /dev/fd0".

3. Mount the first floppy or tape.

4. Type the following **tar** command:

```
tar cfzM /dev/fd0 /
```

This command begins the archiving process, which will prompt you for new media as necessary.

5. When the backup is finished, bundle the volumes together, label them in order, and put them in a safe and easily accessible place.

Related solutions:	Found on page:
Creating A Tar Archive	299
GZipping A File	300
Making A File System	168
Mounting Onto The File System	168

Restoring Full Backups From Tape Or Floppy

To restore a full backup from floppy or tape, do the following:

1. Make backups of any surviving files that are more recent than the archive you are about to restore.

2. Put the first media in the drive.

3. Type the following command to restore your system to its state when fully backed up:

```
tar xfsM /dev/fd0
```

4. Restore any newer files from the secondary backups.

Related solution:	Found on page:
Untarring A File	298

Adding Files To An Existing Tar Backup

To add files to a backup made with tar, use the append flag -r, such as "tar rfz /dev/*device* /*item_to_add*".

Related solution:	Found on page:
Creating A Tar Archive	299

Setting Backups To Run At Specific Times

One tool Linux offers is cron. The cron daemon continuously watches its configuration files for the system and the individual users for when it needs to run specific processes. The configuration files for the systemwide cron are in /etc/crontab and consist of: cron.hourly, cron.daily, cron.weekly, and cron.monthly. The cron configuration files for each user are stored in /var/spool/cron/crontabs and are modified with the crontab program, not by hand.

The basic format for adding a new process to the system cron files follows the following:

```
m h d y w task
```

The timing terms in the format are all numeric. They stand for, in order:

- Minutes after the hour when the task should occur.
- Hour of the day (24 hour format) when the task should occur.
- Day of the month when the task should occur.
- Month of the year when the task should occur.
- Day of the week when the task should occur—beginning with Sunday, which is 0.

These numbers can be used in the following forms:

- Ranges, such as 0-22.
- Sequences, such as 1,3,5.
- Singular, such as 12.
- An asterisk (*), meaning "all".

The *task* term is the name of the program or script you want to run at the assigned time. Include any switches necessary.

For example, perhaps you want to add an item to the weekly cron file that checks disk usage and then mails the results to the root account. This job should run at midnight on the fifteenth and thirtieth of each month. The format used to enter this item would be:

```
00 00 15,30 * * df
```

TIP: *Why not include instructions to mail the output? All output from system cron jobs is automatically mailed to **root**.*

Choosing Backup Software

Quite a few backup packages are available for Linux. Here are some considerations to keep in mind when trying to choose among them:

- Will the software work with your kernel version?
- Will the software work with your hardware?
- Does the software have options that take both your frequency and volume needs into account?
- Does the software support unattended backups?

Automating Backups

To automate the process of making backups, write a script that runs the necessary processes, then add this process to your regular cron jobs. In order to add backup routines to the systemwide cron setup, do the following:

1. Log in as **root**.

2. Change to the /etc/crontab directory.

3. Edit the file corresponding to the frequency you want the backups to run: cron.hourly, cron.daily, cron.weekly, or cron.monthly. For example, if you were attempting to use the Grandfather-Father-Son, you might do the following group of edits:

   • /etc/crontab/cron.daily

   • /etc/crontab/cron.weekly

   • /etc/crontab/cron.monthly

   Although functionally you could just edit the daily cron file, it is helpful to add special reminders in the weekly and monthly files about when to change or save tapes.

4. Add an entry for the backup script or program you want to run in the appropriate cron files (see the section "Setting Backups To Run At Specific Times" for how to format the entries). For an entry to run the backup script /root/bin/backup at 4 A.M., you would add something similar to the following to cron.daily:

   ```
   00 04 * * * /root/bin/backup
   ```

   For just a reminder to set aside tapes after each Sunday backup, consider an entry in cron.weekly such as:

   ```
   00 05 * * 0 echo "Set aside the Sunday tape."
   ```

   Entering this will email that text to **root** at the time specified.

5. Save and exit the file(s).

6. Be sure to put a backup media in the backup drive.

7. Sit back and check to see if the backup is on the media after the job is scheduled. If possible, watch the job run. Remember, any output is emailed to **root**.

Deciding On A Removable-Rack Hard Drive System

A removable-rack hard drive is a familiar concept for some people and unheard of for others. This unit consists of standard hard drives placed into cassettes, which are then plugged into a mounting bay that is installed directly in your computer. A representation of this concept is shown in Figure 20.1.

When planning a removable-rack system, follow these considerations:

- Determine the size of the hard drive(s) you want to mount. The drives are often 3.5 inches, unless they're Ultra-Wide (UW) SCSI.

- Determine the type of drive(s) you need to mount; for example, IDE, SCSI I, SCSI II, SCSI III, or UW SCSI.

- Ensure that you have the drive bay space required. Many rack mounting kits need a 5.25 inch bay, plus approximately one inch of room extra if a fan is included.

- How many drawers might you need? Keep in mind that not all cassettes are compatible with all bays, so it's worth it to order a few extra.

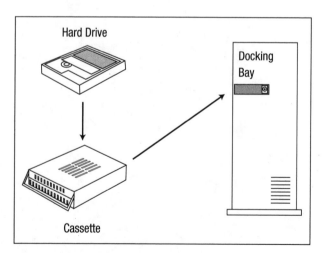

Figure 20.1   Removable-rack hard drives.

Chapter 21

Security Issues

In Brief

Any Internet-connected computer or LAN needs to have at least some security precautions taken against invaders. Some of these precautions are simple to add. They involve knowing the system you are working with and where its initial weak points are; once you find them, you can plug them. Others are subtler, requiring additional software or hardware. The important thing is to know what they are, assess your setup's needs, and implement them correctly.

Firewall Options

Firewalls get a lot of press in discussions about network security, but are by no means a fix-all tool. Their basic function is to filter and block traffic between the network or part of a network and the outside world—namely, the Internet. In the process of doing their job, they interfere with what once would have been routine Internet accesses from inside the network, and from the Internet to the network. See the section "Determining If A Firewall Is For You" for a list of items to help decide whether adding a firewall is the proper solution for your security needs.

IP Filtering Firewalls

Implementing an IP filter firewall involves the *ipchains* package—support for which is available in kernel 2.1 and up. This package manages the IP accounting and firewalling potential of the Linux kernel itself. Your kernel must be compiled with ipchains enabled; if you want to use this function and do not have kernel-level ipchains support, see Chapter 10, which covers compiling the kernel.

To understand the level at which ipchains operates, you need to understand TCP/IP network traffic at the packet level. Packets are chunks of data that include the information necessary to deliver them to their destination point. Think of a packet as a courier package. The packet itself is the data being couriered, and the envelope has all of the headers necessary to deliver the information not only to the right machine, but to the right program. It also contains return address information.

Ipchains is a packet filter. A packet filter is a program that examines the contents of a packet header and, according to a set of rules you created (see the section "Filtering Packets Out" for instructions on how to do this), determines whether to let the packets through and where to send them.

Proxying Firewalls

Implementing a proxying firewall involves downloading and installing the software that controls what services users can reach outside the network and what they cannot. A proxy firewall allows no incoming connections to the machines behind it; there is no packet filtering, it is just a brick wall so far as incoming connections are concerned.

The package commonly used to put a proxying firewall in place is called *SOCKS* (see the section "Installing SOCKS" to obtain and install this program; it does not come with the distributions).

Immediate Solutions

Closing Simple Weak Spots

Whether you installed Red Hat or Caldera, there are some weak spots you can close to help make your system more secure:

1. Deactivate any services you don't intend to use in /etc/inetd.conf by commenting them out (adding a # at the beginning of the line). Each service offered opens one more way for someone to attempt to enter your system, so only use the services you need.

2. Edit the file /etc/issue.net and remove references to the specific hardware and Linux distribution running on the machine. This is the banner that is displayed on login screens during remote login sessions, such as Telnet. Anything that gives such specific information about the machine makes it easy for someone trying to break in to know what weaknesses to look for if they are familiar with the type of setup shown.

3. Assign specific users to the group *console* to give them access to commands to run while physically at the server machine, and disallow anyone else access to those commands. For example, only members of the group *console* should be able to mount disks if there is a high concern for security.

4. View the contents of the file /etc/securetty and be sure that the only devices listed are physical ttys (for example, tty1 through tty8). This file limits where people can log in from as root. Allowing any remote users to log in as root is highly dangerous, because it reduces any potential intruder's steps to break into the superuser account.

5. Be sure that the only writeable part of your FTP server for anonymous users is /incoming.

Listing Logins

To see a list of who last logged in to the system, use the **last** command. If you want more than the default number listed, use the format "last -n *number*" to tell **last** how many logins to display.

TIP: *If this command fails, it means that logins are not being logged. To ensure that they are, type "touch /var/log/wtmp" as root to create the log file.*

Listing Attempted Logins

To see a list of who last failed to log in to the system, use the **lastb** command. As with the **last** command, to see more than the default number of attempts, use the format "lastb -n *number*".

TIP: *If this command fails, it means that logins are not being logged. To ensure that they are, type "touch /var/log/btmp" as root to create the log file.*

Finding Security Breaches

When security has been breached, or you think it has been breached, there is a good chance that telltale footprints have been left in the system logs or elsewhere. Good things to do are:

- The system logs every login and attempted login. See the sections "Listing Logins" and "Listing Failed Logins" for instructions on how to get these lists. The list of failed logins, especially, will let you quickly see if someone has been working hard to gain root access or guess a user's password.

- If you were using the Shadow Suite, look in /etc/passwd to see if the Shadow Suite is disabled—in which case passwords are now stored in /etc/passwd. It requires root access to change this feature, so if it has happened you know that the hacker has root access on the machine.

- Look to see if unfamiliar user accounts have been created that have unusual privileges.

- A hacker who has good tools or knowledge will replace important system functions. Use a standalone machine, or one that you trust has not been compromised, to install a copy of commands like **ls** onto a floppy disk—the best method is straight from the distribution CD-ROM. Then make sure that the creation dates are not recent on the system's versions of the following programs: **ls**, **find**, **ps**, and all of the networking daemons.

- If your networking service logs or any system logs have time holes in them and you know you did not shut off system logging, be very suspicious.

TIP: *If security is of great concern to you, consider writing a program to watch the logs and report suspicious activity.*

Keeping Up With Security Issues

You can keep an eye on a number of places for security advisories and pointers on how to plug newly discovered holes:

- Both the Red Hat and Caldera distributions have announcement mailing lists that offer immediate knowledge of when security updates are uploaded to their sites. Joining one of these lists is highly recommended. To join the Red Hat list, write to the address **redhat-announce-list-request@redhat.com** with the word "subscribe" in the subject line, and leave the body of the message empty. To join the Caldera list, send an email with a blank subject line to the address **majordomo@lists.calderasystems.com**, with the text "subscribe Announce" in the body.

- If you installed the Red Hat distribution, watch their site regularly (weekly or even more often) at **www.redhat.com/errata** for security updates and fixes.

- If you installed the Caldera distribution, surf to the updates from **www.calderasystems.com/support/resources**.

- One of the central clearinghouses for operating system security information on the Internet is the Computer Emergency Response Team (CERT) site. Their Web page is **www.cert.org**.

Determining If A Firewall Is For You

Firewalls are wonderful protection for some sites, but a constant problem for others. Before you implement one, give some thought to whether a firewall is appropriate for your LAN, or whether other options might be better for system security.

Consider Adding A Firewall

You need to at least consider adding a firewall if:

- You have vital business data that you cannot put on a machine that is independent from your network. What would happen if this data were stolen? Erased or changed by intruders? Although good backup techniques can protect against data loss to a certain point, sometimes even a few hours' worth of lost data is disastrous.

- Your Web site is in any way high profile, whether because of the actions of the proprietors or by users. If a particular user is controversial and angers people, or if the site's theme is controversial, somebody might try to break in to "punish the offender." If the site is high profile simply by having a well-known name, somebody might try to break in just to say they did it.

- You need to abstract how many machines are really in your network and which machine has which address in order to make it less appealing to intruders.

Related solution:	*Found on page:*
Choosing A Backup Scheme	365

Improve Security, But No Firewall Needed

The answer to your security needs may not be a firewall at all:

- Does your entire network need to be connected to the Internet at all? Perhaps your office or LAN only needs to have one or two net-connected machines, which don't need to be connected to the rest of the LAN.

- Can the machine with the most vital data be removed from the LAN? That might be all that's necessary.

- Is the Internet connection permanent or on-demand? An on-demand connection generally does not need a firewall, unless the amount of time it is connected is sufficiently close to permanent for a break-in to be possible. This fact is especially true if the Internet connection does not have the same IP address every time.

Firewall Too Cumbersome

For some types of network setups and needs, a firewall is more cumbersome than it's worth. Some examples of these types of situations are:

- The users on your site need access to many different types of services on the Internet. If so, the firewall will eventually be so poked full of holes as you allow data to go in and out that it will be virtually useless; you will waste much of your time debugging the rulesets.

- Some software cannot work through a firewall, but requires special programming to accomplish this. If the software needed within your LAN doesn't function through a firewall, look for another security solution.

Tightening Network Drive Access

When you set up services such as FTP, Samba, or NFS, which allow people to access network drives remotely, you automatically open yourself to potential problems. One rule in security is to assume that, if you offer a network service, someone's going to try to look for a way in. Follow this general process to tighten network drive access:

1. Open the access control files for the service you want to tighten.

2. Examine what exactly you are trying to offer with the service. Are you merely trying to accommodate a few people? A project group? The entire office?

3. Identify the exact range of people you are trying to provide the particular service to, and narrow it down to a spread of IP addresses or specific hosts on a domain.

4. Create precise rules for these groups to use to access the service, and deny access to all others.

Filtering Packets Out

Setting up a firewall with ipchains involves configuring the ipchains packet-filtering aspects. To set this up, do the following:

1. Log in as **root**.

2. Test to see if ipchains is currently installed on your system by typing "rpm -q ipchains". If the package is not installed, see the section "Installing ipchains" and then return to this section at Step 3.

3. Type "ipchains -L" to see the chains that currently exist. What you see if you have never set these options before are the lines:

```
>Chain input (policy ACCEPT):
>Chain forward (policy ACCEPT):
>Chain output (policy ACCEPT):
>
```

4. Choose which chain you want to configure. A chain is a set of rules that pertain to a group of packet types:

   - The *input chain* refers to packets coming into the firewall machine.

   - The *forward chain* refers to packets that came into the firewall and now need to be sent to another machine in the network.

   - The *output chain* refers to packets being sent out.

   Additional specialized chains can be created.

5. Type "ipchains -L *chain*" to list the rules that currently exist within the chain you want to edit. By default, all the chains are empty of rules.

6. Begin a statement to add a new rule by typing "ipchains -A *chain*" to tell ipchains that you want to create a new packet-filtering rule for that chain. For example, you will probably want to create rules for the input chain, so type "ipchains -A input". Don't press Enter yet; you're not done.

7. Now you have to build the statement itself. Perhaps you don't want people to be able to Telnet to any machines behind the firewall except from a specific remote work site. Set the address(es) for the specific rule you are creating with the -s (source) flag in the format:

   - A single full IP address, such as 192.168.152.24.

   - An entire class range of IP addresses, such as 192.168.152.0/ 255.255.255.0, which stands for 192.168.152.0 through 192.168.152.255.

   - Hostname, such as *blue*.

   - Full domain name, such as *blue.colors.org*.

   - A range of IP addresses, carefully constructed with a combination of IP address and netmask.

   For the example, the goal is to only allow Telnet traffic in from three specific machines that have the IP addresses 192.156.12.1 through 192.156.12.3. The address and netmask combination to express this range is *192.156.12.1/255.255.255.252*. Your rule addition statement would now look like:

```
ipchains -A input -s 192.156.12.1/255.255.255.252
```

Don't press Enter yet; you're still not done.

8. If you don't want any incoming traffic allowed through the firewall to the machines behind it unless it comes from those machines, then you're done. However, you can further special-ize the rule by telling ipchains which protocol should be used by the incoming process that is to be allowed in; you do this with the -p (protocol) flag. The Telnet process uses the TCP protocol. Now the rule addition looks like:

```
ipchains -A input -s 192.156.12.1/255.255.255.252 -p TCP
```

Don't press Enter yet.

9. Creating a rule that surrounds a specific protocol is fairly broad. Instead, you can narrow that rule by specifying the port for the process you're referring to, either by adding it onto the end by name or by prefixing the port number with a colon. Look in the /etc/services file to find the port number for any network service. The rule statement now looks like one of the following two lines:

```
ipchains -A input -s 192.156.12.1/255.255.255.252 -p TCP :23
ALLOW
ipchains -A input -s 192.156.12.1/255.255.255.252 -p TCP
Telnet ALLOW
```

Now you can press Enter.

10. This rule is useless unless you actually deny any other kind of traffic. The smartest way to do this—because the goal is to make rules for everything you want to allow—is to use the -P (policy) flag to deny all input. Then ipchains will look for specific rules for what to allow in. Such a policy statement would be:

```
ipchains -P input DENY
```

Installing ipchains

The ipchains package is included as an RPM on your distribution CD-ROM. To install it, do the following:

1. Log in as **root**.
2. Place the distribution CD-ROM into the CD-ROM drive.
3. Mount the CD-ROM with the command "mount /mnt/cdrom".
4. Change to the directory:
   - /mnt/cdrom/RedHat/RPMS on the Red Hat CD-ROM
   - /mnt/cdrom/Packages/RPMS on the Caldera CD-ROM
5. Install the ipchains package by typing "rpm -ivh ipchains*".

Related solutions:	Found on page:
Mounting Onto The File System	168
Unmounting Off Of The File System	170
Installing An RPM Package	295

Saving Packet-Filtering Rules Before Reboot/Shutdown

There is no configuration file that automatically saves your packet-filtering rules to use the next time you boot the machine. It is important to choose a way to do this for yourself; otherwise, you will have to rewrite all the rules from scratch next time. One way to accomplish this task is:

1. Log in as **root**.
2. Use the **ipchains-save** script to save the settings you already have to a file, say to /root/ipchains-settings. For example, type "ipchains-save > /root/ipchains-settings".

Restoring Packet-Filtering Rules After Booting

After you reboot, you need to restore the ipchains settings. To accomplish this task, do the following:

1. Log in as **root**.

2. Use the **ipchains-restore** script to retrieve the settings you already have in a file, say from /root/ipchains-settings. For example, type "ipchains-restore < /root/ipchains-settings".

Installing SOCKS

To install the SOCKS proxying firewall package, do the following:

1. Download the SOCKS source code from **www.socks.nec.com** into a temporary directory.

2. Uncompress the source with the **gunzip** command.

3. Unpack the source with the **tar** command.

4. Change to the new SOCKS directory within the temporary directory with the **cd** command.

5. Read the INSTALL file with the **more** command to ensure that the instructions in the current version are not different from those listed here.

6. Be sure that the C compiler is already installed. To check this, type "rpm -q egcs". If the package is not already installed, it is on both the Red Hat and Caldera CD-ROMs.

7. Be sure that the C libraries are already installed. To check this, type "rpm -q glibc-devel". If the package is not already installed, it is on both the Red Hat and Caldera CD-ROMs.

8. Type "./configure" at the prompt. As the autoconfiguration runs, it prints out each feature it is checking on your machine.

NOTE: *Both this phase and the next can take some time to complete.*

9. To actually compile the SOCKS server, type "make" at the prompt. Compilation messages slowly scroll onto the screen, depending on the speed of your machine.

10. To place the server and its components where they need to go, type "make install".

11. To remove the temporary files generated during the compile process, type "make clean".

TIP: *To find the SOCKS man page, type "man socks5".*

Related solutions:	Found on page:
Untarring A File	298
Viewing Text File Without An Editor	94
Mounting Onto The File System	168
Unmounting A Device Off Of The File System	170
Installing An RPM Package	295

Installing The Proxy Server

The proxy server commonly used on Linux is called *Squid*. You will need this program if you are running a proxying firewall. To install this package, do the following:

1. Log in as **root** on the proxying firewall machine.

2. Mount the distribution CD-ROM with the **mount** command.

3. Change to the distribution's RPM packages directory.

4. Install the squid package with the **rpm** command.

Related solutions:	Found on page:
Mounting Onto The File System	168
Unmounting Off Of The File System	170
Installing An RPM Package	295

Configuring SOCKS

To configure the SOCKS proxying firewall, do the following:

1. Log in as **root**.

2. Open the file /etc/inetd.conf with the **vi** editor.

3. Add a line to ensure that the superdaemon (inetd) opens the proxying server when it is needed. This line should be:

```
socks stream tcp nowait nobody /usr/local/etc/sockd sockd
```

4. Save and exit the file.

TIP: *Type "cd examples" within the directory that contains the SOCKS source code in order to change to the directory that has the sample configuration files for various types of network situations. How you want to configure your setup may be very different from the following example. The assumption here is that you want to allow people inside the network to access anything they want out on the Internet. This is a common setup for firewalls when the only goal is to keep unwanted people out.*

---

5. Type "vi /etc/socks5.conf" to edit the server's configuration file.

6. First you have to tell the server what types of authentication it accepts when trying to verify that users are who they say they are. This statement is done in the format "auth *host port method*", where:

- The *host* is where the request is coming from.

- The *port* is the one that reflects the service the user is requesting.

- The *method* is what type of authentication is acceptable.

Add the following line to allow any form of authentication, so long as authentication is used—the dash is a wildcard denoting "any":

```
auth - - -
```

TIP: *Using no auth statement at all tells SOCKS that any type of authentication is allowed. However, adding the line forces you to at least consider what you are trying to do and contributes to less sloppy setup.*

---

7. To explicitly set who is allowed to access what services, add a permit line in the format "permit *authmethod cmdallowed hostfrom hostto portfrom portto user*", where:

- The *authmethod* is the authorization method(s) accepted.

- The *cmdallowed* assigns the exact command(s) that this permit rule refers to.

- The *hostfrom* is the host(s) the permit rule allows to access the command(s).

- The *hostto* is the host(s) the permit rule allows the command(s) to be executed on.

- The *portfrom* is the port(s) the permit rule will accept the command(s) on.

- The *portto* is the port(s) the permit rule will pass the command(s) to.

- The *user* is the explicit user(s) the permit rule refers to; this is optional.

Add something similar to the following line to allow anyone from within the LAN to access any commands on any ports, assuming for the sake of the example that the LAN covers the range of addresses 192.168.15.*:

```
permit - - 192.168.15. - - -
```

8. Save and exit the file.

9. Restart the superdaemon.

Setting Linux Boxes To Go Through The Proxy

To configure the Linux boxes behind the SOCKS proxying firewall to use the firewall, do the following on each client box:

1. Log in as **root**.

2. Edit the file /etc/libsocks5.conf.

3. Add a line that allows the machines within the protected LAN to connect directly to one another without going through the firewall. To do this, add a noproxy line in the format "noproxy *command hostto portto user server*", where:

- The *command* is the exact command(s) not required to go through a proxy server.

- The *hostto* is the machine(s) the client is allowed to contact without going through the proxy server.

- The *portto* is the port(s) on the machine(s) specified that the client is allowed to contact without going through the proxy server.

- The *user* is an optional component that defines which user(s) may bypass the proxy for the defined line.

- The *server* is an optional component that defines which proxy server to go to for this rule, if one is used.

Add something similar to the following line to allow anyone within the LAN to access any commands on any ports on machines that are also within the LAN without using the proxy server, assuming for the sake of the example that the LAN covers the range of addresses 192.168.15.*:

```
permit - 192.168.15. - -
```

4. Add a line to tell the client machine that it has to go through the proxy server to access anything outside the LAN. Fortunately, all lines within this file are formatted the same way. The only difference is that this line starts with *socks5* to denote that it points to the SOCKS version 5 server. The line will look similar to the following if the proxy server is located on the machine 192.168.15.3:

```
socks5 - - - - 192.168.15.3
```

5. Save and exit the file.

Index